Puffin Bo

FUNNY STORIES

A bumper book of funny stories
from a favourite Australian author

Other books by Morris Gleitzman

The Other Facts of Life
Second Childhood
Two Weeks with the Queen
Misery Guts
Worry Warts
Puppy Fat
Blabber Mouth
Sticky Beak
Gift of the Gab
Belly Flop
Water Wings
Wicked! (with Paul Jennings)
Deadly! (with Paul Jennings)
Bumface
Adults Only
Teacher's Pet
Toad Rage
Toad Heaven
Toad Away
Toad Surprise
Toad Delight
Boy Overboard
Girl Underground
Worm Story
Aristotle's Nostril
Doubting Thomas
Grace
Too Small to Fail
Extra Time
Loyal Creatures
Help Around the House
Once
Then
After
Soon
Maybe
Now
Always
Give Peas a Chance
Pizza Cake
Snot Chocolate
Digging Up Dad
Tweet

MORRIS GLEITZMAN

3 books in one

FUNNY STORIES

AND OTHER FUNNY STORIES

Puffin Books

PUFFIN BOOKS

UK | USA | Canada | Ireland | Australia
India | New Zealand | South Africa | China

Penguin Books is part of the Penguin Random House group of companies
whose addresses can be found at global.penguinrandomhouse.com.

Penguin
Random House
Australia

Give Peas a Chance first published by Penguin Group (Australia), 2007
Pizza Cake first published by Penguin Group (Australia), 2011
Snot Chocolate first published by Penguin Random House Australia Pty Ltd, 2016
This bumper edition, including new story, 'Funny Stories', published by
Penguin Random House Australia Pty Ltd, 2018

Cover and text design by Tony Palmer © Penguin Random House Australia Pty Ltd, 2018
Printed and bound in Australia by Griffin Press, an accredited ISO AS/NZS 14001
Environmental Management Systems printer.

NATIONAL LIBRARY OF AUSTRALIA

A catalogue record for this
book is available from the
National Library of Australia

ISBN: 978 0 14 379338 0

penguin.com.au

For Barney and May, Melanie, and Gracie

Contents

PIZZA CAKE

SNOT CHOCOLATE

Funny Stories

Zac was in big trouble.

So much trouble it isn't funny, he thought to himself miserably.

Sixteen minutes past nine.

Eleven minutes late for assembly.

Zac tried to stay calm. He tried to concentrate on sprinting as fast as he could along the street towards school. He tried not to think about Mr Malone's threat.

At last week's assembly, Mr Malone had stood in front of the entire school and worked himself up into a full-scale Malone cyclone, complete with rain storms of saliva splattering the front rows of kids.

'Punctuality,' he'd said. 'It's an old-fashioned word that means presenting yourself promptly. In this school, punctuality is pathetically poor.'

Half the school looked guilty. The other half looked like they wished they had an umbrella.

'I'm a patient principal,' Mr Malone had stormed. 'But from this point in time, each and every one of you will be punctual or pay the price.'

Everyone, including Zac, knew exactly what Mr Malone meant when he said that.

Paying the price didn't just mean losing a house point or having a parent called to the school. Paying the price meant Mr Malone would put a lot of effort into thinking up a horrible punishment, just for you.

Eighteen minutes past nine.

Zac groaned.

But he knew groaning wouldn't save him.

He dashed across the teachers' carpark towards the school hall.

Maybe, if he was fast and very quiet, there was a tiny chance he could get to his class row without being seen. Please, Ms Patel, Zac begged silently, don't have done roll-call yet. Please, Mr Malone, have your back to everyone, showing them stuff on the overhead screen. Sports results or the addresses of umbrella shops.

Zac knew he'd need a lot of luck.

Since Mr Malone's threat, nobody had been late. It was an amazing achievement. Mr Malone seemed a bit disappointed.

The whole school knew Cyclone Malone was waiting for somebody he could make an example of. A scapegoat. A fall guy. Some clown, as Zac's friend Marty had put it, who was tired of living.

Zac reached the school hall. He stood outside the door and tried to stop gasping for breath.

Then, as slowly and carefully as he could, praying the door wouldn't make any noise, he pushed it open.

The door gave a long and very loud squeak.

Zac froze, but it was too late.

Everyone in the hall was turning and looking at him. Except Mr Malone. He didn't need to turn. He was standing at the front, already staring across all the heads. Directly at Zac.

'Ah,' said Mr Malone. 'Zac Fielding. Welcome. Perfect timing.'

Zac stepped miserably into the hall.

Behind him, as it closed, the traitor door gave another long squeak. A few kids sniggered softly. Mr Malone didn't yell at them. Just smiled at Zac.

'Proceed up here,' he said.

Mr Malone's soft tone didn't fool Zac.

I'm history, Zac thought as he slowly climbed the steps onto the stage and stood silently in front of Mr Malone.

'I was just pointing out,' said Mr Malone, 'how sometimes we can't help being late. And how that's perfectly fine when there's a proper reason. And the reason is explained fully and promptly. In a permission note from a parent.'

Mr Malone wasn't smiling now.

'Do you have a permission note from a parent, Zac?' he said.

Zac shook his head. And not just to get the drops of Mr Malone's saliva off his nose.

'Mum and Dad had already gone to work,' said Zac, 'when it happened.'

There was a silence. Zac could feel about three hundred pairs of eyes watching him.

'When what happened?' said Mr Malone.

Zac knew it wasn't going to sound good. But he reminded himself about something he'd read in a book. About truth being the best defence.

'When Woody fell into the toilet,' he said.

A few kids laughed. But not loudly. It was more like half-smothered spluttering by people who weren't sure if they were allowed to laugh.

You're not allowed to laugh, thought Zac indignantly. This isn't a laughing matter. Woody nearly drowned.

'How does a person fall into a toilet?' said Mr Malone.

'Woody's not a person,' said Zac. 'He's a mouse. And he's only got three legs.'

Mr Malone gave Zac a suspicious look.

'Three legs?' he said.

'He got run over,' said Zac. 'When he was little. By a cheese grater. It fell off the table and rolled over him.'

The laughter was louder now.

Zac would have told everyone to shut up if he hadn't been so concerned about how angry Mr Malone was starting to look.

'I fished Woody out of the toilet,' said Zac, 'and dried him on a towel. But he was shivering badly and Mum had taken her hair dryer to work so I put him in the oven.'

All around the hall, kids were laughing and giggling so much that some of them were squeaking louder than the door.

Zac tried to ignore them.

'I just put Woody in for a couple of minutes,' he said. 'On very low heat. But the oven door jammed and I couldn't get it open. Then I saw what was in the oven with Woody. On the same shelf. It was terrible. Mum must have put it in there so it would finish drying because the tea towel gets ripped if you try to rub it dry.'

Mr Malone was glaring at him.

Zac thought that perhaps it was because he wasn't making himself clear.

'The cheese grater,' said Zac. 'Woody was panicking. I thought he was going to have a heart attack. So I smashed the glass in the oven door with the sandwich toaster.'

Waves of laughter echoed around the hall. Some kids were almost falling off their chairs.

Zac glared at them.

You wouldn't be so amused, he thought bitterly, if you could see poor Woody now. Huddled in his cage at home, trying to pick bits of glass and toasted sandwich out of his fur and brooding about why the cheese grater and me ganged up on him.

Out of the corner of his eye, Zac saw Mr Malone's lips moving.

The laughter was too loud for Zac to hear what Mr Malone was saying, but it didn't matter. He knew. So did everyone else in the hall.

The laughter stopped as suddenly as if someone had switched it off.

Which, in a way, was exactly what Mr Malone had done. By spraying at Zac the four words that every student dreaded.

'See me at lunchtime.'

In class Ms Patel told everyone to sit quietly and read for a few minutes while she stepped out into the corridor to take a phone call.

The moment she left the classroom, everyone crowded around Zac.

'That was great,' said Marty.

'Who'd of thought?' said Sherilee. 'Zac Fielding, good at funny stories.'

Everyone agreed.

Somebody asked Zac if he'd been studying comedy shows online.

Zac was about to tell them he hadn't needed to because it wasn't a funny story, it was the truth. But he didn't. A strange and exciting feeling was starting to tingle inside him. And he was starting to think the same thing as Sherilee.

Who'd have thought?

Me, good at funny stories.

'Maybe,' said Marty, 'getting good at funny stories is one of those things that happens at a certain age, like pubic hair.'

Some of the kids screwed up their faces, but Zac liked the idea. He liked the thought of turning into a person who could always make other people laugh, and who was always popular, and who got invited to lots and lots of birthday parties, and who almost never got pushed into drainage ditches by bigger kids.

'That's bull,' said Gino. 'My brother's only four and he's always telling stories that make our whole family wet themselves.'

Zac wanted to point out to Gino that there was a big difference between being funny and just being cute. But with Gino that would start an argument, and Zac didn't want an argument.

What he wanted, he suddenly realised, was to make Gino laugh.

Zac took a deep breath, threw caution to the wind he got when he was nervous, and went for it.

'Maybe your brother's actually older than four,' Zac said to Gino, 'but he fell in the toilet when he was a baby and it stunted his growth.'

Zac hoped Gino and the others would chortle.

They didn't. They just stared at him. Marty looked shocked. Gino was looking tearful.

I don't get it, thought Zac. They know I don't really mean it. It's just a funny story. They laughed at Woody falling in the toilet.

Sherilee stepped close to Zac and hissed at him. 'Say sorry, you idiot.'

Even more confused, Zac looked at her.

And then remembered.

Gino's younger brother. The one who fell into a swimming pool at the age of two and drowned.

Zac felt terrible.

'Sorry,' he said to Gino.

Gino ignored him.

Zac wondered if he should try to explain that he hadn't meant to hurt anyone's feelings.

He decided not to. Because now that he thought about it, as well as very unkindly forgetting about Gino's dead brother, he'd also managed with one not very funny story to be hurtful to Gino, his younger brother, and Woody.

Accept it, said Zac to himself miserably. You're completely hopeless at funny stories. Which is why you will never try to tell another one, ever.

The other kids were going back to their desks, all ignoring him. But at the same time managing to give him really disgusted looks.

Zac wished it was lunchtime, so he could get out of there. Even though he was dreading what Mr Malone would have waiting for him when lunchtime did arrive.

Zac peered into the toilet bowl.

The stench was horrible. His stomach heaved.

He held his nose, but it didn't make any

difference. So he used both hands to grip the toilet brush and scrub at the lumpy stains.

While he scrubbed, he tried to take his mind off feeling nauseous by feeling indignant. Mr Malone would be sitting in his office right now probably, thinking what a clever punishment this was. Someone tells him a toilet story that he thinks is fake, so he gives the offender real toilets to clean, a whole boys' block full of them.

Not so clever actually, thought Zac. These toilets won't be very clean if I throw up. Would have been smarter to give me cheese graters to clean. Or mice.

'Excuse me,' said a voice behind Zac.

'Sorry,' said Zac, without looking up. 'The toilets are closed for cleaning.'

'We don't need the toilets,' said the voice.

Zac turned round.

And stared.

On the floor in front of him was something that hadn't been there when he'd come into the toilet block a couple of minutes ago.

An electric sandwich toaster.

'We need your help,' said the voice.

As the voice spoke, the two halves of the sandwich toaster opened and closed, like a mouth. The voice seemed to be coming from inside it.

Zac felt stunned and confused and a bit scared.

The sandwich toaster opened itself, as if it was going to say something else. Zac peered inside. It was empty. Which was a relief. Or maybe not a relief, now he'd started wondering how an empty sandwich toaster could talk.

'Please,' said the sandwich toaster.

Then Zac realised what was going on.

'Good one, Marty,' he said. 'But if Cyclone Malone catches you doing a practical joke in the middle of my punishment, we'll both be in the poo.'

He tried to sound as stern as he could, but he was impressed. Marty had never done a practical joke this complicated before. The sandwich toaster wasn't even plugged in. Zac couldn't see a single cable or power lead attached to it. Must be a bluetooth sandwich toaster. That was impressive, even for Marty.

'How did you get in here, Marty?' said Zac. 'I locked the door behind me.'

That was impressive too.

'I'm not Marty,' said the sandwich toaster.

Zac rolled his eyes. Always taking things too far was Marty.

'Neither am I,' said another voice.

An air-conditioning unit appeared next to the sandwich toaster.

Zac blinked. It was a big air-conditioner with a double fan. Out of nowhere. Nobody carrying it, or dragging it, or pushing it.

A wave of panic hit Zac.

Marty couldn't have done a stunt like that. Not with something that size. His place wasn't even air-conditioned.

'What's going on?' Zac stammered.

His mind was racing. Maybe the smell of the caked-on poo was affecting his brain. Maybe he was seeing things.

That didn't seem likely. Cleaning out Woody's cage could be almost as whiffy, but it had never made him see electrical appliances that weren't there.

'Sorry to startle you,' said the air-conditioner.

Zac tried to make sense of it all.

He'd seen things this weird in movies, but he was pretty sure movie special effects were done on computers, not in toilets. The only time he'd seen this kind of thing done in real life was on those TV comedy shows that trap people into embarrassing situations. Except no way would Mr Malone allow a TV comedy show into the boys' toilets . . .

Unless . . .

Zac remembered what Mr Malone had mentioned once in assembly. That his wife spent a lot of time working in her studio. Zac had assumed he meant a small shed in the backyard where she did water-colour paintings and pottery.

What if I was wrong, thought Zac. What if Mrs Malone works in a TV studio, or even owns one. What if Cyclone is using a TV comedy show from her studio to punish me for trying to fool him.

By fooling me back.

It was possible. The couple of times he'd met Mrs Malone, she was clearly, to the puzzlement of the whole school, deeply in love with Mr Malone.

'What channel are you on?' said Zac to the sandwich toaster and the air-conditioner.

'Channel?' said the sandwich toaster. 'We're not on any channel.'

'Are you online?' said Zac.

'We're not on anything,' said another voice.

A big-screen TV suddenly appeared. Hovering a metre above the floor.

That's pretty amazing, thought Zac. Specially for a TV show that hasn't even been launched yet.

'By channel,' said the TV, 'I assume you mean a dense-matter teleportation channel. That's old technology. Where we come from, we haven't used that for a thousand years.'

Zac digested this. Mrs Malone's scriptwriters obviously read a lot of science fiction.

'Where exactly is that?' said Zac. 'Where you come from?'

'The future,' said yet another voice.

A strange-looking object appeared next to the other appliances. It was a sort of curved black rubbery thing on the end of a stick.

Zac realised what it was.

A toilet plunger.

He grinned. You couldn't help grinning when you met something as dopey and funny as a toilet plunger claiming to be from the future.

Peering around, Zac tried to see the hidden cameras that were recording all this. He couldn't.

But that was probably normal with hidden cameras.

'We don't usually look like this,' said the air-conditioner. 'But when we were planning this trip, we decided we shouldn't let people see us for real. Us humans have changed a lot since your time, and we were worried we'd scare the pants off you. And we know what that's like, because mostly we don't wear pants.'

Zac grinned again.

Not bad scriptwriters

'So we thought it would be best,' said the sandwich toaster, 'if we turned up as things that people of your time really like. Household appliances.'

Zac was starting to enjoy this. It was going to make a really funny story when he told people about it. Plus, maybe he'd even get paid for being on the show. If he did, he'd be able to buy Woody a bigger cage.

'I've met a lot of household appliances,' said Zac to the four of them. 'But you're the funniest.'

He was pretty sure that TV producers would like guests who were also funny, so he jiggled his toilet brush as if it was feeling enthusiastic.

'I think my friend likes you,' he said to the plunger.

Zac waited for the appliances to chuckle, or rather the actors doing their voices, now they saw that their guest could be funny too.

While he waited, he had a crazy thought.

Maybe, when the producers saw he had comedy

talent, he'd get a regular spot on the show. Then he could buy Woody a titanium leg as well.

Except the appliances weren't laughing.

They were still and silent.

'You're very kind,' said the sandwich toaster. 'But you've put your finger on our problem. The reason we're here. We're not funny at all.'

Zac stared at them.

'Yes, you are,' he said. 'If you weren't, they wouldn't put you in a comedy show.'

'This isn't a comedy show,' said the plunger. 'We wish it was. But where we're from there aren't any comedy shows. People stopped laughing hundreds of years ago.'

Zac wasn't sure what to say.

The script was suddenly getting less funny.

'We know this is a lot for you to take in,' said the TV. 'It might help if we show you what we mean.'

The sandwich toaster moved towards Zac until it was in front of his feet.

'Just touch me with your fingertips,' said the sandwich toaster. 'Anywhere you like except for my on/off light.'

Zac hesitated. Was this the big comedy climax where he got an electric shock or something?

'Please,' said the sandwich toaster.

There was something in the sandwich toaster's voice. Something gentle and pleading that made Zac throw caution to his wind again.

He reached out, slowly, and placed his fingertips

onto the sandwich toaster's metal lid. And gasped and snatched his hand away.

He took a step back, trembling from the shock.

Not an electric shock.

An awful surging shock of sadness. Followed quickly by an equally surging shock of realisation. That this wasn't a TV show.

'Sorry about the sadness,' said the sandwich toaster. 'But it's like that all the time now where we come from.

'We've got really amazing technology,' said the air-conditioner. 'Toilets that clean themselves. And the rest of the bathroom.'

'That's right,' said the toilet plunger. 'And they automatically clean your bottom too.'

'But somewhere along the way,' the sandwich toaster said sadly, 'we humans forgot how to make each other laugh. We had robots to do it for hundreds of years, but they got bored and won't do it any more.'

'We're hoping you can remind us,' said the TV.

'Me?' said Zac.

The appliances didn't say anything. Just waited quietly. And, it seemed to Zac, hopefully.

His mind whirled as he tried to think of a funny story. Or at least a joke. Anything, as long as it was hilarious.

Yes, he had an idea.

'If I had a toilet that automatically cleaned my bottom,' said Zac, 'I'd be laughing all the time.'

Silence.

Zac felt sweat running down his back.

'You know,' said Zac, 'because I'm ticklish.'

More silence. The TV gave a little cough, or maybe it was just static.

'Earlier,' said the sandwich toaster, 'your school hall lit up on our laughter map. When we zoomed in on our screen, you'd just finished telling a funny story.'

'A very funny story,' said the air-conditioner, 'from the amount of laughter we picked up.'

'Can you tell that funny story to us?' said the TV.

'Please,' said the toilet plunger.

Zac hesitated.

For a second he saw himself, standing in the school toilets, about to tell a funny story to a group of human household appliances from hundreds, maybe thousands of years in the future.

Their warranties would be expired for a start.

Zac didn't say that.

They wanted the funny story from earlier, so that's what he gave them.

Silence.

The funny story was over and the appliances weren't saying a word. Not a spare part was moving. Not one of them was laughing.

At least say something, begged Zac silently.

'That poor mouse,' said the air-conditioner. 'He could have drowned in that toilet.'

'Or had a heart attack in the oven,' said the sandwich toaster.

'How bad would the poor cheese grater have felt then?' said the toilet plunger. 'I was almost a cheese grater for this trip.'

'I hate to say this,' said the TV, 'but that wasn't a funny story at all.'

Zac sighed.

'I know,' he said.

'Have you got another one?' said the sandwich toaster.

Zac shook his head.

'Just meeting you guys,' he said. 'And you probably wouldn't find that funny either.'

Another silence.

'Sorry I couldn't help you,' said Zac. 'Perhaps you should try a comedy club. Or watching TV or something. A different TV to your friend, I mean.'

The sandwich toaster gave a sigh too.

'Thanks for trying,' it said.

'I have to go,' said Zac. 'If I'm late back to class, Ms Patel will tell Mr Malone and I'll be cleaning these toilets for the rest of the year.'

'Actually,' said the plunger, 'it's not technically possible to be late. People who think you're late don't understand that time is circular.'

'That's right,' said the TV. 'It's one of our most useful discoveries. That and price stickers that don't leave gunk behind when you peel them off.'

Zac stared at them.

Time, circular?

'Time can't be circular,' said Zac. 'It starts, then it carries on, then it ends.'

'When does it end?' said the sandwich toaster.

Zac thought about this. He realised it wasn't a very good example of how time can't be circular. He looked around for a better example.

The toilets. Of course.

'If time was circular,' said Zac, 'when you have a pee, the pee would be coming out and going back in at the same time.'

Another silence.

Then the air-conditioner started to shudder.

For a moment Zac thought it had switched itself on. But then the toilet plunger started to shudder too, and it didn't have a switch.

The sandwich toaster was shuddering as well now, and the TV.

They were all making the same sound, softly at first and then louder and louder.

It was laughter.

Zac stared at them. Then he started laughing too, from relief.

'Out and back in at the same time,' spluttered the plunger. 'That is so funny.'

The appliances were laughing so hard they had to lean against each other.

'Thank you,' gasped the sandwich toaster to Zac. 'Thank you so much.'

* * *

Zac blinked.

Why was he standing in front of the bathroom mirror, just staring at himself?

In the reflection he saw Woody, behind him, scampering up onto the edge of the toilet bowl and sitting there, cleaning his tail.

'Careful, Woody,' said Zac. 'You know you get wobbly sometimes doing tail maintenance.'

He turned to lift Woody down to safety, but before he could, he froze.

It all came back to him. Everything. Woody's terrible experiences in the toilet and the oven. Being on stage with Mr Malone. Hurting Gino's feelings. The not-so-clever toilet-cleaning punishment.

And the household appliances.

Was that yesterday? wondered Zac.

He looked at the date on his watch.

No, it was today.

'Bye, Zac,' yelled a couple of distant voices, and Zac heard the front door close. Mum and Dad going to work. Again.

How could that be?

On the rim of the toilet bowl, Woody started to wobble. Zac reached out to grab him, then hesitated, his mind alive with possibilities.

If time really was circular, he could let this whole day happen again, as many times as he liked, making his funny stories funnier each time until everyone agreed, now and in the future, that his were the funniest stories ever.

Zac smiled.

That would be awesome.

Woody started to slip, frantically scrabbling at the rim of the toilet bowl.

Zac felt a pang and thought of Gino's poor brother drowning in the swimming pool. Time hadn't been very circular for him.

Zac shivered.

And reached out and caught Woody, warm and quivering, in his cupped palm.

It must have been the combination of surprise and relief, Zac thought later, that made Woody do what he did next. Something he'd never ever done before.

Zac stared at the warm pungent liquid dripping through his fingers. Coming out and definitely not going back in.

He smiled.

Then he kissed Woody to show him there were no hard feelings, gently washed him, carefully dried him till he stopped shivering, put him into his cage, and gave him some breakfast.

'Bye, Woody,' said Zac. 'See you this arvo.'

He hurried off to school, looking forward to the day so much it wasn't funny.

Did he have a story to tell.

GIVE PEAS A CHANCE

Mission Impossible

'Your mission,' said Dad to Jake, 'if you choose to accept it, is to take full command of this operation and to achieve victory using only cunning, daring, ruthlessness and cotton buds.'

Dad didn't use those exact words.

What he actually said was, 'Jake, could you keep an eye on things for a couple of hours? The twins kept me and Mum awake most of the night and we're pooped.'

Jake knew exactly what Dad meant.

He and Mum needed sleep.

A motel could be a noisy place, specially when you owned it and lived in it and never got away from it.

Mum and Dad needed him to keep things quiet. It was a big responsibility for someone who'd recently been voted the biggest daydreamer in year six.

'I accept the mission,' said Jake.

Dad gave Jake a grateful but weary smile and tiptoed into the bedroom.

Jake held his breath, hoping Dad wouldn't trip over yesterday's underpants and wake the babies.

He didn't, and the babies were still asleep a few minutes later as Jake sat in the big leather chair in the office and reviewed the situation.

Everything was quiet.

The guests were all checked out or at the beach. Sharnelle and Patsy who cleaned the units had finished and gone. *Out Of Order* signs in Jake's neatest writing were on the ping-pong table, the laundry, the ice machine, the swimming pool and the crazy golf, all three holes. The rattly door on the cold drinks cabinet in the office was wedged firmly and silently shut with cotton buds.

Jake glanced at the clock.

Two-fifteen.

With a bit of luck, nobody would want to check in for at least two hours. Everything would stay peaceful as long as a sea breeze didn't spring up and make the sheets on the line flap too loudly.

Mission accomplished.

Jake couldn't hear a peep from Mum and Dad's room.

Not even a snore.

He looked proudly through the office window at the big sign out the front.

Off-Highway Motor Lodge.

Quietest Motel In Town.

Which it is, thought Jake, when I'm running it.

He wondered whether to quietly get the ladder and a red texta and underline the *Quietest Motel In Town* bit. Before he could, three cars roared past the reception window and screeched into the parking area.

Jake leaped out of the chair with the lithe grace and superb reflexes of Tom Cruise. Or would have done if he hadn't hooked his foot in a worn patch of carpet and gone sprawling.

Jake picked himself up, glared at the carpet with the silent indignation and bruised elbows of Tom Cruise, spat out a bit of carpet fluff and peered through the window at the cars.

At first he thought they were the very thing he didn't want. A gang of early check-ins. Then he saw he was wrong. They were the other thing he didn't want. Units 7, 8 and 9 back early from the beach.

Several mums and dads and lots of little kids were getting out of the cars. Slamming the doors. Chattering loudly.

Jake's thoughts raced so fast he didn't even have time to compare them to Tom Cruise's.

Perhaps, he said to himself, units 7, 8 and 9 have just forgotten their sunblock. Perhaps if I help them find it they'll go back to the beach.

Jake hurried outside.

A mum in a green beach smock and sun-visor

slammed one of the car boots, turned, saw Jake approaching and glared at him.

Jake hoped he'd got that wrong. He hoped she was actually glaring past him at the sign out the front and realising that this was the quietest motel in town and thinking that her kids shouldn't be dragging their plastic spades along the ground so noisily.

She wasn't.

She was glaring at Jake.

'Oi,' she said, jabbing her finger at him. 'Why didn't you tell us that beach hasn't got a shark net?'

Jake was stunned.

Shark net?

The beach was the shallowest beach on the coast. It was famous for its shallowness. If you walked the length of three footy fields out to sea, the water was still only up to your ankles. A shark would need a lift from the rescue helicopter to get anywhere close to the beach.

Jake started to explain this.

Then he stopped.

The rest of the adults and kids were heading for the swimming pool.

'This sign reckons the gate's out of order,' one of the dads was saying. He pushed the pool gate open. 'Seems OK to me.'

They all crowded into the pool enclosure.

Jake hurried after them.

He knew he had about five seconds to think

of something before they all started throwing themselves into the water and yelling and splashing and waking up Mum and Dad and Gwen and Mabel and making Jake's mission completely impossible.

Dirty water.

That's it, thought Jake.

I'll tell them the pool water's dirty and not safe to swim in.

Except there was one little problem. The pool was clear and blue and sparkling. Dad was a genius with pool chemicals. He liked to say you could eat your dinner off his pool if you didn't mind soup.

Jake stood helplessly in the pool enclosure, surrounded by adults and kids stripping down to their swimmers. He wished he had Tom Cruise's Hollywood screenwriters to tell him what to do next.

But he didn't.

And one of the little girls was clambering onto the diving board.

Before Jake could stop her, one of the mums did.

'Charlene,' said the mum. 'Get off that. You'll hurt yourself. Come over here in the shade.'

'But I want to swim,' said the little girl.

Several of the other kids were sitting on the edge of the pool, dangling their legs in the water.

'Come away from there,' said one of the dads. 'That water could be filthy. You can never tell with motel pools. Not without a microscope.'

Jake looked admiringly at the dad.

Brilliant, he thought. You should be a Hollywood screenwriter.

The kids didn't look like they thought it was brilliant. They whinged and moaned and dragged themselves away from the pool. They stood dejectedly around the feet of the adults, who were stretched out on sun lounges under umbrellas.

'Can we do crazy golf then?' said one of the little boys.

Jake looked anxiously at the Hollywood screenwriter dad. He seemed to have fallen asleep. Jake scrambled to think of something. *Out Of Order* signs didn't work with this lot.

To his relief, he saw that one of the other mums was on the case.

'No crazy anything,' she said to the little boy. 'I'm not having you taking your eye out.'

'Ping-pong then,' said one of the little girls.

'Too dangerous,' said another dad. 'I read about a kid who choked on a ping-pong ball.'

Jake stared at him, grateful but also puzzled.

Choked on a ping-pong ball?

You'd have to have a windpipe the size of a spa bath waste duct.

Then Jake realised what was going on.

He'd heard Mum and Dad talking about this. How the modern world was making everyone feel scared, parents included. Mum reckoned it was because of global warming and terrorism and war and crime and pollution. Dad reckoned it was also because of bushfires and drought and those TV ads about germs that live on insects and kids.

Mum and Dad are right, thought Jake. People are even bringing their fears on holiday with them.

Jake thought that was a shame, but at least it made people nice and quiet.

He tried to hurry away before the green-smock mum started yelling at him about something else and woke Mum and Dad and the babies.

He almost made it, but one thing stopped him.

The sight of all the little kids sitting under umbrellas, miserable and bored.

Poor things, thought Jake. Not much of a holiday.

He wondered if there was anything he could do to cheer them up.

Quietly.

'Psst,' he said to the kids, kneeling down. He signalled for them to kneel down next to him.

Rows of tiny sugar ants were streaming out of the cracks in the concrete. The kids crowded around, curious.

'Those aren't bull ants, are they?' called an anxious dad's voice from a sun lounge.

'No,' said Jake, trying to demonstrate that it was possible to have a conversation in a quiet voice. 'They're coastal racing ants. But they're very shy and they only race if the conditions are right. They need lots and lots of absolute silence.'

He let one of the ants clamber onto his finger.

'This is my champion,' he whispered to the little kids. 'Antelope Flyer. He can beat any ant here.'

The little kids' eyes lit up.

They chose an ant each and Jake marked out a race track in the dust.

'They're off,' he whispered. 'Shhh.'

The race started.

Jake was impressed. As the ants scampered, the little kids were busting with excitement, but not one let out a squeak.

Brilliant, thought Jake. I should have thought of this ten minutes ago.

Then suddenly there were lots of squeaks. Jake looked behind him. The squeaks weren't coming from the little kids. They were coming from the mums and dads who were all crowding around as well.

Oh dear, thought Jake with a twinge of panic.

He silently begged the parents to control themselves.

They didn't.

'Go,' yelled one of the dads at his daughter's ant. 'Go, go, go, go, go.'

'That's us in the lead,' yelled a mum. 'Hey, not fair. Your brute of an ant kicked our ant.'

'That's not your ant,' shouted another mum. 'That's our ant. Charlene trod on your ant.'

Jake's panic was more than a twinge now.

'Please,' he hissed at units 7, 8 and 9. 'Argue quietly.'

They didn't hear him.

Jake prayed things would quieten down once the race was over.

'Go faster,' he whispered to the ants.

Things didn't quieten down once the race was over.

'Nathan's ant won by a mile,' yelled a dad.

'No way,' yelled another dad. 'That's Nathan's loser ant back there going round in circles.'

Jake felt like throwing himself in the pool and just letting himself sink. And taking the whole noisy bunch with him.

This was all his fault.

'Loser, eh?' Nathan's dad was yelling. 'Well you won't say loser when Nathan thrashes your lot at table tennis.'

Before Jake could stop them, the whole group stampeded over to the games room and crowded around the ping-pong table where four kids slugged the ball at each other and the adults whistled and cheered.

Jake was frantic.

The games room was even closer to Mum and Dad's room than the pool.

'Please,' he begged the group. 'Two babies and two exhausted parents are trying to sleep and they can't use sleeping pills because Mum's allergic and Dad only uses herbal medicine.'

But units 7, 8 and 9 weren't listening.

The game ended and a bitter dispute broke out

about the score-keeping. The parents of the losing team flung out a challenge to the parents of the winning team and suddenly the whole group was surging towards the crazy-golf course.

Jake had a disaster-movie-sized jolt of anxiety.

The first crazy-golf hole was right outside Mum and Dad's window.

Jake hurried after units 7, 8 and 9 as their voices echoed around the entire motel.

He could kick himself.

He should have seen this coming.

Dad was saying only recently that some parents' global fears were making them incredibly competitive about their kids. Wanting their kids to always come first so their kids would be better at surviving in a tough world.

Something like that.

Mum had been a bit doubtful, but Jake could see now that Dad was right.

These mums and dads from units 7, 8 and 9 were fearful, but they were also very competitive.

Olympic competitive.

AFL grand final competitive.

Nicole Kidman and Katie Holmes playing crazy golf in Hollywood competitive.

Jake knew he had about five seconds to think of something before a golf ball smashed through Mum and Dad's bedroom window.

He had an idea.

He flung himself into the middle of units 7, 8

and 9, who were squabbling noisily over who got to use the crazy-golf club first.

'Listen,' he yelled as loudly as he could, but facing away from Mum and Dad's room. It was a trick he'd learned from teachers. Sometimes, to get quiet, you had to make a lot of noise first.

Units 7, 8 and 9 went quiet.

Jake knew he had about two seconds before they went noisy again. This had to be good. Unlike Tom Cruise, he didn't have a special effects team to fake it.

He pointed over to the sign at the front of the motel.

'See where it says *Quietest Motel In Town*?' he said. 'Well, there's another motel over the other side of town who reckon they're quieter than us.'

It was true.

When Dad had put the sign up, the Parkside Slumber Inn had complained to the council.

'That's why,' said Jake, 'we at the Off-Highway Motor Lodge offer a prize each day to the quietest family staying with us.'

Units 7, 8 and 9 thought about this.

'What prize?' said one of the kids.

Jake gulped. He hadn't got quite that far with the idea.

Then he saw that the parents didn't care what the prize was.

'You've lost,' said the green-smock mum to the other parents. 'My kids can be quieter than your kids any day.'

The parents all glared at each other.

Silently.

So did the kids.

Jake held his breath, hardly able to believe it. The whole group were making their way back towards their units on tiptoe, kids with their hands over their mouths, parents pausing only to slip off squeaky shoes.

Jake grinned.

Let's see Tom Cruise have an idea like that, he thought. Even with Nicole Kidman and Katie Holmes to help him.

It was fantastic.

The whole bunch of them, the yellers and the moaners and the arguers, weren't making a peep.

Jake glanced up at the motel sign.

Have to change that now, he thought.

Quietest Motel In The World.

Then suddenly the silence was shattered. Not by the parents and kids of units 7, 8 and 9. By a noise far louder than anything they'd come up with.

Two babies howling.

Everyone froze.

Everyone looked at Jake and frowned.

Jake glanced at his watch.

Ten to three.

Oh well, he thought. Forty-three minutes unbroken sleep is better than nothing. Mum and Dad are always saying that.

Tomorrow he might be able to get them an hour.

For now, though, he had a motel to run.

Units 7, 8 and 9 were muttering to each other.

Jake thought fast.

The important thing was to make sure nobody went into the office and pestered Mum and Dad while they were getting up and feeding the bubs.

Easy.

'Hey,' Jake yelled to units 7, 8 and 9. 'You lot might be good at ant racing and ping-pong and crazy golf, but I'm the fastest swimmer round here.'

Jake took his t-shirt off and sprinted over to the pool. He glanced back, saw he had a crowd of competitors at his heels, smiled to himself, and dived in.

Paparazzi

I crouch inside the front door, waiting for Kevin. I'm pretty nervous. That's why I'm chewing my nails. Yuk. This new nail polish looks good but it tastes revolting.

I've never done anything like this before. Usually on a Saturday afternoon I'm hanging out at Madonna's place or somewhere. But a friend needs me, that's why I've decided to do this. I just have to be careful I don't ruin everything by being seen.

There are paparazzi everywhere.

That's what Kevin reckons they're called. People who chase after you with cameras, desperate to get your picture, tripping over things, bumping into each other, invading your privacy, yelling at you to pull a funny face or sing something.

Why do families always do that?

Paparazzi sounds like an Italian word. I don't know what the *razzi* bit means, but I bet the *papa* part is because the person at the front with the biggest camera is usually your dad.

My mobile's ringing.

Two rings.

That's Kevin's signal. He must be almost here.

I open the front door and check for grown-ups. I hate to think what Mum and Dad would do if they saw me like this.

When I checked earlier, Dad was in the back yard trying out his new handicam. Mum was taking snaps of him on her digital cause she reckoned he looked so funny trying to video insects and walking into the washing.

From the sound of her giggles he must still have a bra on his head.

I hope they don't wake Daniel. Dan's not really into photos, but he'll always grab a couple with his mobile if there's a chance of getting his little sister into trouble.

The front yard is clear.

I pull the paper bag over my head and half walk half run down the front path.

Oh no, I haven't made the eye holes big enough.

I can't see anything either side of me.

My main worry is Mrs Kyneton next door. Her son got her a six megapixel 3G Nokia for Christmas and she's been putting the whole suburb on her blog ever since.

I don't think she's seen me.

I can't hear anyone yelling 'say cheese'.

What I can hear is Kevin's brother's car wheezing and spluttering as it gets closer.

I hope Kevin's right about it being more mechanically reliable than it sounds. It looks fantastic, a gleaming light-blue 1982 Valiant that always gets photographed at car shows, but looks aren't going to help us today.

The car squeaks to a stop. Kevin's in the front next to his brother. He winds down the window.

'Haul butt,' he says.

Even though I'm sweating with tension, I smile inside my paper bag. Kevin's got hair gel on. He thinks it makes him look like Brad Pitt. It does a bit, but his voice is even squeakier than the car.

'Hurry up,' says Kevin, starting to sound panicked.

I yank the back door open and scramble inside. The car roars away at high speed. That's what I wish it was doing. Actually it chugs away slowly.

'G'day Nat,' says Holly.

Holly is lying across the back seat, her head in a pillowcase. She squeezes over and I lie down next to her so nobody can see us from outside the car.

'Hi Natalie,' says Madonna.

Madonna is lying on the floor behind the front seats. She's got her head wrapped in a towel. It's her sister's sports towel from school. I can see the name tag. Beyonce Crutchley.

'Is it me,' says Madonna, 'or is it hot in here?'

'Sorry,' says Kevin's brother. 'Heater's jammed. I can't turn it off.'

'This isn't hot,' says Kevin. 'I had a go in a spin-dryer once and it was much hotter than this.'

None of us say anything.

Kevin is known all through grade six and most of grade five for exaggerating. It's what you have to do when you're the youngest of eight.

Suddenly the brakes slam on and I roll off the back seat onto Madonna.

'Ow,' she says.

'Sorry,' I say, and try to shift my bony bits.

'Does anyone know anybody with a yellow Corolla?' says Kevin's brother. 'It's blocking our way. There are people inside with cameras and they're waving at us. I think they want us to get out.'

My paper bag deflates. So does my chest.

It's my rellies. They must have come round the corner and seen me as I was getting into the car.

'It's my nan,' I say. 'And my Auntie Pru and Uncle Andrew. They've come over to take pictures of the Christmas clothes they gave me, but they're not meant to be here till this evening.'

'Paparazzi,' says Kevin. 'They don't care whose lives they wreck. I'll handle them.'

He gets out of the car.

'Kevin's amazing,' says his brother. 'He can lie his way out of anything. I've got videos of him doing it.'

Carefully I kneel up, not on Madonna, and peep out the window.

Kevin is yelling at Nan through the windscreen of the Corolla.

'It's an emergency,' he shouts. 'We've got to get to the hospital.'

Me and Holly look at each other through our paper bag and pillowcase eye holes.

Why is he telling them the truth?

In the Corolla, Nan looks puzzled too. She might not have her hearing aid turned up.

Auntie Pru winds down her window and points her camera at Kevin. It's the big one she uses for her wildlife photos on holiday. Kevin sees her and puts his hands up over his face and scurries back into our car.

'Don't worry, Kevin,' says Holly. 'You tried.'

'It's not my fault,' says Kevin indignantly. 'Look at the size of that zoom lens.'

None of us say anything, but we all know how he's feeling. We've all been caught by paparazzi not looking our best. We've all had our pimples and baggy track pants plastered across family slide nights and aunties' websites.

'They're backing up,' says Kevin's brother.

We chug off again.

I flatten myself onto the back seat, hoping they didn't hear what Kevin said about the hospital.

Why didn't he say we were going to the mall or somewhere?

It's not Kevin's fault. He must have panicked. I'd probably have done the same. Dealing with the paparazzi is just so stressful. I don't know how Angelina Jolie and that lot cope.

'Nat, keep your head down.'

Holly is hissing at me because I'm peeping out the car window.

I know she's right, but I can't help it. We're passing what's left of Tara's house and even though I've seen it heaps of times since the fire I can't stop myself looking.

Tara is the only kid in our class whose house has ever burned down.

A great big house turned into a pile of scrap and ash by a bunch of candles.

'Sheesh,' says Kevin's brother, slowing down and staring. 'I wouldn't mind getting a picture of that.'

'Not now,' pleads Kevin. 'We're on a deadline.'

'Yeah, yeah, I haven't forgotten,' says Kevin's brother. 'Keep your gel on.'

We don't stop.

I puff out my paper bag with relief.

But I don't blame Kevin's brother for wanting a picture. Each time I see the remains of Tara's burnt house I'm shocked because it's so much worse than I remember.

For example, I'd forgotten that the tiles in Tara's upstairs bathroom were pink. They're stacked up on the front lawn now, and most of them are singed and scorched and black round the edges.

Which is really sad because it was one of the

nicest bathrooms I've ever been in.

But of course it's not as sad as what's happened to Tara.

'Poop.'

Kevin's brother is swearing.

The car's stalled and he can't get it started again. He pumps the pedal and the engine whines like a kid with pillow hair who doesn't want to be in a family photo.

'Are we out of gas?' says Kevin, who likes to use American words whenever possible.

'Battery's going flat,' says his brother. 'I need a push.'

'I'll handle it,' says Kevin and jumps out.

We don't even wait for him to try. Kevin's built like a TV aerial and even if he could move the car on his own he'd probably rupture one of his very skinny internal organs.

Plus we've got to be at the hospital in less than ten minutes.

'Keep your heads covered up,' Holly says to me and Madonna as we get out of the car.

She doesn't have to remind me. My paper bag is firmly on. To be sprung now would be a disaster.

We all push as hard as we can and the car starts moving.

'Hey,' yells a voice. 'Look. Kev's girlfriends have gone Islamic.'

I recognise the voice.

Rocco Fusilli.

I swivel my head and glare at him through my eyeholes. The one kid from school I hoped would be somewhere else today. Like Antarctica. But there he is, taunting us with his mates. They've got their mobiles out and as we break into a trot, pushing the car, they chase us and take pictures.

'Ignore them,' mutters Holly.

'You're invading our privacy,' Kevin yells at them. 'It's against the law. My dad's a cop and he's watching you on the police satellite.'

Rocco and his mates just laugh.

Kevin is always doing that, exaggerating about the surveillance capacity of the police. Everyone knows that compared to rellies with cameras, most law enforcement agencies can't compete.

The car gives a big jolt and the engine splutters into life.

'Get in,' yells Holly.

We all clamber in and chug away from Rocco and his paparazzi pack.

I flop down in the back with Holly and Madonna. Inside my paper bag I'm sweating.

Just my luck.

I've got the most important photo session of my life coming up and I think my make-up's running.

We bump and totter into the hospital lift. Just the four of us because Kevin's brother has to stay with the car in case it gets scratched.

There are two nurses in the lift.

They stare at us.

I can feel Madonna shuffling nervously behind me and I know why. What if there's a hospital security regulation forbidding visitors to have their heads in bags or pillowcases? What if the nurses ring an alarm bell? What if security guards are waiting for us when the lift doors open and we don't even get to see Tara?

'Hi ladies,' says Kevin to the nurses, who glare at him sternly.

He's got courage, Kevin, for a skinny youngest kid in a big family.

'Don't be alarmed,' he says to the nurses. 'We're here to make a patient feel better.'

The nurses think about this, then both grin at him.

'Fair enough,' says one. 'They say laughter's the best medicine.'

'Which is why,' says the other, 'I predict a complete recovery when the patient sees your hair.'

The lift doors open and we drag Kevin out before he can get defensive about his gel.

As we hurry along the corridor I catch a glimpse of Tara's dad up ahead, going into Tara's ward.

I take a deep breath and keep going.

We knew Tara's rellies would be here for such an important occasion. The surprising thing is that her dad hasn't got his camera round his neck. Out of all our parents, he's the biggest photo fanatic. That's why Tara's house had so many burning candles in it, so their Christmas family pictures would look extra atmospheric.

On second thoughts, after what happened, he's probably gone right off photography.

We stop outside Tara's hospital room and peek cautiously in.

And nearly die.

It's not just Tara's rellies who are crowded around her bed. My mum and dad are there too. And Holly's. And Madonna's.

Kevin's aren't, but with eight kids they never are.

Mum and Dad and the others are staring at us.

None of them have got their cameras.

It's OK, I say to myself. Stay calm. We knew there was a chance this might happen. Everyone must have decided to keep cameras away from Tara.

I glance at Kevin. He pats his pocket.

'It's cool,' he says.

'G'day Nat,' says Mum uncertainly. 'Auntie Pru told us you were coming here and we guessed it must be Tara's special time so we thought we'd come and help cheer her up too. Why have you got a bag on your head?'

I don't say anything, partly because I'm a bit dizzy now the big moment is close and partly because a doctor is bending over Tara's bed, slowly unwinding the bandage from around her face.

We all stop looking at each other and anxiously

watch the doctor and Tara.

It feels like nobody's breathing in the room, except Kevin who's looking a bit pale and like he might faint.

The last bit of bandage drops away from Tara's chin.

'Good,' says the doctor. 'That is good. It is. It's very good.'

Nobody else says anything.

It's as bad as we thought it would be.

The beautiful smooth skin on Tara's face isn't smooth any more and it hardly even looks like skin. It's bright red and cracked and flaky. And her hair, her long fair hair which was probably the most photographed hair outside Hollywood despite how Tara used to come up with some really clever hiding places to get away from her dad's camera, her hair isn't long any more.

It's short and very patchy.

You can see bits of her scalp.

'Give it a few weeks,' says the doctor to Tara. 'Few weeks and you'll be right as rain. Two months tops.'

Slowly, her hand shaking, Tara picks up the mirror on her bed and looks at herself.

I have a weird thought.

Can people whose faces have been burnt still cry?

They can. Tara's eyes are filling with tears as she looks at her reflection. I glance at Holly and Madonna through my eyeholes.

This is the moment.

I pull my paper bag off my head and Holly removes her pillowcase and Madonna unwraps her towel. We all stand there in front of Tara and let her see us.

I've prepared a speech about how she'll always be our friend no matter what she looks like. But when I see the expression on her face as she stares at us through her tears I know I don't need to say anything.

I glance at Holly and Madonna.

I was right, our make-up has run, but I reckon we still look pretty good. Madonna's mum prefers orange lipstick, so Madonna's face isn't as red as Tara's, but Holly's is. And because we smeared the lipstick onto our faces really thickly and blasted it with our hairdryers, it's cracked and flaky and looks exactly like the real thing, specially on our foreheads.

I'm so glad we decided to give ourselves these short and patchy haircuts and shave our eyebrows off.

We look at Tara.

Tara looks at us.

Yes. It's working.

Tara isn't crying any more. She's even managing a smile.

'Thanks,' she whispers.

Mum and Dad and the other parents are staring at us like the doctor has just given them a really strong anaesthetic that knocks you out with your eyes open.

When it wears off there's a good chance they'll be totally furious. Me and Holly and Madonna know this, but we think it's worth it.

The colour has come back into Kevin's face. Not as much as we've got, but at least he won't need oxygen.

I give him a nudge and he fumbles in his pocket. He pulls out his dad's camera and pushes it into Tara's dad's hands.

Then me and Holly and Madonna and Kevin go over and hug Tara and sit on the bed with our arms round her so the grown-ups, when they recover, can take our photo.

Greenhouse Gas

Today is a very big day for our family.

Me and Grandpa are both getting honoured. Grandpa's been voted Australian Of The Year and I've been voted Young Australian Of The Year. Plus we're getting a ten metre high concrete tomato. Nobody in our family's ever won anything before except scratchies so everybody's very excited.

But there's a problem.

Grandpa has jumped into the sea again and I'm out in the boat trying to find him.

'It's one-thirty, Grandpa,' I yell. 'You're being honoured in an hour and Mum reckons if you're not in your best pants by two-fifteen she's gunna get Andy Wicks to demolish the big tomato with his bulldozer and use the bits of concrete to build a new toilet block in the caravan park.'

I pause, out of breath.

All around me the calm surface of the sea

shimmers in the sunlight like a massively large plasma telly lying on its back. I used that description in my history project, but I only got six out of twenty.

I stare at the water.

I'm looking for bubbles.

Grandpa had fried tomatoes for breakfast as usual. When he goes snorkelling in the ocean after breakfast you can sometimes spot his gas bubbles. You have to make sure they're his bubbles, though. Once I tried to tell a big jellyfish it was morning nap time.

'Grandpa,' I yell again. 'Dad said to remind you that this is the proudest day in the entire history of our town, so try not to blow off at the ceremony.'

I peer at the sea.

'I'll try not to, young Dougie,' says a voice behind me. 'But my botty wind is the least of our worries.'

I turn round.

Grandpa is hanging onto the other side of the boat, treading water and pushing his snorkel mask up from his face.

'I wish you hadn't found me,' he says quietly.

I nod.

I know what he means.

I wish I hadn't found him either, not yet. I wish I could stay out here for another few hours looking for him. I wouldn't even mind chatting with a jellyfish or two. That way me and Grandpa could both miss the ceremony.

Grandpa drags himself into the boat.

Sadly I help him.

We don't have to look at each other to know we're both feeling the same thing.

We don't want to be Australians Of The Year.

I row the boat towards the jetty.

'Careful, Dougie,' says Grandpa as we get into shallow water.

He always says that. It's because of the barbed wire fences just below the surface. This part of the sea used to be all sheep paddocks.

'It's OK, Grandpa,' I say quietly as I steer us past the roof of a submerged shearing shed. 'You can trust me.'

I always say that.

Grandpa usually smiles to himself and says 'yeah, I know', but today he doesn't.

He's frowning and concentrating on picking a bit of seaweed out of his ear. I can tell he's thinking about things.

I know how he feels.

I'm thinking about things too.

'We'll have to own up,' says Grandpa. 'Tell them we don't deserve to be Australians Of The Year.'

My guts go tighter than a sheep fence when a shark swims into it.

But I know Grandpa's right. If we accept these honours we'll spend the rest of our lives feeling guilty.

'If we confess,' I say, 'what'll happen to us?'

'Don't know,' says Grandpa.

Nor do I.

I don't want to think about it. Instead I concentrate on helping Grandpa tie the boat to the jetty.

'We'd better hurry,' I say. 'Mum's having a meltdown.'

I point over towards the house.

Mum's on the verandah, waving to us like an octopus stuck on a windmill. I used that description in my English assignment, but I only got seven out of twenty.

'Three cheers for Noel and Dougie Webber, the tomato heroes of Australia,' says the woman from the government.

There's a big crowd in front of the stage next to the surf club and they all give big cheers. Including my teachers, who still don't understand how a person who's never got more than eight out of twenty can be Young Australian Of The Year.

They don't have to worry.

I can't be.

I wish I could sneak off this stage and creep out of town and never come back. But I wouldn't make it. Hundreds of friends and neighbours are watching, and thousands of city folk from the caravan park.

Anyway, I can't leave Grandpa here to confess on his own.

The cheers die down, almost. Then Mum and Dad realise they're the only people still cheering and stop too. It's not their fault. They're just so proud. When they heard somebody was coming down from Federal Parliament House in Alice Springs to give us our prizes, they nearly cacked themselves.

I wish I didn't have to do this to them, but I do.

Grandpa, who's standing next to me, squeezes my hand.

'You OK?' he whispers.

'I think so,' I say.

The woman from the government is speaking into the microphone again.

'We may have lost the battle against global warming and melting ice-caps and rising sea levels,' she says. 'We may have lost our big cities, but thanks to Noel and Dougie Webber, we haven't lost the battle to feed ourselves.'

The crowd cheers again.

From up here I can see that heaps of people are having picnics and doing their cheering with their mouths full. I can see tomato pizzas and tomato sandwiches and lots of sun-dried-tomato burgers dripping with tomato sauce.

As the cheering dies down, I can also hear the faint sound of thousands of puffs of gas escaping from thousands of bottoms. It's what happens these days when crowds get excited.

And, to be honest, even when they don't.

'Five years ago,' says the government woman,

'a very clever little boy found something very special in his dad's paddock. A native Australian tomato plant that had never been discovered before. The boy's grandfather put its seeds into pots and, thanks to his skill as a gardener, got them to grow. And did they ever grow. They produced ten times more tomatoes per plant than any other type of tomato anywhere. And the rest, as we know, is history.'

I can feel myself blushing, partly because the whole crowd is clapping me and Grandpa, and partly because in a moment I'm going to have to confess to a very big lie.

'Last year,' continues the woman from the government, 'Australia exported nearly a million tonnes of tomatoes to help feed the world.'

More cheering.

More gas escaping from well-fed tummies.

As usual, nobody even notices. That's the thing about botty gas. People start off being polite and pretending it's not happening, and then after years of ignoring it they don't even notice it any more. Not even when it's erupting all around them.

Me and Grandpa notice it.

We notice it a lot.

Mum and Dad do as well, probably because Grandpa goes on about it when he's had a few glasses of tomato wine.

'It gives me great pleasure,' says the woman from the government, 'to unveil this monument to two very special Australians.'

Her assistant puts down his briefcase and grabs hold of the ropes attached to the big tarpaulin. He pulls on them and the tarpaulin slides down and ends up in a heap at his feet.

A bit like my insides.

That's what it feels like.

We all stare up at the Big Tomato. It's the tallest man-made structure in town except for the surf lifesaving tower, and it's definitely the brightest. Ken Bullock in the hardware store was mixing red paint for days.

When the crowd quietens down, as much as any crowd these days can, the woman from the government steps closer to Grandpa.

'And now,' she says, 'please welcome this year's Australian Of The Year, Noel Webber.'

She holds the microphone out to Grandpa, who doesn't even see it.

He's staring over at the shimmering ocean with a smile on his face, which is what he spends most of his time doing when he's not actually swimming or snorkelling. Mum reckons his brain might be a bit waterlogged, but I know that's not it.

Think about it. For the first sixty years of Grandpa's life, this town was hundreds of kilometres inland. Grandpa only ever saw the sea on telly. Now, thanks to melting ice and rising sea levels, we're a coastal resort.

Grandpa can't believe his luck.

None of us can.

We're happier than wallabies in wellies, which is a description I included in my science essay, but I only got four out of twenty.

I give Grandpa a nudge. He sees the microphone and takes it. We look at each other. Neither of us feels very happy right at this moment.

In front of the stage, lots of media cameras are pointed at us.

'Ladies and gentlemen,' says Grandpa. 'Thank you for your kindness, but I can't accept this honour. I don't deserve to be Australian Of The Year.'

People are gasping.

Bits of tomato sandwich are dropping from open mouths.

'We told a lie about where the new tomatoes came from,' says Grandpa. 'My grandson didn't really find a tomato plant in a paddock. What really happened was that I took an ordinary everyday tomato plant and did a bit of cross-pollinating in my greenhouse. Then I made up the paddock story so people would think the new tomato was natural and just as nature intended.'

The crowd has gone dead silent. All I can hear is the sound of the sea and the gulls and the gas escaping from multiple bottoms.

'We're sorry,' says Grandpa.

I nod to show I am too.

The woman from the government is looking a bit shocked. She pulls herself together and puts her hand on Grandpa's shoulder.

'We accept your apology,' she says into the microphone. 'The fact remains, you created a wonder tomato for the benefit of the world, and we want to honour you for that.'

The crowd applauds and whistles.

'Thank you,' says Grandpa. 'But there's another reason we can't accept this reward. It's hard to put into words, but every time somebody eats one of our tomatoes somewhere in the world, that's reward enough for us.'

I nod to show I agree.

The crowd is looking sort of puzzled. You know, like the eskimos when their igloos started melting and they knew they hadn't left the oven on. In social studies I wrote a letter to Iceland to say sorry, but when I showed it to Grandpa he made me tear it up, which meant I got nought out of twenty.

'I hope you understand,' Grandpa says to the crowd.

They just stare back at him.

I don't think they do.

Grandpa has been controlling himself very well so far, but now he stops clenching his buttocks and blows off big time.

I know what he's doing. Trying to give everyone a clue to help them understand.

The woman from the government is looking totally confused.

'Please,' she says. 'Just accept the honour.'

'Sorry,' says Grandpa. 'I'd rather not.'

'Me neither,' I say. 'It wouldn't be right.'

'But I don't understand,' says the woman, putting her hand over the microphone. 'You don't get any money from the tomatoes. What reward are you talking about?'

The crowd, which is frowning and muttering and giving off a lot of gas, obviously doesn't understand either.

I feel sick with nerves, but I take the microphone to explain to them.

'Our reward,' I say, 'is that our tomatoes make people fart.'

Some people in the crowd look shocked. But only because I used a rude word. They still don't get it.

Before I can continue, Grandpa takes the microphone from me and switches it off.

'Careful, Dougie,' he murmurs.

At first I think Grandpa means the rude word too. Then I realise what he's saying. We've done the right thing and confessed. No point getting ourselves in extra trouble.

'It's OK, Grandpa,' I reply quietly. 'You can trust me.'

I bite into a big red juicy tomato and sit back in my favourite chair, the cane one in Grandpa's greenhouse with the view out to sea.

I blow off, a long slow one that fills the greenhouse with a sweet tomatoey smell.

Grandpa doesn't mind. He's sitting next to me in his favourite chair doing the same.

He points down the hill towards the surf club.

'They're nearly finished,' he says.

He's right. The painters working on the Big Tomato have nearly finished painting it white.

'That was a clever idea of your mum and dad's,' says Grandpa. 'Turning it into the Big Golf Ball. When you've got the biggest caravan park in Australia, adding a beachside golf course is a top idea.'

Grandpa is right, it was a top idea. And a kind one.

A lot of the city folk in the caravan park need cheering up. It can't be easy, living in your four-wheel drive and spending all your time staring miserably at the sea and thinking about the place you used to live in that's now under water. Perhaps a bit of golf will help them feel better.

I hope so.

Grandpa has stood up and is pottering about up the other end of the greenhouse, watering his special plants. The onion weed and the kelp and the soy bean bushes and all the others. The ones he cross-pollinated with the tomato plants to get the side-effect he was after.

Grandpa's quite old and old people like to keep things for nostalgia. I'm young, but I know how he feels. We owe a lot to those plants.

Grandpa sits back down.

'Talking of clever ideas,' he says. 'Remember five years ago when the sea was still a hundred kilometres away and it didn't look like it'd ever reach us and all we had here was a drought-struck town full of dead sheep and unemployed people?'

I nod.

I'll never forget it.

Mum and Dad didn't have a job for the first six years of my life.

Grandpa's getting that misty far-away look in his eyes that old people get when they're having happy memories.

'Remember the day you asked me why the sea wasn't coming here any more?' says Grandpa. 'And I explained the ice had stopped melting because global warming was slowing down. Coal was running out and petrol was scarce and electricity was very expensive and people weren't making so much greenhouse gas and . . . what was it you said?'

When Grandpa's having these memories he likes me to say exactly the same words I said five years ago.

I don't mind. I know them off by heart.

'You've got a greenhouse, Grandpa,' I recite. 'Why don't you make some greenhouse gas?'

Grandpa stares out to sea with a big smile on his face and I know what he's thinking.

About the millions of people all over the world who've been eating our tomatoes for the last five years and blowing off.

I smile too because I know what he's going to say next and it always makes me feel happy. Even being Young Australian Of The Year wouldn't make me feel happier. The only time I feel happier is when I see Mum and Dad busy and content in their caravan park by the sea.

'That greenhouse gas idea was brilliant, Dougie,' says Grandpa. 'Twenty out of twenty.'

Think Big

MY SCIENCE PROJECT
BY
TRACY SPICER
6W, ORCHID COVE PUBLIC SCHOOL,
NORTH QUEENSLAND, AUSTRALIA, THE WORLD,
THE SOLAR SYSTEM, THE MILKY WAY GALAXY,
THE VIRGO SUPERCLUSTER, POSTCODE 4879.

PURPOSE

The purpose of this science project is to collect data, do research, carry out an experiment, and with a bit of luck get Mum off that dopey diet Aunty Bev has got her on.

INTRODUCTION

Things are really crook. Mum's gone mental about

food. She reckons everything goes to her thighs. Even fish fingers. I tried to explain scientifically that's bull. Food goes to your tummy, then your bum tube. But Mum won't listen and I'm desperate. I haven't had chips for weeks. Mum steams everything. Even fish fingers.

I asked Dad to help me with the project. But he reckons getting people to do your homework is dishonest and could lead to a life of crime. It's OK for him, he goes fishing every night after work, then has a fry-up in the shed. He does offer to share his fish with me, but I can't eat them because of the tiny bones. Is there a biological reason why fish can't have drumsticks?

Anyway, I kept on at Dad about helping me. I read somewhere that a good scientist never takes no for an answer. Finally Dad blew his top and told me the scientific reason why he doesn't want to help. He hates taking sides between me and Mum. He reckons he'd rather suck snake venom out of Doug Walcott's big toe. Which he did once, so I suppose he knows what he's talking about.

DATA COLLECTED SO FAR

1. When your Dad calms down and gives you a hug, it feels really good. Even when he's on the way to the shed and he's got a coral trout inside his shirt.

2. Mum will never be as thin as Aunty Bev. It's not scientifically possible. Aunty Bev has worn skin-tight pink jeans all her life and they've stopped her leg flesh from spreading. Plus she does that trick supermodels do. You know, wears really big dangly plastic earrings to make her body look smaller.

3. Aunty Bev has started a local Weightwatchers group. Except Weightwatchers won't let her use their name because she swore at them on the phone. So she's calling her group Think Small. It meets at our place on Thursday nights after that show on telly about fat people.

4. Mum doesn't want to be on a diet. Most of the time these days her face is longer than a school term. Plus she's got chocolate fingers hidden in her bra drawer. Aunty Bev is making Mum starve herself. She's Mum's big sister measured in years, but she's always nagging Mum about Mum being the one who's bigger measured in fat globules.

5. I hate seeing Mum unhappy.

6. I'm also worried that Mum might want us to move away. Up here in the tropics 99.999% of people wear shorts and t-shirts so your body can breathe. (The other 0.001% of people wear skin-tight pink jeans.) Now that Mum thinks she's fat she'll probably want us all to move to some

cold place where people cover up with heaps of clothes. My friend Keith lives in England and some days it's so cold there he wears three pairs of jeans. Under his school pants.

7. Dad reckons Mum's fatness is all in her head and I think he's right. Mum is actually quite small if you compare her to the average height for a human. And her average weight is definitely not heavier than average. It's not Mum's fault she's deluded and obsessed. Aunty Bev can be harder to shake off than stringy snot. Which is why I'm using science to help Mum see the truth.

RESEARCH METHOD

My research method consists of lying on the back lawn looking up at the stars and having dinner. I do that a lot. I love outer space. Plus Mum can't see what I'm eating. Aunty Bev can if she's got a torch.

I started my research with a research question like you're meant to. My research question was, *If Aunty Bev has her way and nobody in our family ever gets to eat another sausage and onion sandwich after the one I'm eating now, how will we cope?*

Sometimes research questions can make scientists feel a bit upset and they have to gather more data till they feel better.

I started gathering data about stars and planets. By counting them. Except as every scientist and person lying in a backyard knows, there are too many to count completely. But it does calm you down and help your digestion. It also helps you have a ripper of an idea for an experiment.

THE EXPERIMENT

A scientific method of demonstrating to a non-fat mother who's gone a bit mental that she is not too big in any way, shape or size.

THINGS YOU NEED TO DO THE EXPERIMENT

1. Birthday money (all of it).
2. Both of Mum's large shopping bags.
3. Fast walking to the supermarket and back so nobody notices you're gone.
4. Hiding place for the shopping bags as soon as you get home.
5. Big bone to distract Buster so he doesn't find the shopping bags behind the lounge and eat what's in them. He's got a few bits missing (one leg, half an ear, some of his tail), but that doesn't mean he's slow. His nose works super well, specially when there are large amounts of lollies in the house.

EXPERIMENT METHOD

A laboratory wasn't available for this experiment so I used our lounge room which was better because that's where the Think Small lot were meeting.

I waited till they'd started, then walked in. Mum was there, and Aunty Bev, and Mrs Newman from the post office, and Mrs Newman's daughter Gail who works at KFC, and Doug Walcott who's been depressed and off his lollies since the snakebite. All lollies, not just jelly snakes. His wife reckons he's already lost weight. Aunty Bev doesn't. She reckons he's still pretty porky.

I asked if I could join in. Mum looked doubtful, but Aunty Bev beamed like big plastic earrings were on special and said I could as long as I waited my turn.

Mrs Newman finished telling the others her Think Small Experience Of The Week. It was about how if you steam snow peas for too long they go mushy and you don't want to eat them and you go even thinner.

The others came out with their Think Small Experiences. Each one was about not eating something or else chewing it nine million times. Everybody in that room must have been starving.

Then it was my turn.

'Trace, do you have a Think Small Experience?' said Aunty Bev. I nodded and dragged the shopping bags out from behind the lounge.

'Behold,' I said, which I think is a scientific word. 'The Milky Way.'

I ripped open a bulk bag of chocolate peanuts and tipped them on the floor. I didn't use real Milky Ways because they're the wrong shape.

Everyone stared. Not at me, at the chocolate peanuts rolling across the carpet.

'Imagine those are planets in space,' I said.

I emptied out another bag of chocolate peanuts and then lots of bags of chocolate sultanas, chocolate macadamias and chocolate hundreds and thousands.

'Our galaxy's got even more planets than that,' I said, once the floor was covered. 'There are loads we can't even see.'

Mrs Newman bent forward and peered under the coffee table. I opened a big tin of Milo and tipped it onto the carpet. Mum gave a kind of squeak, which I hoped showed she was getting my drift.

'Each grain of Milo,' I said, 'is a planet in our galaxy too.'

Mrs Newman's mouth was moving silently like she was praying. Or eating. I don't think she was thinking about steamed snow peas, but. Doug Walcott's eyes were bigger than really swollen big toes. (I've never seen any, but Dad told me.) Aunty Bev was standing up, ropeable, looking like she was gunna do me.

I had to move quickly. I pointed to all the chocolate planets on the floor.

'Our whole galaxy,' I said, 'is in a cluster with hundreds of other galaxies.'

I held up a piece of chocolate nut cluster to illustrate the point.

'There are thousands of galaxy clusters in the universe,' I said, chucking fistfuls of chocolate nut clusters into the air. 'And there are even clusters of galaxy clusters.'

Before I could get on to how they're called superclusters and there are ten million of them in the universe, Aunty Bev grabbed me. She didn't look as amazed as I'd hoped she would. I could see I had to finish the experiment fast.

I looked around at the other stunned faces in the room. Then I concentrated all my look on Mum.

'Millions of planets in millions of galaxies in millions of superclusters,' I said to her. 'Makes you feel really small, doesn't it.'

RESULTS

1. I got sent to bed.
2. After the others had gone, Mum spent ages out the back staring up at the stars and planets. Dad

was with her. I peeked and saw them. Then they went into the shed.

3. Next morning all my chocolate planets and galaxies had vanished. I didn't ask Mum where they were and she didn't say.

4. I felt a bit depressed. What if the experiment had been a flop? I needed chocolate to give me hope. But there weren't even any asteroids under the coffee table.

5. I needn't have worried. That night me and Mum and Dad all had dinner together in the kitchen. Sausage and onion sandwiches. Even the bread was fried. And chocolate nut clusters for dessert. It was out of this world.

CONCLUSION

Science is really good, and I'm not just saying that to suck. Next project I'm going to attempt an even harder experiment. See if I can get Aunty Bev into shorts.

Odd Socques

Macques was dreading the spelling test.

The minute he walked into class and saw the substitute teacher sitting at Ms Conway's desk, he knew there'd be one.

Substitute teachers always did spelling tests.

'Good morning 6C,' said the substitute teacher. 'Ms Conway is away today. My name's Mr Green.'

Macques could see something bulging in Mr Green's jacket pocket.

Spelling test prizes.

'Good morning, Mr Green,' chanted the class.

'OK, 6C,' said Mr Green. 'I've heard you're very good at maths and spelling. Would you rather have a maths test or a spelling test?'

Macques sighed gloomily.

He knew exactly what was coming.

'Spelling,' yelled the class.

Mr Green looked around at all the shining

eyes and excited faces. He allowed himself a quiet smile.

A spelling class.

He'd spotted it the minute they walked in.

Then Mr Green spotted something else. A boy up the back, a boy with brown hair and a sad face, who didn't seem very delighted at all.

Can't be helped, thought Mr Green. Every class has at least one bad speller.

He pulled the bag of mini chocolate bars from his jacket pocket and waited for the cheer a teacher with lollies always got.

It didn't happen.

Mr Green looked around the class, surprised.

'A mini chocolate bar for every word you get right,' he said, in case this lot were a bit slow and didn't get how substitute teacher spelling tests worked.

Still no cheer.

Mr Green felt a moment of panic.

But only a moment. The class were still looking excited and enthusiastic. Eyes still gleaming and lots of smiles. Except the boy up the back.

How unusual, thought Mr Green. This lot seem to like spelling tests more than they like lollies.

He decided to keep the words simple, in case he was right the first time and they were a bit slow.

'OK,' he said. 'First word. Pivot. Hands up.'

Hands shot up.

Mr Green chose a girl at the front.

'P-I-V-O-T,' said Jane Dillon.

'Good,' said Mr Green and tossed her a chocolate. 'Next word, diesel.'

Sam Webster got it right.

Over the next few minutes the class also got snail, patch, gravity, blood, digital, drought, tickle and splash.

Macques wasn't surprised. He knew from experience the class were good spellers.

They'll probably get every single one, he thought gloomily. Until Mr Green asks them the one they're waiting for.

Which, a few minutes later, Mr Green did.

'Fax,' he said, taking another mini chocolate bar from the bag. 'Listen carefully. Not facts, fax.'

Every hand in the room shot up. Except Macques's.

Mr Green pointed to Tina Walsh.

'F-A-C-Q-U-E-S,' said Tina.

Mr Green looked at her, his hand frozen in mid-toss, the mini chocolate bar still between his fingers.

Strange, he thought. I wasn't told about any special needs students in this class. Perhaps she's just a comedian.

He gave her a quick frown, then pointed to the boy next to her.

'You have a go,' he said. 'Fax.'

'F-A-C-Q-U-E-S,' said Garth Spence.

Mr Green felt his face going hot.

OK, he knew what this was. Not a spelling test. A substitute teacher test.

Mr Green took a deep breath. He prided himself on always passing such tests. Well, almost always. There was the one unfortunate incident when he'd shouted at a boy for several minutes from a distance of about three centimetres, but that was months ago.

Mr Green unwrapped the untossed chocolate bar, popped it into his mouth and savoured it like he was at a wine tasting.

This didn't get the laugh he'd hoped for, but at least he was showing them he was in control.

'Let me help you,' he said to the class. 'Here's another word very similar to fax. Sax. It's short for saxaphone, my favourite musical instrument. Any jazz fans here?'

Everybody put their hands up, except the sad boy.

Mr Green had a feeling this class probably weren't jazz fans, but he pressed on.

'You,' he said, pointing to a girl. 'The word is sax.'

'S-A-C-Q-U-E-S,' said Lilly Potter.

Mr Green hestitated, not sure what to do next.

Move on to 'tax', or a maths test?

'Sir,' said a boy at the front. 'There is one person in the class who might know. His name is . . .'

The boy was trying not to giggle and he spluttered the name as he said it, but Mr Green was pretty sure it was 'Max'.

Mr Green smiled to himself. Perhaps this was a trap, perhaps it wasn't. Either way he'd win. Always easier to punish one ringleader than a whole class.

'Thank you,' he said to the boy at the front. 'Max, where are you? Stand up please.'

Slowly Macques stood up.

He didn't try to explain. He'd tried with too many other substitute teachers and he always got the blame anyway.

He knew the rest of the class were watching him. He knew they were struggling not to laugh. They always preferred to do their laughing a bit later, after the substitute teacher had got angry.

'Max,' said Mr Green. 'Spell your name for us please.'

'M-A-C-Q-U-E-S,' said Macques, wishing for the millionth time in his life that his parents hadn't done this to him.

As usual, Macques walked home from school on his own.

Near the corner of his street he heard somebody running up behind him.

Macques told himself to relax. He reminded himself that the bullying almost never happened this close to the house. But when he turned to see who it was, he still felt a jolt of anxiety.

It was Sam Webster.

'That sucked,' said Sam. 'When that substitute teacher yelled at you. Unfair.'

Macques glanced nervously up and down the street. Sam Webster usually hung out in a gang and he didn't usually have anything to say to Macques. So why was he here now?

Macques could only think of one reason. The street sign a couple of metres away. The one showing the name of Macques's street.

Knocques Avenue.

Macques glared up at the sign like he did every afternoon. He wished he could rip it down. If only someone had done that ages ago, before its stupid spelling had inspired Mum and Dad when they were looking for baby name ideas.

But it was still there and now it was the perfect mocking spot.

Max braced himself for a mocking.

Then he saw that Sam was glancing nervously up and down the street too.

'Can you keep a secret?' muttered Sam.

Macques peered around again. He couldn't see anyone else from school lurking about. He hesitated for a moment, wondering if Sam was for real. Could you trust a kid who flicked snot at substitute teachers behind their backs?

There was a kind of haunted look on Sam's face that made Macques want to trust him.

'Yes,' said Macques quietly. 'I can keep a secret.'

'Let's keep walking,' said Sam. 'I don't want anybody to hear this.'

They walked along Macques's street.

Macques waited for Sam to speak.

Sam looked as though he was having some sort of pain, possibly in the guts. Macques wondered if Sam had an allergy to mini chocolate bars.

Poor bloke, he thought, that'd be a bit rough.

Finally Sam spoke.

'I've got a dumb name too,' he muttered.

Macques looked at Sam, surprised.

Sam wasn't a silly name, nor was Webster, so it must be a secret middle one. Parents did all sorts of bad things with middle names. The worst ones were usually from dead pop singers or footy players. Elvis and Archibald, stuff like that.

Macques waited for Sam to unburden himself.

'Sam isn't spelt S-A-M,' said Sam, staring at the footpath. 'It's spelt S-A-H-M.'

Macques looked at him, even more surprised.

'My parents didn't want me to have an ordinary name,' said Sahm gloomily. 'They wanted me to be special and different and um, what's that other thing, unique.'

Macques knew all about parents wanting that.

'But . . .' said Macques. 'How did you . . . I mean how come nobody knows? How come you don't get the same treatment as me?'

Sahm glanced up and down the street again.

'I was lucky,' he said. 'When I enrolled in school the office got it wrong. They thought S-A-H-M was a spelling mistake, so they put me down as S-A-M. My parents never found out. Nor did the other kids.

But next year we go to high school. Nobody gets that lucky twice in a row. What can I do?'

Macques thought about this.

'How come your parents haven't spotted that the school is spelling your name wrong?' he asked. 'The school sends letters home all the time.'

Sahm didn't seem to hear the question.

Macques wasn't suprised.

Sahm's face was desperate and pleading. Obviously all he could think about was avoiding six years of high school bullying and misery.

Macques knew exactly how Sahm felt.

For a few seconds Macques hesitated.

Should he tell Sahm his secret? It was risky. He hadn't told anybody his confidential plan to survive high school. If it got into the wrong hands, the whole thing would be ruined and the next six years would be as bad as the last six had been.

But Sahm needed his help.

'Listen,' said Macques quietly. 'I've been talking on a chat site to some other kids with tragic names like ours. They reckon they know people who can hack into any school computer in Australia. These people charge a lot, but I'm saving up. Once I've enrolled in high school, I'm going to chuck my student card away, pay them to hack in and change my name to the proper spelling, then get a replacement card.'

Macques realised he was out of breath, even though he and Sahm had reached Macques's front gate and had stopped walking.

Sahm's eyes were shining.

'It's two hundred dollars,' said Macques. 'Can you save that much?'

Sahm didn't reply. He stuck his hands into his pockets.

'If they do yours at the same time as mine,' said Macques, 'perhaps I can get them to charge you a cheaper price.'

Sahm still didn't say anything.

Macques understood. Sahm was probably in shock about how expensive a safe and happy high school education was these days. Macques was feeling very stressed himself. If any of the kids at school found out about this . . .

Suddenly Sahm gave a big relieved grin.

'Thanks,' he said, and slapped Macques on the back.

'Think about it,' said Macques. 'If you want to give it a go, let me know.'

'I will,' said Sahm. 'Thank you so much. You're a legend.'

For a second Macques thought his new friend was going to burst into tears. Sam was struggling to keep his face under control.

Poor bloke, thought Macques. I won't invite him in. Give him a bit of time on his own to calm himself down.

He gave Sahm a wave and headed for the front door.

On his way there, he had a nagging thought. The way Sahm had slapped him on the back. Kids at school didn't usually do that. Not unless . . .

At the front door Macques turned and glanced back at Sahm. And saw the giggling faces of the rest of the gang, crouching in the hedge.

Sahm, or rather Sam, didn't look tearful any more. He was laughing even harder than the others.

Macques managed to get the key in the lock. Inside, once the door was shut, he squeezed his eyes closed and struggled with his own tears.

Real ones.

Then he wiped his eyes and checked his back in the hall mirror. He wasn't surprised to see something stuck there.

A yellow post-it note with two words scrawled on it.

Tricqued You.

Macques waited until dinner time to have another go at Mum and Dad.

'Please let me change my name,' he begged. 'Please let me spell it M-A-X.'

Mum and Dad looked at each other.

They both sighed, but they didn't say anything until they'd finished chewing their mouthfuls of pan-seared swordfish with balsamic vinegar and pink peppercorns.

'Darling,' said Mum. 'We've explained this to

you so often. Macques is a lovely name. It's special and distinctive and unique. Like you.'

'Forget those pea-brains at school,' said Dad. 'Once you're out in the big wide world, you'll be glad you've got a name that people notice. In those hospitals or TV stations or nuclear research facilities or wherever you end up working, there'll be all the ordinary Maxes, but only one Macques.'

Mum and Dad both glowed.

Macques wasn't sure if it was from pride or pink peppercorns.

'I want to be an ordinary Max,' he said.

This time Mum and Dad didn't wait till they'd finished chewing.

'That is crazy talk,' said Mum. 'You are not ordinary.'

'I am,' said Macques.

'Rubbish,' said Dad. 'When you were born we decided we weren't going to let you be ordinary. That's why we didn't give you a boring ordinary name like our parents gave us.'

'Eric and Joan are nice names,' said Macques.

Mum and Dad both sighed crossly.

'When will you get it into your head?' said Dad. 'You won't stand out in the crowd if people think you're ordinary and boring.'

'Why do you think me and Dad go to so much trouble?' said Mum.

Macques knew what was coming next.

Mum swung her feet out from under the table,

pulled up the legs of her black tracksuit and pointed to her socks. One was pink, one was orange.

'I'm the only person at the gym with odd socks,' she said. 'Nobody there thinks I'm ordinary.'

Dad twanged his braces. They had green sheep on them.

'One look at my braces,' said Dad, 'and everyone in my office knows I'm not ordinary.'

'Do you see, Macques?' said Mum. 'Do you see what we're saying?'

Macques replied through gritted teeth.

'Yes,' he said. 'You're saying that the reason you drive the same foreign cars as everyone else and wear the same designer clothes as everyone else and eat the same swordfish with balsamic vinegar and pink peppercorns as everyone else is so everyone will think you're not ordinary.'

'Macques,' said Mum.

'Careful, young man,' said Dad.

'But you are ordinary,' said Macques. 'I am too.'

Macques realised he was standing up and shouting and several of his pink peppercorns were on the handwoven Icelandic tablecloth.

He didn't care.

'I just want us to be an ordinary family,' he pleaded.

'Macques,' yelled Mum. 'Stop yelling. We do not yell in this house.'

'Go to your room,' said Dad with icy calm. 'Have a long hard think. I don't want to see you or hear a peep from you until you come to your senses.'

'Nor do I,' said Mum.

Macques threw himself onto his bed and buried his face in his Scandinavian-style organic goose-down pillow.

I can't take it any more, he thought desperately.

He used to think he could.

He used to think that if he got through life one day at a time, he could make it to his eighteenth birthday and then leave home and change his name.

Not any more.

'Help,' he whispered into his pillow. 'I need help.'

Then he stopped. One thing he'd learned in life was that pillows couldn't help with the really big problems. Small ones, like being tired or having a stiff neck, yes. Big ones, like war and disease and having a stupid name, no.

The other reason Macques stopped was that somebody was tapping at his window.

He jumped up.

Even before he opened the curtain, Macques felt anger burning through him.

Sam Webster and his gang. Still loitering in the front yard. Still hoping to get a bit more taunting and mocking in before bedtime.

Thank you Sam, thought Macques grimly. You don't know it, but I'm very glad you're still here.

When I haul you in through that window and drag you down to Mum and Dad, then maybe they'll understand.

Macques flung the curtains open.

And stared.

It wasn't Sam and his mates.

Four other kids were standing outside looking at Macques through the glass. It was dark out there, but the light from the room shone on their faces. Two boys and two girls, all wearing white overalls. Macques had never seen any of them before.

One of the boys signalled to Macques to open the window.

Macques hesitated. Then he saw that the boy had a name tag on his overalls. It said *Nickless.*

Max opened the window.

'G'day,' said the boy. 'Unfair Name Rescue Squad. Are you Macques spelled M-A-C-Q-U-E-S?'

Dazed, Macques nodded.

'We're here to rescue you,' said the boy.

Macques didn't understand.

He saw that the others had name tags too. The other boy's said *Shorn.* The girls' were *Jeen* and *Kaitye.*

'Sorry we've taken a while to get to you,' said Jeen. 'Big backlog.'

'Unfair Name Rescue Squad?' said Macques.

Then he realised what was going on. It was another trick. The most complicated piece of bullying and mockery yet. These kids weren't even from his school. Somebody must have paid them.

'Do you want to be rescued?' said Kaitye.

Macques nodded.

He could see they'd even got a taxi waiting out in the street. It was perfect. He'd pretend to go along with them, and when they all got to the taxi he'd yell for Mum and Dad. Then Mum and Dad would see the sort of thing an unfair name did for you and they really would understand.

Macques opened the window wider.

'No need to bring anything,' said Shorn.

This lot are very good, thought Macques as they helped him down from the window. Perhaps they're a high school drama group.

As he hurried across the front yard with them, Macques had a thought. A quick flash of a thought that was stupid but he had it anyway because it felt so good even just for a fleeting moment.

How incredible and amazing and wonderful it would be if the Unfair Name Rescue Squad was real.

No.

Impossible.

Don't even hope.

Then Macques saw the lit-up sign on the roof of the taxi.

TACQUESI.

'Don't worry,' said Nickless, who was sitting next to Macques in the back of the taxi. 'This won't take long.'

'Only round the block,' said Jeen.

'Just as well these rescues are quick,' said Shorn from the front. 'We've got three more jobs tonight.'

Macques felt a stab of panic as they sped away down the dark street, partly because he'd always promised Mum and Dad he'd never get into a taxi with people he didn't know, and partly because Kaitye was driving and he was pretty sure she was too young to have a licence or third-party insurance.

At the top end of Macques's street they turned the corner.

'Where are you from?' asked Macques.

He wanted them to be real, he did so much, but part of his brain kept saying *TV show* and *I wonder where the camera's hidden*.

'The UNRS operates all over the world,' said Nickless. 'Thousands of us. And we're all flat out.'

'Dunno who kicked off this craze for dodgy names,' said Jeen. 'They should be locked up.'

The taxi turned another corner.

'Where are we going?' asked Macques.

'Home,' said Shorn.

'Your home,' said Kaitye.

Macques didn't understand.

'Your real home,' said Nickless.

Macques still didn't understand.

He was still trying to work out what they meant, and wondering if the TV show host was in the boot, when the taxi made the final turn of the block into the bottom end of Macques's street.

Macques knew it was his street because through the taxi window he could see the street sign, clear as anything in the light from a street lamp.

Knox Avenue.

Macques stared.

'Look,' he said. 'The spelling's changed. It's Knox, K-N-O-X.'

'That's right,' said Jeen.

Macques felt dizzy. Not in a horrible I'm-going-to-throw-up way. In a nice this-is-very-weird-but-I-don't-want-it-to-end way.

The taxi stopped outside Macques's house.

'That's it,' said Nickless. 'We're done. You're rescued.'

Nickless got out.

Macques realised he was meant to get out too, but he was finding it hard to actually move.

'Go,' said Shorn. 'We're on a schedule.'

Macques got out.

'How do I know this isn't all a dream?' he heard himself say to Nickless.

Nickless smiled and Macques had the feeling Nickless got asked that question a lot.

'How do you know all that stuff before we arrived wasn't a dream?' said Nickless.

Macques wished his thoughts weren't so scrambled. He felt like one of those characters in a science fiction movie who gets taken at warp-speed into another dimension and arrives with bulging eyes and sticking-out hair and a smoking brain.

He put his hand to his head. His hair felt fine. But then he had only been round the block.

'Hope you like your parents,' said Nickless, getting back into the taxi and pulling the door shut.

Macques wasn't sure he'd heard that right. But it was too late to check. The taxi was driving away.

He gave the Unfair Name Rescue Squad a wave and watched the lit-up sign on the top of the taxi disappear into the darkness.

TAXI, it said.

Inside the house, everything looked exactly the same.

Well, almost. The wallpaper was a bit different, and the carpet, and there was a pine dresser in the hallway Macques didn't completely remember.

Macques stared at his reflection in the hall mirror.

His face looked the same and he felt wide awake.

There was nothing stuck to his back.

'Dinner's ready,' sang out Mum's voice.

Macques went into the living room. Mum and Dad were sitting at the table. They looked exactly the same too.

Well, almost.

They both looked slightly plumper and Mum's hair was curly instead of straight.

Macques started to feel a little bit panicked.

Then he saw something that made the panic go away. The big loving smiles on Mum and Dad's faces.

'Tuck in,' said Mum.

On the table were three plates of fish and chips. Mum was already stuffing quite a few chips into her mouth at once.

'Come on,' said Dad, winking at Macques. 'Make the most of it. You'll probably only be living at home for another ten years or so. Get Mum's cooking into you while you have the chance.'

Macques did just that. It was the best fish and chips he'd ever tasted. The more chips he put into his mouth, the happier he felt.

There were lots of questions buzzing around in his head, but they could wait till later.

Except one.

After a few more mouthfuls, Macques decided to get it over with.

'Mum and Dad,' he said. 'Can you test my spelling?'

Mum and Dad looked a bit nervous.

'OK,' said Dad. 'But we're pretty ordinary spellers.'

Macques couldn't help smiling to himself. Last time he'd asked Mum and Dad for a spelling test, they'd given him words like vicissitude and extracurricular and had gone on for hours about how important a big and impressive vocabulary was.

'You give me the word,' said Macques, 'and I'll spell it.'

'OK,' said Mum.

'Start with my name,' said Macques.

'You kind thing,' said Mum. 'Letting us all kick off with an easy one.'

'OK,' said Dad. 'Here goes.'

'Max,' said Mum.

'M-A-X,' said Macques.

He held his breath.

'Correct,' said Mum and Dad, grinning at him. 'Very good.'

Max grinned back. They were right, it was very good.

As Mum leaned over and gave him a hug, Max took a peek at her socks.

Both grey.

They were ordinary and they matched.

Ashes To Ashes

It's the last half-hour of the fifth cricket test. I can hardly breathe.

I feel almost as woozy as poor Grandad must have felt a month ago when his insides packed up and his innings finally came to an end.

The whole Ashes test series is hanging in the balance. We've won two matches and England have won two.

This is the decider.

It'll all be over soon. England need twelve more runs and they're batting well. Australia need one more wicket and they're bowling like year threes. And I'm sitting here in the northern stand holding something that could help Australia win this match, and the whole series, and the Ashes.

I'm holding some other ashes.

Grandad's ashes.

'Whoo,' says Pino, 'Look at her.'

My friend Pino isn't interested in cricket. He's only interested in girls. He's been that way for most of year seven. He only agreed to come to the cricket today because he reckons it's a top place to meet girls who aren't your sisters or aunties.

'Nice,' says Pino, leaning forward in his seat. His eyes are so wide the green and yellow stripes on his face are going bendy.

I asked Pino to come today because he's brave and reckless. You'd have to be to talk to girls who are complete strangers. When I try and do it, my mouth stops working and my fingers go all twisted like a spin bowler's.

But I'm not here for girls today, I'm here for something much more important. That's why I asked Pino. I need his help to do something even more dangerous than talk to girls.

'That one,' says Pino, nudging me so hard I almost drop the urn. 'The one with her dad.'

I try to see who he's pointing at. I can't. There are sixty thousand people in this stadium and about six thousand of them are girls with their dads.

'If I'm not back in five minutes,' says Pino, 'tell my mum I'm getting married.'

I try to stop him. I try to remind him that his parents don't even think he's mature enough to use the slicing machine in their deli, so it's unlikely they'll agree to a wedding.

'Come with me,' says Pino. 'She might have a friend.'

I shake my head.

Even the thought of it makes my hands go all googly.

'Tragic,' says Pino, looking at me not very sympathetically.

Then he's gone.

And time's running out.

Relax, I tell myself. He'll be back soon. He's left his lollies.

England score two more runs.

I check the breeze. And nearly have a serious Grandad-sized heart failure. The wind has changed direction. It's blowing towards us now. We'll have to go all the way over to the other side of the stadium to do what we have to do.

'Don't worry, Grandad,' I whisper to the urn. 'We'll make it.'

I try to sound more confident than I feel.

Pino comes back, frowning.

'I was wrong,' he says. 'She's not very nice. Neither's her dad.'

I can see them both now. They're looking across at Pino and laughing at him in an unkind sort of way.

I should be a good friend and tell Pino that the face paint probably isn't helping, or the hanky he's got tied round his head with *England sucks* scrawled on it.

But there isn't time.

'Change of plan,' I say. 'We have to go over to the other side and scatter my grandad's ashes there.'

Pino stares at me.

'Why?' he says. 'Your grandad just wants to be laid to rest on hollowed turf. Why does it matter which side?'

'Hallowed,' I say. 'Test cricket turf is called hallowed.'

'Whatever,' says Pino. 'In his will your grandad just asked to be scattered on a test cricket pitch, that's what you said. He didn't mention anything about which side.'

'Actually,' I confess, 'he didn't mention anything about a test cricket pitch either. But I know it's where he'd want to be. He loved cricket even more than beer.'

I shudder as I think what Mum and Dad will do when they find that Grandad's urn isn't on the kitchen shelf any more. That's if they notice. They're probably still too busy arguing about where to scatter him.

'Look at it this way,' says Pino. 'People don't care which side of the glass they drink beer from and they don't care which side of a test cricket pitch they're scattered on. It's gunna be hard enough fighting our way onto the pitch with everyone else at the end of the match. At least over this side we're close to the fence.'

I start to explain to Pino that the plan has changed from the one I told him this morning. That we're going to do more than just lay Grandad to rest on hallowed turf. Much more. And we don't need to be near the fence to do it. The most important thing now is wind direction.

Then I stop.

We're running out of time.

'The girls over the other side might be nicer,' I say.

Pino follows me without another word.

In the tunnel that leads to the other side of the stadium, I explain the new plan.

'Scatter the ashes in the air?' says Pino. 'Why?'

'So Australia can win,' I say.

Pino looks puzzled.

We can't see the pitch, but I can hear the England supporters cheering. England must have scored more runs.

I explain the new plan in detail.

'There are millions of bits of Grandad in here,' I say, shaking the urn. 'With the wind behind them, chances are at least one of the bits will end up in an English batsman's eye.'

Pino thinks about this.

'So he can't see properly,' says Pino.

'Yes,' I say.

'So he gets bowled,' says Pino.

'Exactly,' I say.

'So Australia wins,' says Pino.

'Spot on,' I say.

He's pretty smart for someone who doesn't know much about cricket.

'That is so stupid,' says Pino.

I look at him.

Smart, but not very confident about the future.

I think it must come from talking to girls.

When we hurry out of the tunnel I look across at the scoreboard.

England only need six more runs.

'Come on,' I say to Pino. We run up the steps.

I reckon the highest part of the stadium will be the best place for scattering ashes. I can see big sliding windows behind the back row of seats. They're open for ventilation, and a strong breeze is blowing through them and gusting towards us as we climb higher.

'Anyway,' pants Pino. 'Why would your grandad want Australia to win? He was from England, wasn't he? That's like my dad wanting Italy to lose at soccer. My whole family would put their heads in the meat slicer before they'd want that.'

I explain about Grandad.

'He wanted England to lose at everything,' I say. 'He hated the place because he had such an unhappy childhood there. His parents were very strict. He got bullied a lot by other boys. Girls thought he was a nerd.'

'Sounds pretty normal,' mutters Pino.

More applause from parts of the crowd. England have scored two more runs.

We reach the back row of seats.

'Right,' I say to Pino. 'Go over there and do

something that'll make everybody look at you.'

Pino hesitates, uncertain.

'People mustn't see me scattering Grandad,' I say. 'It's a serious crime, temporarily blinding a tail-ender batsman.'

Pino thinks about this.

'OK,' he says. 'But if you get arrested, I'll have to pretend I don't know you. Or your grandad.'

'Of course,' I say quietly.

Pino goes along behind the seats.

Clutching Grandad to my chest, I loosen the lid of the urn and unscrew it with as little movement as possible and slip the lid into my back pocket.

'What have you got there?' says a voice.

I try and stuff Grandad out of sight as well, but my t-shirt's not baggy enough.

'We did that once,' says the voice.

It's a girl.

She's about my age and she's sitting at the end of the back row, staring at the urn and grinning.

I try to control my panic. I also try to remember if Australia has won any other test series because a tail-ender batsman got something in his eye.

'Our cat Warnie died,' says the girl. 'He loved cricket, but he'd only ever seen it on telly, so we brought his ashes here for a squiz.'

I don't know what to say. It's the same as always. Whenever I try to have a conversation with a girl, my brain feels like Ricky Ponting has whacked it with his bat. Must be a gene I inherited from

Grandad. The nerd gene. Actually I think I'm even more of a nerd than he was. At least Grandad ended up married. I'm probably going to end up on my own, babysitting Pino's kids.

'Pretty funny, eh,' says the girl, still looking up at me. 'Bringing ashes to see who wins the Ashes.'

She's got the friendliest grin I've ever seen.

I open my mouth, trying to think of something to say to her that can't be used against me later in court.

Before I can speak, a commotion starts up further along the row of seats. It's Pino, yelling and clapping.

'England sucks,' he chants. 'England sucks, England sucks, England sucks.'

Everyone, including the girl, turns to look at him.

I don't waste a second.

'Bye, Grandad,' I whisper.

I grip Grandad in both hands and swing the urn in a big movement so all his ashes fly out into the wind. Which, I realise too late, isn't blowing towards the pitch any more. It's changed direction again. It's blowing towards me, and towards the huge ventilation windows behind me.

Grandad swirls around the back of the stand for a few seconds, then disappears out through the windows.

Frantic, I dive after him, but it's too late.

I stick my head through one of the open windows.

I can just make out the dusty cloud that is Grandad, getting fainter by the second as he's blown down into the busy street below.

He's being scattered among people who don't even know he's there. People getting on with their busy lives. Squabbling about parking spaces. Laughing at other people who've dropped their shopping. Walking past a charity collector and ignoring her.

I can see bits of Grandad landing on a mother who is smacking her crying toddler. And on several big kids who are chasing after a small kid.

Instead of laying Grandad to rest on hallowed turf, I've dumped him in the middle of people doing nasty things.

Things that aren't cricket.

Suddenly, behind me, the crowd roars and groans all at once.

I turn round.

England have scored a boundary.

Four runs.

Both English batsmen are standing with their arms in the air. Our players have slumped. Some are crouching with their heads in their hands. Others are sitting dejectedly on the grass as if they've just tried to talk to a girl and been laughed at.

We've lost.

England have won the match. And the whole test series. And the Ashes.

I turn back to the window. I can't even see

Grandad down in the street now. Not one single tiny bit of him.

'Well,' says Pino, coming over. 'That was successful.'

'Sorry, Grandad,' I whisper.

We head towards the exit. Most of the departing crowd are looking unhappy. I bet they don't feel as unhappy as me.

Losing a test series is bad, but not as bad as what I've done.

Pino isn't looking happy either. There were groups of England fans up the back of the stand when he was chanting, and he's worried about what they'll do to him if they see him. He's taken his *England Sucks* hanky off and stuffed it in his pocket.

We're in the street now.

I look down, just in case there are any specks of Grandad on the footpath. It's no good, my eyesight isn't strong enough. Anyway, even if I did see some bits of ash, how would I know it was Grandad and not the remains of a cigarette or a cricket-loving cat?

'Sorry, Grandad,' I whisper again. 'Sorry you ended up somewhere you didn't want to be.'

Grandad always hated crowded streets. He was always worried someone would jostle him and he'd drop his shopping. And if someone squabbled with him about a parking spot, he'd always give in.

I look up from the footpath.

All around me, people are rubbing their eyes.

The mother who was smacking the toddler is rubbing hers while the toddler chuckles happily.

The big kids who were chasing the small kid are rubbing theirs while the small kid disappears into a side street.

The people who were laughing at the dropped shopping are rubbing theirs with both hands. One of them is dropping his shopping while he does it.

This is weird.

I should be feeling guilty, but instead I'm getting a strange feeling. A feeling that this is where Grandad wants to be. I can't explain it. But the more I look around, the stronger I feel it.

Then I see something else.

'Look,' I say.

Pino ducks behind a bus shelter. He thinks I've seen some England fans. But that's not what I'm pointing at.

It's the girl from the back row of the stand. She's with a man who's bent forward with his hands over his eyes.

'Careful, Dad,' she says. 'Let me try and get it out.'

'Gently, love,' he replies. 'It feels like grit.'

Before I have a chance to think what I'm doing, I grab the hanky from Pino's pocket, lick the corner and go over to the girl and her father.

'Um,' I say. 'Excuse me. My dad's a demolition contractor and he works with dust all the time. This is something my grandad taught us.'

I gently hold one of the father's eyes open with my thumb and forefinger, and dab away the tears with Pino's hanky. A bit of the texta Pino used for the writing gets on the father's eye socket, but I'm sure he won't mind.

With the corner of the hanky I flick a couple of bits of Grandad out of the father's eye. Then I do the other side.

Once the girl's father can see again, he gives me a grateful look.

'Thank you very much, young man,' he says.

Oh no. Now he's peering at me as if he's seen me before but he's not sure where.

I hope the girl won't tell him. I hope she won't say anything about bringing ashes to the Ashes and unpredictable wind changes. If the people in this street hear, they'll lynch me.

She doesn't.

'Thanks,' she says to me, grinning again. Then she steps very close and murmurs something else. 'Next time you bring a member of your family to the cricket, give the rest of us some warning, OK?'

'OK,' I say.

She turns to Pino, who's staring at us both, stunned.

'What's your friend's name?' she asks him.

'Um . . .' he says.

'Mark Smalley,' I say, amazed how easily the words come out.

'I'm Alice,' says the girl.

'G'day Alice,' I say.

'Well, Mark,' says Alice's father. 'If you end up being an eye doctor, let us know. We'll be your first clients.'

'Actually,' I say, 'I'm planning on being a Porsche dealer. Or a test cricketer.'

Alice doesn't laugh, or mock, or chuck me one of those 'as if' looks. She just gives me another friendly smile.

'See you around,' she says, and I can see she means it.

'Thanks again,' says her father.

'Nice to meet you,' I say as they head into the crowd.

Pino seems to have lost the power of speech.

I, on the other hand, suddenly feel like I could rabbit on till midnight. With Alice or any one of the other five thousand nine hundred and ninety-nine girls leaving the cricket stadium.

But I don't. What I want to say only needs two words.

'Thanks, Grandad,' I whisper.

101 Text Messages You Must Read Before You Die

DEAR RO HERE IT IS MY FIRST ONE WITHOUT YOUR HELP PRETTY GOOD EH JEEZ FINDING THE LETTERS TAKES AGES ANYWAY MY TEXT MESSAGE IS CAN I HAVE A CUP OF TEA PLEASE
LOVE DAD

RO ARE YOU THERE

DAD TO RO BUNG THE KETTLE ON

COME ON RO ITS THIRSTY WORK HERE IN THE ORCHARD NOW WEVE DECIDED TO GO ORGANIC AND STOP USING SPRAYS AND I HAVE TO YELL AT THE BUGS TO GET OFF THE APPLES

RO WAKE UP IM DRYER THAN A WALLABYS WASHING

OOPS DOPEY ME YOU CANT READ THIS IF YOURE STILL ASLEEP AND I DONT BLAME YOU IF YOU ARE AFTER WHAT THOSE CHEESE BRAINS DID TO YOU AT SCHOOL LAST NIGHT

DONT WORRY LOVE IM COMING UP TO THE HOUSE

GET OFF THAT APPLE YOU MONGREL

SORRY RO NOT YOU

OOPS JUST REMEMBERED WHAT YOU TOLD ME ABOUT KEEPING THE WORDS SHORT IN TXTS

TRBLE IS WHN I DO I CANT UNDRSTND WHT IM SAYNG ITS A CMPLT MNGRL

BACK TO BIG WORDS NO SWEAT IVE GOT STRONG THUMBS I CAN HANDLE IT I DONT KNOW HOW YOU KIDS CAN UNDERSTAND ABBRV ABBRIV SHORT WORDS

HEY IM GETTING FASTER AT THIS ALMOST AT THE HOUSE NOW IGNORE THIS IF YOURE STILL SNOOZING

YOURE NOT STILL SNOOZING WHERE ARE YOU LOVE YOUR BEDS EMPTY AND SO ARE YOUR JARMIES AND YOURE NOT IN THE SHOWER OR THE KITCHEN OR THE HALL CUPBOARD

I BET YOURE UP THE BACK PADDOCK GIVING THE LONG GRASS A WALLOPING AND PRETENDING ITS MR CHEESE BRAIN GLOSSOP GOOD GIRL HE DESERVES TO HAVE HIS EDGES TRIMMED AFTER WHAT HE DID TO US LAST NIGHT

THE MONGREL

THIS CROOK MOBILE RECEPTION IN THE BUSH IS A PAIN IN THE APPLES I MEAN IF A BLOKE WANTS TO RING UP HIS DAUGHTER BY VOICE TO SEE IF SHES OK HE CANT YEAH I KNOW TEXTS ARE BEST FOR YOU RO BUT IT STILL GETS UP MY NOSE

GIVE THAT BACK PADDOCK AN EXTRA WHACK FROM ME LOVE BUT SEND ME A TEXT FIRST SO I KNOW YOURE OK

HANG ON IM UP ON THE ROOF NOW AND I CAN SEE THE BACK PADDOCK AND YOURE NOT THERE

ALSO YOURE NOT IN THE FRONT PADDOCK OR THE SIDE PADDOCK OR THE PACKING SHED

OH NO THE TRACTOR ISNT IN THE PACKING SHED EITHER

RO URGENT URGENT URGENT WHEREVER YOU ARE STOP DRIVING THE TRACTOR NOW AND TURN THE ENGINE OFF COMPLETELY AND GET AWAY FROM IT I KNOW YOURE ALLOWED TO DRIVE IT BUT THIS IS DIFFERENT SEE NEXT MESSAGE

DANGER FUEL TANK LEAKING

ITS FROM WHEN I ACCIDENTLY BACKED INTO THAT FOOTY CLUB BUS AFTER THEY LAUGHED AT YOU FOR SPEAKING WITH YOUR HANDS

OK I SHOULD HAVE GOT IT FIXED BUT I HAVENT HAD TIME WHAT WITH HELPING YOU PRACTISE FOR THE SCHOOL DEBATE AND LEARNING ORGANIC APPLE GROWING METHODS SO I PATCHED IT UP BUT IF THE CHEWY GIVES WAY IT COULD BE A BIT DANGEROUS

VERY DANGEROUS

THE TRACTOR COULD BLOW UP LOVE

TURN THE ENGINE OFF NOW RO OH JEEZ WHY ARENT YOU ANSWERING MY MESSAGES

IM ON THE GROUND WITH MY EAR IN THE DIRT TRYING TO HEAR WHICH DIRECTION YOUVE GONE BUT I CANT HEAR ANY ENGINE VIBRATIONS CAUSE THE GRASSHOPPERS ARE TOO LOUD

IF YOUVE TAKEN THE TRACTOR OVER TO NEXT DOORS ORCHARD TO PULL SCARY FACES AT THEIR INSECTS I WONT BE CROSS

RO TALK TO ME TELL ME WHERE YOU ARE TELL ME YOUVE DITCHED THE TRACTOR PLEASE

IM RUSHING ROUND THE HOUSE LIKE A MANIAC SEEING IF YOU LEFT A NOTE BUT THERE ISNT ONE IN THE KITCHEN OR THE LOUNGE OR TIED TO THE DOG WHY DO YOU CHOOSE A DIFFERENT PLACE EACH TIME

FOUND IT I SHOULD HAVE LOOKED ON THE TOILET DOOR FIRST OFF OK LETS SEE WHERE YOU ARE

OH JEEZ RO NO NO NO TAKING THE TRACTOR TO TOWN IS TOO FAR LISTEN ITS A BIT TECHNICAL BUT IF THE CHEWY OVERHEATS AND FUEL SPLASHES ONTO THE INTAKE MANIFOLD YOURE HISTORY

IM IN THE TRUCK IM COMING AFTER YOU

NO IM NOT THE TRUCK WONT START

IM SURE I PUT THOSE NEW SPARK PLUGS IN THE BATHROOM CABINET DID YOU MOVE THEM

FOUND THEM MY FAULT THEY WERE IN MY SOCK DRAWER

IM COMING AFTER YOU YOUR TYRE TRACKS IN THE DRIVEWAY LOOK FRESH SO I HOPE YOURE NOT TOO FAR AHEAD STOP DRIVING RO PLEASE

WICH WAY DID YOU GO MAIN ROAD OR BAK WAY SORRY ABOUT THE SPELING IM TEXTING ONE HANDED I REKON THE BAC WAY CAUSE YOUR A KID AND KIDS DRIVING TRACTRS ON MAIN RODS STIK OUT LIKE MOTHS BALLS

THATS BETTER STEERING WITH MY KNEES NOW BOTH HANDS FOR TEXTING RO ANSWER ME BUT FIRST PLEASE STOP THE TRACTOR AND RUN

OH NO ITS JUST HIT ME WHY YOURE NOT ANSWERING AND WHY YOU DON'T WANT TO STOP DRIVING INTO TOWN

REVENGE

LISTEN RO I AGREE WHAT THAT CHEESE BRAIN GLOSSOP DID LAST NIGHT WAS A CROOK THING

I DONT MEAN SNEERING AT MY ORANGE AND PURPLE COWBOY SHIRT I MEAN CHUCKING A BRILLIANT DEBATER OFF THE TEAM JUST CAUSE SHE WAS BORN WITH HER VOICE MISSING AND SHE HAS TO DEBATE WITH HER HANDS

IT WASNT YOUR FAULT THAT AMANDA WAS BEING REALLY SLOW TELLING THE OTHER TEAM WHAT YOU WERE SAYING SO I HAD TO HELP OUT

OK I WAS A BIT LOUD AT FIRST BUT THATS CAUSE I WAS STANDING UP THE BACK OF THE HALL

I WAS ONLY TRYING TO HELP

WHERE ARE YOU RO STOP THE TRACTOR PLEASE

I CANT STAND THIS EVERY TIME I GO ROUND A CORNER I THINK IM GUNNA SEE A BIG CLOUD OF SMOKE AND A BLOWN UP TRACTOR AND A BLOWN UP DAUGHTER

OK I DID GET A BIT CARRIED AWAY LAST NIGHT BUT ONLY BECAUSE OF THE DEBATING TOPIC

WHAT SORT OF DEBATING TOPIC IS WORDS SPEAK LOUDER THAN ACTIONS

WHAT AN INSULT

THERE YOU WERE SITTING ON THAT STAGE A TOP LIVING BREATHING EXAMPLE OF HOW ACTIONS ALWAYS SPEAK LOUDER THAN WORDS AND THEY STILL RECKONED THEY HAD TO DEBATE IT

SO I SAW RED APPLES AND DID SOME THINGS I SHOULDNT HAVE

ITS LIKE CARLA TAMWORTH SAYS IN HER CLASSIC SONG ABOUT THE BLOKE WHO DOESNT WANT TO ADMIT HES GOT A BOIL ON HIS BUM SO HE SITS ALL DAY ON HIS HORSE IN AGONY

YOUVE GOT TO STAND UP FOR THE TRUTH

ID SING IT TO YOU IF YOU WERE HERE JEEZ YOU MUST BE A LONG WAY IN FRONT IM DRIVING LIKE A MANIAC

NO IM NOT RO DONT WORRY IVE GOT VERY SAFE KNEES

PLEASE RO WHY DONT YOU STOP AND TURN THE TRACTOR OFF AND LET ME CATCH UP WITH YOU SO I CAN APOLOGISE

IM SORRY I WENT UP ON STAGE LAST NIGHT AND MUCKED UP THE DEBATE

I JUST WANTED TO MAKE SURE THEY GOT THAT BRILLIANT THING YOU SAID ABOUT ACTIONS SPEAKING LOUDER THAN WORDS EG PARENTS WHO MIME COUNTRY AND WESTERN SONGS TO THEIR KIDS IN THE BATH

THAT WAS ONE OF THE BEST DEBATING ARGUMENTS
IVE EVER HEARD AND THE ONLY REASON I SANG AT
THAT POINT WAS TO GIVE THEM AN EXAMPLE

I WOULD HAVE NICKED OFF THEN LIKE MR GLOSSOP
TOLD ME TO IF THAT CAPTAIN OF THE OTHER TEAM
HADNT GOT PERSONAL

WHEN HE SAID AN EXAMPLE OF WORDS SPEAKING
LOUDER THAN ACTIONS WAS PEOPLE WHO WORE
DUMB BELT BUCKLES WITH THE WORDS LOVE AND
DEATH ON THEM EVERYBODY IN THAT HALL KNEW
HE WAS TALKING ABOUT ME BECAUSE GLOSSOP
WAS WEARING BRACES

AS YOU KNOW I BOUGHT THAT SKELETON ON A
HARLEY BUCKLE TO WEAR AT YOUR MUMS FUNERAL
AND ITS VERY PRECIOUS TO ME SO I HAD TO
DEBATE HIM BACK

IM SORRY IT GOT US CHUCKED OUT AND IM SORRY
I SAID THAT STUPID THING DRIVING HOME ABOUT
HOW SOMEONE SHOULD TOW GLOSSOPS FLASH
NEW CAR INTO THE RIVER

I SHOULD NEVER HAVE SAID THOSE WORDS IN
FRONT OF A PERSON WHOS SO TOP AT DOING
ACTIONS

DONT DO IT RO IF YOU TRY AND TOW ANYTHING WITH THAT TRACTOR YOULL OVERSTRESS THE CHEWY

OH JEEZ IF THE TRACTOR BLOWS UP ILL NEVER FORGIVE MYSELF

WHERE ARE YOU LOVE I DONT GET IT IM PULLING INTO TOWN NOW AND THERES NO SIGN OF YOU.

DID I PASS YOU IN A DUST CLOUD ON THE DIRT TRACK AND NOT SEE YOU CAUSE THE TRACTOR HAD ALREADY BLOWN UP AND ALL THE BITS OF YOU ON THE ROAD WERE TOO SMALL

OH NO

BLACK SMOKE

DIRECTLY OVER THE SCHOOL CARPARK

NO PLEASE NO IF YOURE STILL ALIVE LOVE JUST LIE STILL DONT TRY TO MOVE IM GETTING TO YOU AS FAST AS I CAN

WHY DO PEOPLE HAVE SO MUCH GARDEN FURNITURE IT MAKES THEIR BACKYARDS REALLY HARD TO DRIVE THROUGH

HANG ON RO

HOW OFTEN AT P AND C MEETINGS HAVE I SAID THE SCHOOL CARPARK NEEDS A BACK ENTRANCE NOW ILL HAVE TO DRIVE THROUGH THE PETROL STATION FENCE

OUCH ITS OK IM NOT HURT

SHOULD HAVE LOOSENED MY BELT BUCKLE BEFORE THE IMPACT BUT ITS ONLY A FLESH WOUND

SMOKE EVERYWHERE NOW

RO WHERE ARE YOU

I CANT LOOK DON'T BE DEAD

WHAT HAVE I DONE

EVERYTHING I DO IS TO TRY AND PROTECT YOU THATS THE ONLY REASON I STOPPED THE SPRAYING PLUS AS YOU CORRECTLY POINTED OUT WHEN THE WIND BLOWS THE SPRAY ONTO THE WASHING IT ROTS THE ELASTIC IN MY UNDIES

BE ALIVE RO PLEASE

I WANT TO HAVE LOTS MORE DEBATES WITH YOU ABOUT WHETHER ORANGE GOES WITH PURPLE AND THE BEST RECIPE FOR APPLE FRITTERS EVEN THOUGH THE DOG WONT EAT THEM WHEN YOU PUT SALT IN THEM AND

WAIT A SEC

THAT SMOKE ISNT FROM THE TRACTOR ITS BLOWING ACROSS FROM DOUG THE WRECKER BURNING OLD TYRES OUT THE BACK OF HIS PLACE

I CANT EVEN SEE THE TRACTOR IN THE SCHOOL CARPARK ONLY GLOSSOPS CAR AS FLASH AS EVER AND NOT IN THE RIVER

OH JEEZ RO

THERES THE TRACTOR PARKED IN THE PETROL STATION WORKSHOP AND THERES YOU SHOWING THE FUEL TANK TO THE MECHANICS

YOU DROVE IT IN TO GET IT FIXED

YOU KNEW I WAS BUSY IN THE ORCHARD TELLING THE WEEVILS OFF SO YOU DID IT TO HELP ME OUT

OH LOVE I DUNNO WHAT TO SAY

AS YOUR DAD I SHOULD BE TELLING YOU OFF FOR RISKING YOUR LIFE BUT INSTEAD IM HAVING A BLUB

I LOVE YOU RO

THERES ONE THING I DONT GET BUT

YOUVE SEEN ME AND YOURE GRINNING AND WAVING BUT YOURE NOT LOOKING AT YOUR PHONE JEEZ RO WHY HAVENT YOU ANSWERED MY MESSAGES AND WHY ARE YOU POINTING AT MY PHONE

I GET IT YOUVE SENT ME A TEXT MESSAGE OK ILL READ IT

G'day Dad. Actions speak louder than words with texts too. You have to remember to press send. Love Ro xx :)

Give Peas A Chance

'Ben,' said Mum. 'Eat your veggies.'

Ben didn't hear her. He was too busy staring gloomily at the dead kids on TV.

'Come on, mate,' said Dad. 'A few carrots and zucchini won't kill you. Bung some tomato sauce on them and pretend they're sausages.'

Ben didn't hear him either. This was the third lot of dead kids just on tonight's news.

'Watch out, young man,' said Mum. 'If you don't eat those vegetables now, you might get them cold for breakfast tomorrow. With milk. And only one spoonful of sugar.'

Ben still didn't take his eyes off the TV.

The small blood-stained bodies were lying on a stone floor, arms and legs flopped in different positions like the kids were asleep. Except they weren't asleep, they were dead.

'Ben,' said Dad. 'Did you hear what your

mother just told you?'

Angry men were standing next to the small bodies, yelling and waving guns. Ben could tell they were upset about the dead kids. But this didn't make him feel any better. The men looked like they were yelling for revenge, so by tomorrow night other kids in Iraq would probably have bullets in them too.

'Ben,' said Dad in a voice like a gun going off.

Ben realised the others were all looking at him. Mum wearily, Dad crossly and Claire with that you-are-such-a-der-brain expression big sisters liked so much.

Claire leaned towards him.

'You won't lose any weight skipping veggies,' she said. 'I went on a veggie-free diet last year. Waste of time. You end up eating extra ice-cream to get the vitamins.'

Ben sighed. How could a whole family not see what was happening to the world? Specially now they all had their new contact lenses.

'I don't understand, Ben,' said Mum. 'You like veggies.'

Ben had to admit she was right.

But that was before.

Dad tossed a two-dollar coin onto the table near Ben's plate.

Ben stared at it. Then he realised what Dad was doing. Giving him tomorrow's tuckshop money now. Hoping the thought of tomorrow's jam donut or cream lamington would be enough to help him force down tonight's veggies.

It wasn't.

'Sorry,' said Ben. 'I can't.'

He hadn't planned any of this. It was just sort of happening.

'Why not?' said Dad with that about-to-explode expression dads liked so much.

'Because,' said Ben, 'I'm not eating any more vegetables until people stop shooting each other.'

Later that evening, after Mum and Dad calmed down, Ben explained that his strike wasn't just vegetable-based.

'I won't be tidying my room either,' he said quietly. 'Or clearing the table or taking the bins out or doing homework or being polite to relatives.'

Dad ran his big raw butcher's hands through his thinning hair.

Ben hoped all this wasn't going to make Dad's hair go even more thinning.

For a fleeting moment, Ben was tempted to tell Mum and Dad he was only joking. But he didn't, because he wasn't.

Now I've started this, he thought grimly, I have to keep going.

'This is crazy, Ben,' said Mum. 'People can't change the world even if they want to. Not unless they're Bono or that bloke who invented the iPod. You'll feel different in the morning. Have an early night, there's a good boy.'

'I'm not being a good boy any more,' said Ben. 'Not until grown-ups get rid of all the guns and bombs.'

'Why us?' moaned Dad. 'We haven't got any guns.'

Mum went out to the kitchen and came back. In one hand she had the gas gun for lighting the stove. In the other she had the kitchen waste-bin. She dropped the gas gun into the bin.

'There,' she said to Ben. 'Will you eat your veggies now?'

Ben shook his head.

'Those Iraq and Africa and Palestine people aren't killed by kitchen appliances,' he said.

Mum ran her slim office-manager's hands through her lightly-permed hair.

Ben hoped all this wasn't going to make Mum's hair go even more permed.

At bedtime, Claire came into Ben's room for a chat.

'You're making a big mistake, you know,' she said. 'You might think this is a clever way to get out of eating veggies and clearing the table and all that other stuff, but it's not.'

Ben could hear the distant sound of gunfire in the living room. Mum and Dad must be watching the late news.

'I tried something like it last week,' said Claire. 'I told Mum I wasn't going to stop biting my nails unless she let me wear nail polish. So she let me wear some and I forgot and my finger got glued to my mouth.'

Ben looked at his sister's frowning face and, he now saw, her slightly-green teeth.

'You must know why I'm doing this,' he said to her. 'You watch the news. Every night there's more and more people being killed in wars. Doesn't it make you upset?'

Claire thought about this.

'Not really,' she said. 'I don't look. Not when I'm eating.'

Ben wished he had that skill.

'When I see those dead people,' he said, 'it makes me think how I'd feel if it was you or Mum or Dad or my friends.'

Claire gave him the der-brain look.

'Don't worry,' she said. 'When the kids at school find out you're behaving like a complete psychiatric, you won't have any friends.'

The kids at school didn't think Ben was behaving like a complete psychiatric.

When he told them he was on strike and wouldn't be eating veggies or clearing the table or tidying his room or taking the bins out or being polite to rellies or doing homework, their part of the playground went quiet and they all looked sort of impressed.

And thoughtful.

'That is such a great excuse, guns and bombs,'

said Skye Borlotti. 'When I want to get out of doing all that stuff, I can only think of things like headaches and pet allergies, and we haven't got any pets.'

'I'm gunna tell my parents they have to get rid of guns and bombs and spiders,' said Shane Moore. 'Our bathroom's a death-trap.'

Several of the other kids started discussing what they were going to add to the list.

Water pistols.

Sticks.

Aunties who kiss.

Ben was a bit worried some of the kids might be missing the point.

He explained about the thousands of people around the world who were killed each day by bullets and explosions, and what it must feel like to have a bullet or a piece of shrapnel go through your head or your mum's head.

The kids all stared at him, even more thoughtful than before.

Shane started to ask how many people were killed by spider bites, then changed his mind.

That night, Ben sat in front of a large plate of steaming vegetables.

He peered at them.

The peas and broccoli looked new, but those carrots and zucchini looked like last night's.

'They are last night's,' said Dad. 'And if you don't eat this lot, they'll be on your plate with tomorrow night's lot.' He shrugged. 'Up to you how long this goes on for.'

Ben frowned as he chewed a mouthful of chop.

He didn't know how long it would go on for, but he was pretty sure the plate probably wouldn't be big enough.

Mum came in from the kitchen, also frowning.

'That was Jean on the phone,' she said. 'Jason's on strike. Veggies, bins, rellies, same nonsense as Ben.'

Dad got his about-to-explode look.

'Typical,' he said. 'There'd have to be one other clown and it'd have to be Jason.'

'Not one,' said Mum. 'Jean's the seventh school parent I've had ringing up complaining tonight.'

Dad stared at her in surprise.

Then Claire gave a yell.

'Look.'

She pointed to the TV. The news had started. On the screen was a headline. Ben had to read it three times to make sure he was seeing it right.

Kids On Strike.

'A text-message craze swept the country today,' said the newsreader. 'Thousands of children have gone on the offensive against what one nine-year-old described as weapons that hurt people'.

A girl Ben had never seen before appeared on the screen. She was standing in a milk bar with her arms folded. Behind the counter, looking on proudly, were her parents.

Ben hoped the girl wouldn't say anything about spiders or aunties who kiss.

She didn't.

'I'm not helping in the shop any more,' she said. 'Plus I'm not eating hamburgers, chips, toasted sandwiches or any other hot food or snacks. Not until there's world peace.'

The girl's mother looked even prouder.

Ben felt dazed.

Incredible.

He wanted to hug someone. But he didn't. The available people in the room were all staring at the TV, mouths open.

'Police are investigating,' said the newsreader. 'They say that with the aid of phone records, they will eventually trace the person or persons behind what some commentators are calling un-Australian behaviour.'

Ben had trouble swallowing his mouthful of chop.

Police? Investigating?

Mum, Dad and Claire were all staring at him now with grim faces.

'I tried to warn you,' said Claire.

Ben stayed home the next day.

'I don't want you running around at school causing more trouble,' said Dad as he left for work. 'Keep your head down here till it all blows over.'

'If a SWAT team busts in looking for you,' said

Claire as she grabbed her school bag, 'you can hide in my wardrobe.'

'Don't answer the phone,' said Mum, zipping up her briefcase. 'Your veggies are in the microwave.'

Ben felt too excited to be hungry.

He spent the day on his computer, checking the news sites.

It wasn't blowing over.

Kids all around the country were staying home from school as part of the strike. Others were being driven to school by parents but refusing to get out of the car. Others were sitting in the playground, saying teachers would have to carry them into the classroom. Teachers were refusing because of their backs.

Grown-ups were getting very upset.

Ben felt sorry for them, particularly the vegetable shop owners who were saying they'd go broke if the major world powers didn't seriously rethink their armaments policies.

He knew the same could happen to Dad if kids started not eating meat.

Ben pushed the thought out of his mind. He clicked to another news site.

Incredible.

Kids were going on strike in New Zealand too.

And Japan.

Suddenly Ben felt a bit faint. He wondered if his blood sugar levels were being affected by the speed of the whole thing and how big it was getting.

He went to the kitchen and got a cold sausage from the fridge.

'It'll blow over,' said Dad. 'Just watch.'

Ben looked at the pile of vegetables in front of him. Claire had just done a huge sneeze, but the five nights of veggies heaped on Ben's plate weren't even wobbling.

Ben realised Dad didn't mean the veggies.

'There were crazes when I was a kid,' Dad was saying. 'Pointy shoes. Disco. Smurfs. Hoola hoops. Mohawk hairdos. They all blew over.'

Mum gave Dad a look. She pointed to the TV screen, where a classroom full of Tibetan students were sitting at their desks, ignoring the bowls of yaks-milk porridge going cold in front of them.

'Didn't you hear what the news just said?' demanded Mum. 'Two hundred and thirty million kids in eighty-six countries have gone on strike. I don't think mohawk hairdos were ever quite that popular.'

Dad stared at the screen too.

His shoulders sagged.

He turned to Ben, not looking cross any more, just very worried.

'Why couldn't you have eaten your veggies?' he said pleadingly.

Ben didn't know what to say. He was feeling a bit stunned. He also hated seeing Mum and Dad unhappy, but that was partly why he was doing this, so it would be a safer happier world for them to grow old in.

The front door bell rang.

Claire went to answer it.

She came back looking frightened.

'It's the federal police,' she said.

After posing for photos with Ben on the steps of Parliament House, the Minister for Defence spoke briefly to the crowd of reporters.

'I salute the vision of this young Australian,' he said. 'The government shares his desire for a peaceful world. But unfortunately guns and missiles and our new fighter-bombers with their laser-tracking capability are a necessary evil. To have peace we must be well-armed.'

Ben took a deep breath and spoke up.

'Excuse me, your honour,' he said. 'But if nobody else was armed, why would we need to be?'

The defence minister smiled for quite a long time.

'Young people get confused,' he said to the cameras. 'It's up to you, parents of Australia. Explain it to them.'

Ben saw that Mum was looking a bit doubtful.

'Could you just run through the main points?' she said to the defence minister.

The minister hesitated, then smiled some more.

'I know it's not easy,' he said to the cameras. 'I'm a parent too.'

Dad was looking thoughtful.

He nodded towards Ben.

'If you were his father,' Dad said to the minister, 'how would you get him to eat his veggies?'

For a horrible moment Ben thought the minister was going to announce a new law with on-the-spot fines for kids who wouldn't eat all their dinner.

Instead, Claire spoke up.

'Do you think any countries'll get rid of their guns?' she asked the defence minister, loudly so the reporters could hear.

The defence minister stopped grinning and shook his head.

'Not a chance,' he said.

The first country to get rid of its guns was Iceland.

Ben stared at the TV, struggling to stay calm, a piece of roast pork unchewed in his mouth.

Mum and Dad and Claire stopped chewing too.

'Unreal,' said Claire.

'We're doing it for our children,' said the Icelandic prime minister, standing next to a big drilling machine that was drilling into the ice. 'We've decided to bury our weapons in this glacier, so future generations of young Icelanders will be able to see them in the ice and think about how much better off we are without them.'

'And are you also doing it,' said one of a large group of journalists, 'so the current generation of young Icelanders will get out of bed and start eating fish again?'

'Yes,' said the Icelandic prime minister. 'That as well.'

Ben realised the rest of the family had stopped looking at the TV and were all looking at him.

So were the reporters outside the lounge room window.

Dad reached over and squeezed Ben's shoulder.

'Incredible,' he said in a stunned voice.

'Well done, love,' said Mum to Ben, sounding pretty stunned herself. 'Now will you eat your veggies?'

'Not yet,' said Ben.

Other countries tried to keep their guns.

'Hey,' yelled a reporter to Ben. 'Egypt has banned all pictures of shot and blown-up people on their TV. Any comment?'

Ben knew he wasn't meant to answer journalists who yelled at him through the lounge room window. But Mum was in the bathroom and he couldn't resist.

'If I was an Egyptian kid,' he yelled back, 'I'd draw a picture in coloured crayons of what happens when a toddler gets hit by a machine gun bullet and I'd stick the picture on my parents' TV screen.'

Two days later, the same journalist was yelling at Ben again.

'Two million Egyptian kids followed your suggestion,' he shouted. 'Any comment?'

'See what you've done now, Ben,' said Mum in

an exasperated voice as she pulled the curtains. 'I told you not to talk to the media.'

The next country to get rid of its guns was Taiwan.

'Good on you, Taiwan,' said Dad as he turned up the sound on the TV.

Mum glanced at Ben's plate.

Ben pretended not to notice.

'We're doing it for our economy,' said the Taiwanese president, standing next to a brand new recycling plant for ferrous and non-ferrous metals. 'Melting down these guns will allow us to make many more MP3 players.'

'And are you also doing it,' said a journalist, 'so the young people of Taiwan will get out of bed and start buying MP3 players again?'

'Yes,' said the Taiwanese president. 'That as well.'

Ben helped Dad find Taiwan in the atlas.

'It's next to China,' said Mum.

Dad put a big tick with a texta on the map of Taiwan.

'Two down,' said Dad, studying the list of countries in the front of the atlas. 'A hundred and twenty-three to go.'

'I wish they'd hurry up,' said Mum, staring wearily at the huge pile of uneaten veggies on Ben's plate.

When China saw that Taiwan didn't have any guns, they decided to invade.

Millions of Chinese children lay down in front of the war planes and tanks. The Chinese authorities arrested the parents of every child involved. And the aunties, and the uncles, and the people who weren't really relatives but helped out with child-minding after school.

'Any comment?' yelled the reporters in Ben's front yard.

Ben didn't have any comment.

Not to the reporters.

Silently he worried that things might be getting a bit out of control, and that it was all his fault.

'I'll send an email to the Chinese embassy,' said Claire. 'Remind them they've got the Olympics coming up.'

Soon the Chinese authorities started releasing people from jail.

Chinese children stayed on strike.

China started getting rid of its weapons.

'They had to,' said Claire to Ben. 'Most of their athletes are under eighteen. Plus who'll vacuum the Olympic stadiums if all the adults are in jail?'

'Thanks, Claire,' said Ben. 'I'm glad you're on our side.'

When the other countries saw China had got rid of its weapons, they did too.

America was last.

They made excuses and broke promises and pretended they didn't have enough recycling depots.

'That's bull,' said Mum indignantly. 'They can turn all their gun shops and missile silos into recycling depots.'

Ben grinned. Trust an office manager to get things organised.

Finally the US Congress persuaded the president to sign the disarmament bill by explaining the terrible damage that would be done to the US economy if American kids continued not to eat McDonald's.

'Come on, Ben,' said Mum. 'You've got no excuses now. Eat your veggies.'

Ben knew it was Mum from her voice. He couldn't actually see her because of the mountain of vegetables on the serving platter in front of him.

She sounded tired.

Ben wasn't surprised.

They were all tired after weeks of living in the media spotlight. Thank goodness the footy season had started and a couple of coaches had been sacked and the media had all gone to their front yards.

'Look,' said Claire, pointing to the TV screen.

Ben peered around his veggies.

On the TV news, the last gun from the last warship in the world was being melted down in San Diego.

'You heard your mother, Ben,' said Dad. 'You've got your own way, you've brought peace to the entire planet, now you have to keep your side of the bargain. Eat those veggies.'

Ben looked at Dad's proud grin and the relieved expression on Mum's face.

World peace felt good.

He stuck his fork into a big lump of much-microwaved broccoli, put it into his mouth and started chewing.

All next day at school, even while people were saying how nice it was to have him back, Ben couldn't stop thinking about how long it was going to take him to eat that pile of veggies.

About a year, probably.

Longer if he kept getting sick of their fridge-taste as quickly as he had last night.

But later, when Ben sat down at the dinner table, he stared in surprise.

The mountain of veggies had been divided into four smaller piles. Mum, Dad and Claire each had a pile on their plate. They were eating the veggies as fast as they could.

'Thanks,' said Ben.

What a generous family.

'We're not doing it for you,' said Claire through a mouthful of spinach.

She pointed to the TV screen.

Ben stared. The news report was describing how two hours ago America had invaded Iran. On the screen, American warplanes and bombers hurtled over Tehran.

'But they haven't got any guns or bombs,' said

Ben. 'How can they declare war?'

'Veggies,' said Dad grimly.

At first Ben didn't understand. Then he saw what the bombers were dropping from high altitude onto the panicked Iranian people.

Cauliflower.

Pumpkin.

Mashed potato with really big lumps in it.

'That is disgusting,' said Mum. 'Targeting kids like that.'

On the TV a fighter plane roared low over a block of flats. Every window exploded into shards of glass under a hail of frozen brussel sprouts and sweetcorn.

Ben stared in horror.

'Don't just sit there gawking,' said Claire. 'Eat your veggies.'

'The more we can eat,' said Mum through a mouthful of carrot, 'the less there'll be to injure innocent civilians.'

Ben nodded.

He looked at his family, all doing their bit to make the world a better place.

Then he stuffed a big forkful of peas into his mouth and chewed as fast as he could.

Good Dog

Veronica looks horrified when I arrive at her party.

She stands at the front door, her mouth open. The fluffy balls on her party dress wobble with alarm. The fake jewels on her tiara tremble with panic.

'Happy birthday,' I say.

She's not even looking at me, she's staring at Anthony.

'Woof,' says Anthony.

'A dog?' squeaks Veronica. 'Ginger, why did you bring a dog? My dad's not good with dogs.'

'I couldn't afford a present,' I explain. 'So I brought Anthony. You've been saying all week you hope your party will be a success. Well Anthony's here to help. He's a party dog.'

Veronica gives a little whimper.

'Don't worry,' I say. 'I know Anthony's big, but he's friendly. He won't hurt your dog.'

Veronica glances nervously over my shoulder.

'Our dog isn't here,' she says. 'My dad's in the park, training it.'

She doesn't have to tell me. I can hear Mr Pobjoy's angry voice drifting over from the park across the road.

'Bad dog,' he's yelling. 'Bad dog.'

I swap a look with Anthony.

Mr Pobjoy should be in the army. We live two streets away and most evenings I can hear him roaring at that poor dog even over the noise of Mum and Dad's music in the kitchen.

Anthony hates hearing another dog being treated like that. Usually he sticks his head under one of our cats so he doesn't have to listen to it.

Now he just wants to get inside.

'Stop,' says Veronica to Anthony. 'Come back.'

Anthony has squeezed past her into the house.

'Party dogs hate having to wait outside,' I explain. 'They want to get in and start partying.'

We hurry inside after Anthony.

The party is in the family room. About ten kids are on leather chairs in front of a huge TV. The boys are fighting and the girls are complaining and they're all throwing party food at each other.

'Good grief,' says Veronica's mum when she sees Anthony. 'That's all I need.'

Mrs Pobjoy is very stressed. Her fashionable clothes have got quite a lot of marshmallow dip on them. Her very fashionable hair, which Mum reckons would cost more to have done than some countries spend on food, is looking a bit sweat-affected.

'Is that your dog?' Mrs Pobjoy says to me.

'Yes,' I say. 'His name's Anthony. I'm Ginger. I sit next to Veronica in class.'

I hold out my hand to shake Mrs Pobjoy's. She doesn't see it.

'Pets were not invited,' she says to Veronica.

'I didn't invite it,' says Veronica miserably. 'She just arrived with it.'

'It's OK,' I say to Mrs Pobjoy. 'Anthony's here to help.'

Mrs Pobjoy still looks stressed.

I explain to her how Anthony was already a party expert when I got him. How when I first saw him in the pound he was playing What's The Time Mr Wolf with all the other dogs. Letting them creep up behind him, then turning and chasing them till they nearly wet themselves with excitement.

'That is the stupidest thing I've ever heard,' says Mrs Pobjoy crossly.

'It's not,' I say. 'Anthony's a mixture of wolfhound and English sheepdog. Wolfhounds are very fun-loving and English sheepdogs have to organise a lot of party games out in the fields to keep the sheep warm in winter.'

'Get it out of here,' says Mrs Pobjoy.

'Look,' says Veronica, pointing.

Anthony is already rounding up the kids for

the first game, nudging and nuzzling them off the couch. When someone doesn't want to move, Anthony grabs a corner of their party frock or best shirt between his teeth and gently drags them.

Some of the kids are screaming and trying to run away. Others are trying to hide under the chairs. This always happens when Anthony arrives at a party. Kids get over-excited.

'The first game's Hide And Seek,' I say to the screamers and runners. 'It's fun. Do what the others are doing. Hide somewhere you don't think Anthony will find you.'

Kids hurl themselves into cupboards and clamber up onto shelves.

Soon everyone is hidden. Except for Mrs Pobjoy, who is outside in the barbeque area, glowering at Anthony and talking very fast into her mobile.

Anthony starts finding everyone.

Some people are so worked up they almost faint when Anthony sticks his big head into the laundry basket or nest of tables they're hiding in. He does have very big teeth, which can be a bit of a problem for a party organiser.

But when he licks your face, which is his way of saying *good hiding place, but I found you*, you know he wouldn't hurt a fly. Not even an over-excited fly who's had way too many lollies.

By the end of the game, some kids are grinning. Even Veronica isn't looking so upset, probably because she won by hiding in her dad's wine cellar.

'Good on you,' I whisper to Anthony.

He made sure he found Veronica last. That's the advantage of being a mixture of breeds. You get to be not only clever, but also kind on birthdays.

'What's next?' someone yells.

Anthony is already organising the next game, wagging his big tail and herding everybody into a line.

'Musical Chairs,' I say, grabbing the dining chairs and putting them into a line too.

Anthony starts singing. Well, howling really. He can sort of do some of Mum and Dad's Rod Stewart tunes. Well, bits of them.

A few of the kids look like they want to go back to playing Hide And Seek.

I know why. When Anthony sings, he does spray quite a lot of saliva around. It's the one other problem he has as a party organiser.

But his timing's great. He waits for me to whisk another chair away, then stops howling at really unexpected moments. Each time he does, kids are laughing and falling over each other to get their bums on a seat.

Veronica is laughing too. She can see her party's going really well.

Then a loud voice booms out.

'Whoa. What's going on here?'

The room goes quiet. We all turn and see a man in a business suit standing in the doorway. He's got a mobile phone in one hand and a very small white dog in the other.

'It's OK, Dad,' pleads Veronica. 'We're having a really good time. Anthony's a really good party org . . .'

Her voice trails off. Mr Pobjoy is glaring at her.

'Bad girl,' he says.

Veronica tries to shrink inside her party dress.

Mr Pobjoy points at Anthony.

'What are you thinking, Veronica,' he says, 'bringing a brute like that in here? It could tear Flossy Evangeline Diamante to pieces. Good grief, you know how much we paid for Flossy.'

Veronica is close to tears.

'Two thousand dollars,' she says in a tiny voice.

The rest of us stare at the little white dog in amazement. That must work out at more than a thousand dollars a kilo. Even Anthony is looking stunned.

'Poor little Flossy,' says Mr Pobjoy. 'Look at her. She's trembling. She's terrified.'

No she's not. She's curled up contentedly and looking down at Anthony with keen interest. Veronica's the one who's trembling and upset.

Suddenly Flossy jumps down from Mr Pobjoy's hand, trots over to Anthony and starts sniffing his bottom. Well, sniffing his legs, because there's no way she can reach his bottom without a small ladder.

'Flossy,' snaps Mr Pobjoy. 'Come back here.'

Flossy ignores him.

'Bad dog,' he yells at her. 'Bad dog.'

Flossy still ignores him.

Anthony gives her a sniff because that's the polite thing to do. And also, I can tell, because he feels a bit protective. She's a small dog being yelled at by a big man.

'Bad dog,' roars Mr Pobjoy again.

Anthony tilts his head down next to Flossy's and gently licks her ear a few times. It's almost like he's whispering to her.

Suddenly Flossy trots back over to Mr Pobjoy, who gives an angry but satisfied nod.

Flossy stops right next to his feet and pees on his shoes.

'Bad dog,' yells Mr Pobjoy, jumping back and trying to shake the pee off his feet, his voice going squeaky with outrage.

The rest of us are trying not to laugh. Several of the kids aren't managing it very well. I see Anthony looking at me with his big brown eyes and something in his expression gives me an idea. I speak up before Veronica's dad sends us all home.

'Mr Pobjoy,' I say. 'I'm quite experienced with dogs and I know how hard it can be to train them. One thing that's worked really well for me is a party game called Good Dog Bad Dog.'

Mr Pobjoy looks at me long and hard.

I can see that what he really wants to do is chuck us all out so he can yell at Flossy and Veronica in private. But he's been trying to train Flossy for weeks. Underneath his expensive suit and his hair transplant, I'm guessing he's desperate.

'Please, Dad,' says Veronica. 'Give it a go.'

'Good Dog Bad Dog?' mutters Mr Pobjoy, not sounding convinced.

Mrs Pobjoy has been off and changed her clothes and she's looking a bit less stressed.

'You might as well give it a go, Vince,' she says wearily to her husband. 'You've said yourself Flossy is a difficult dog.'

Mr Pobjoy frowns suspiciously.

'How does this game work?' he says.

'It's simple,' I say. 'For the next five minutes, all we're allowed to say is either *good dog* or *bad dog*.'

Mr Pobjoy looks doubtful.

Please, I urge him silently. Give it a go.

My plan is dead simple. To show Mr Pobjoy that kindness gets better results than yelling. Though you'd think a top business manager like him would already know that.

'OK,' I say. 'Let's start.'

I look at Anthony to make sure he understands what we're doing. I can tell from the way he looks at me that he does.

I'm going to say *good dog* to him lots of times and he's going to do lots of clever tricks and obedient things to show Mr Pobjoy that *good dog* always works better than *bad dog*.

Flossy is sniffing Anthony's leg again. Anthony

starts licking Flossy's ear again in a murmuring sort of way.

Before I can get my first *good dog* out, Mr Pobjoy, whose shoes are still wet, turns to Anthony.

'Bad dog,' he snaps.

Anthony looks at him for a moment, then does something that isn't really what you'd expect from a good dog.

He leans forward, opens his huge jaws, places them around Flossy, and closes them.

Flossy disappears.

Inside Anthony's mouth.

Veronica screams.

So do the other kids.

Mrs Pobjoy clutches the pool table.

I feel faint. I can hear the distant echo of something a dog-hater once said to me. That you can never trust pound dogs. That sooner or later they always turn vicious.

Then I see Anthony is looking at me. He isn't chewing or swallowing, just looking at me patiently. The bulge in his mouth is still moving.

Suddenly I know what he's doing.

He isn't turning vicious, he's just playing Good Dog Bad Dog his way.

'No,' howls Mr Pobjoy. 'Flossy. That brute has eaten Flossy.'

I turn to Veronica, whose fluffy party-dress balls are trembling almost as much as her lips.

'Rescue Flossy,' I whisper to Veronica. 'You won't

get hurt, I promise. Just say *good dog.*'

Veronica stares at me.

I can see this isn't the birthday party she was hoping for.

'Better hurry,' I whisper. 'Flossy's running out of air in there.'

Veronica goes nervously over to Anthony. She has to step around her father, who is yelling insulting things at Anthony again.

'Bad dog,' he's shouting. 'Bad dog. Bad dog.'

Anthony ignores him and turns to face Veronica, his jaws still closed.

I can just make out faint tremors of movement inside his mouth.

Veronica hesitates. Then I see Anthony looking into her eyes and I know everything's going to be OK.

Veronica can hardly get the words out.

But she does.

'Good dog,' she whispers to Anthony.

'Mr Pobjoy,' I say. 'Look. Veronica's saving Flossy.'

And she is.

'Good dog,' she says, and Anthony slowly opens his mouth. Veronica puts her hands inside and lifts out a soggy, bedraggled, stunned-looking Flossy.

'Woof,' says Flossy.

'Good dog,' says Veronica.

'Thank God,' says Mr Pobjoy, taking Flossy from Veronica. 'Flossy, sweetie. It's OK, you're safe. Good dog. Good dog.'

He hugs Flossy.

'Good dog,' he says, over and over.

Then he hugs Veronica.

'Good girl,' he says to her. 'Good girl.'

Veronica is tearful again, but in a way that lets us all see this is the best party she's ever had.

'Good on you,' I whisper to Anthony.

Mr Pobjoy stops hugging Flossy and Veronica, and looks over at me and Anthony.

'I think it's best,' he says tersely, 'if you both leave.'

Then he goes back to hugging his dog and his daughter.

I don't argue.

On the way out, Veronica's mum catches up with us.

'Thank you,' she says. 'Thank you both so much. Veronica's cousin is having a party next week. I don't suppose you and Anthony can come?'

'That's very kind,' I say. 'I think we can.'

I check with Anthony.

He licks my hand.

I can see he likes the idea of another party.

We both do.

Cornflakes

That morning I didn't have the faintest inkling my life was about to change forever. So I just did what a ten-year-old boy normally does first thing. Padded sleepily to the toilet and had a pee.

I watched it spurt out.

Why, I wondered, does the first pee of the day always look like chicken soup?

I hadn't had any chicken soup for weeks. So if it was chicken soup, why had it taken so long to reach my willy? And why would chicken soup only drain out first thing in the morning?

Gradually, as the pee trickled out of me, so did my sleepiness.

My thoughts got clearer.

I realised it probably wasn't chicken soup. It didn't smell like chicken soup, and there were no vegetables in it.

*

Now, all these years later, I know the truth.

My pee wasn't chicken soup, it was much more interesting than that.

Like all human urine it was a deadly aqueous solution of salts, minerals, vitamins, corpuscles, uric acid, nitrogenous waste products, organic compounds, and chemicals from lollies.

When it splashed into the toilet bowl, there was widespread carnage. Most of the hundreds of millions of tiny organisms who had spent the night floating in the toilet water without a care in the world were killed instantly.

Peed to death.

Please don't blame me.

I didn't know then.

My family didn't know either.

My mother didn't have a clue, as she cleaned her shoes over the kitchen sink, that she was wiping out a microbe population bigger than the human population of Australia, including Tasmania.

My big sister Sarah had no idea, as she delicately removed a wax-based community from one of her ears with a fingernail and ate it, that she was a mass-murderer of mind-boggling proportions.

My father didn't suspect, as he waited for the toaster to finish its work, that he was searing and scorching countless tiny bread creatures and turning them into, well, toast.

The only member of the family who did suspect

something was my little sister Nell.

'Nell,' said Mother. 'Eat your cornflakes, love.'

Mother pointed to me.

'Look,' she said, 'Timmy's eating his.'

Nell pushed the bowl away.

In those days, I thought Nell was just a cute little kid who didn't know much.

I was wrong.

Nell already suspected that if she ate her cornflakes, innocent creatures would die. But it wasn't the millions of cowering proteobacteria trying not to draw attention to themselves on the surface of the milk in her bowl that she had in mind.

'Nell,' said Mother. 'Why don't you want to eat your cornflakes?'

'Because of the fairies,' said Nell.

Mother and Father looked at each other and tried not to smile.

One thing I did know was that adults could sometimes be a bit hurtful, even when they were loving parents who didn't mean to be, and that sometimes little sisters needed a brother on their side.

'Fairies?' I said to Nell. 'Where?'

'In the cornflakes,' said Nell. She pointed to a picture of a fairy on the cornflakes box. 'See?'

Now Mother and Father did smile.

'You're so funny,' said Sarah, giving Nell a tickle. 'And dopey.'

I've never approved of younger sisters being

called dopey, so I gave Sarah a look. And I gave Mother and Father one too, just in case they were thinking of using the same word.

'Nell,' I said gently. 'We've taken the fairy out, remember?'

I pointed to the plastic fairy standing next to Nell's dish, plastic wand raised, plastic wings bejewelled with cornflake dust.

'Not that fairy,' said Nell, getting annoyed. 'The other fairies. The tiny ones. In the cornflakes.'

Sarah struggled not to laugh. She put her hand over her mouth and millions of finger microbes found themselves having a travel experience they hadn't expected.

I spoke up quickly before somebody said something else that hurt Nell's feelings.

'There's only one fairy,' I explained gently to her, pointing to the side of the cornflakes box. 'It says so here.'

Because Nell couldn't read yet, I did it for her.

'*One fairy per carton.*'

Nell didn't look convinced.

'Come on sweetie,' said Father. 'Eat up.'

Nell shook her head.

'The box is wrong,' she said.

'Those cornflakes manufacturers are mean,' I said to Nell. 'Only putting one fairy in each box.'

'Tell you what,' said Mother to Nell. 'How about Timmy has the first spoonful of your cornflakes to prove there are no more fairies?'

I wasn't sure about this. I felt like we were all ganging up on Nell. But Mother and Father were both looking at me pleadingly.

I scooped some of Nell's cornflakes and milk onto my spoon and lifted it to my mouth.

Nell's pudgy little jaw started to quiver and behind her blonde curls her dark eyes filled with tears.

I hesitated.

I wanted to help, not hurt.

'If you scare fairies by trying to eat them,' said Nell fiercely, 'they make you sneeze.'

I looked at Mother and Father to see what I should do.

Father gave a little nod of encouragement.

I put the cornflakes into my mouth and chewed.

Up my nose, chaos broke out. Several million nasal-passage microbes, alarmed by the sudden proximity of the proteobacteria in the milk, tried to crowd into my sinuses.

My mucus membranes got seriously trampled, my cilia became inflamed, the whole subcutaneous region went tickly, and I sneezed a spray of cornflakes and milk across the table.

Nobody moved. Except Nell, who picked a bit of soggy cornflake off her face and put it back into her bowl.

'See?' she said.

Nobody else said anything for a moment.

I stared at the bowl of cornflakes, and in that instant I felt my whole life change.

Then Father spoke.

'It's OK, sweetie,' he said to Nell. 'You don't have to eat your cornflakes if you don't want to.'

'Oh dear, Timmy,' said Mother. 'I think you might be coming down with something. I'm going to make you some chicken soup.'

I didn't reply.

I was too busy staring at the cornflakes and wondering if I had enough money in my junior saver account to buy a microscope.

Many years later, when I was a professor at university, I told a class of students about Nell and how she'd changed my life.

I brought my first microscope along to show them, and as I took it out of its battered old box, I knew exactly what they were going to ask. So I gave them the answer before anyone even spoke.

'Not powerful enough,' I said, shaking my head and giving my dear old junior microscope a fond polish.

I don't teach at the university any more. I went on to become a research scientist, and I've been one for over thirty years now.

Last year one of my ex-students came to visit. He was very kind and congratulated me on being what he called one of the most brilliant research scientists in the world.

'I'm not really,' I replied. 'Not compared to my little sister Nell. She's the one who is truly brilliant.'

I could see the ex-student thought I was just being modest. He'd forgotten what I'd told him that day in class about how I owe my whole career to Nell.

He's remembered now.

A few months ago Nell won the Nobel prize for her work developing the most powerful microscope ever. The one that uses fixed orbiting satellites to increase its focal length.

That ex-student was one of thousands of people who sent Nell messages congratulating her on the prize.

She deserves it.

It isn't easy being the youngest. You get a bit overshadowed. Specially when everyone thinks your older brother is the brilliant one, plus your older sister owns the biggest pest-exterminating business in the world.

It hasn't been easy for Nell as a scientist, either.

When you're doing research that's a bit different, other scientists can sometimes be hurtful even when they don't mean to be, and sometimes little sisters need a brother on their side.

I was with Nell in the lab yesterday when she finally did the thing our colleagues said could never be done.

She turned from her microscope, eyes shining with excitement.

'Look,' she said.

I looked into the microscope, the one Nell had invented. I looked for a long time.

'I knew you'd do it,' I said.

Scientists aren't meant to get emotional, but we both laughed and shouted and danced. Which can sometimes happen when scientists have a breakthrough in the research project they've been working on for years.

Then we went to our favourite restaurant and celebrated with chicken soup.

I can't go into too much detail about our breakthrough because the official announcement hasn't been made yet, but I can say it's a remarkable discovery involving cornflakes.

My First Ever Go At Bomb Disposal

A Play by Ned Timms

NOTE *– If you do this play at home or in class, please make sure the part of Mum is performed by somebody under 35 as she's getting a bit sensitive about her age.*

SCENE ONE
ME AND MUM SITTING IN A TRAIN AT CENTRAL STATION WAITING TO GO TO AUNTY KATH'S IN LEURA FOR AFTERNOON TEA AND HUNDREDS OF HOURS OF GROWN-UP TALK. THE TRAIN ISN'T LEAVING FOR ANOTHER SIX MINUTES AND I'M BORED ALREADY.

ME I'm bored already.

MUM Don't start love. Read your book.

ME I forgot it.

MUM Well listen to your MP3.

ME I forgot that too.

MUM I left it on the kitchen table for you. How could you forget it?

ME I must have put my book on it.

MUM DOES ONE OF THOSE LOOKS SHE DOES WHEN SHE FORGETS THAT PEOPLE ARE ONLY HUMAN.

MUM Right young man well you're not sitting here for a two-hour train trip whingeing the whole way so you'll have to think of something else to do. You didn't forget your imagination did you?

ME No Mum.

MUM Well use it.

ME How do you mean?

MUM I don't know Ned it's your imagination.

MUM STARTS READING HER BOOK WHICH IS ALL RIGHT FOR HER, SHE HASN'T INHERITED DAD'S BAD MEMORY.

ME I spy with my little eye something beginning with X.

MUM DOESN'T ANSWER. SHE HATES I-SPY.

ME Xpress train.

A MAN GETS ON THE TRAIN AND SITS A FEW SEATS AWAY FROM US. HE HAS QUITE DARK SKIN AND A BLACK MOUSTACHE AND A BRIEFCASE AND FOREIGN CLOTHES. I LOOK AT HIM FOR A WHILE. SOME OF THE OTHER PASSENGERS LOOK AT HIM TOO. SUDDENLY I HAVE A SCARY THOUGHT.

ME (WHISPERING) Mum.

MUM Mmmm?

ME What if that man's a terrorist?

MUM Eh? What man?

ME (POINTING) That man sitting over there.

MUM Don't be silly. And don't point.

ME He could be. He's foreign and he looks like the terrorists on telly and he's wearing a terrorist kaftan thing like you used to wear when you didn't want people to see you were fat.

MUM Ned. Enough.

ME Maybe we should tell somebody.

MUM Be quiet.

MUM HAS GOT HER TEETH CLENCHED LIKE SHE'S STRUGGLING NOT TO PANIC. SHE GIVES THE MAN AND THE OTHER PASSENGERS A FAKE SMILE.

MUM I'm sorry, please excuse my son.

THE MAN SMILES BACK. IF HE'S A TERRORIST HE MUST BE REALLY WELL-TRAINED BECAUSE YOU CAN'T TELL IF HIS SMILE IS FAKE OR REAL.

MAN Is OK. Is happy time to travel with children.

MUM Mmmm.

THE MAN STOPS SMILING. SUDDENLY HE LOOKS VERY SAD LIKE HE'S THINKING OF BAD THINGS HE'S DONE IN THE PAST FOR EXAMPLE BLOWING UP BUILDINGS, OR ELSE BAD THINGS HE'S PLANNING TO DO IN THE FUTURE FOR EXAMPLE BLOWING UP THIS TRAIN.

MUM Say sorry Ned.

ME Sorry.

MUM Not to me, to the gentleman.

BEFORE I CAN, THE MAN JUMPS UP.

MAN Please to protect my seat.

THE MAN GETS OFF THE TRAIN.

MUM I despair of you sometimes Ned. You've hurt his feelings and the train's leaving in four minutes.

I STARE AT THE MAN'S EMPTY SEAT WHICH ISN'T AS EMPTY AS I'D LIKE IT TO BE.

ME Mum, look.

I POINT. MY FINGER IS TREMBLING. SOMETIMES WHEN YOU STRUGGLE TO STAY CALM ALL THE PANIC GOES TO YOUR FINGER.

MUM An innocent businessman, and just because he comes from Iran or Iraq or somewhere . . .

ME He's left his briefcase.

THE MAN'S BRIEFCASE IS SITTING ON HIS SEAT. MUM STOPS YAKKING. SHE STARES AT THE BRIEFCASE JUST LIKE I'M DOING AND SEVERAL OF THE OTHER PASSENGERS ARE DOING TOO.

ME What if it's a bomb?

A COUPLE OF THE OTHER PASSENGERS MOVE TO OTHER SEATS.

MUM Don't be silly.

ME It could be, you don't know.

MUM Ned I'm losing patience.

ME Ring the army bomb disposal squad. Or the police if you haven't got the army bomb disposal squad's number.

MUM Ned . . .

ME On the platform it said we should report all unattended luggage. (POINTS) That luggage is totally unattended.

MUM Ned, sit down and stop pointing.

SOMETIMES MUM GETS A TONE IN HER VOICE THAT IS VERY SCARY. NOT AS SCARY AS A BOMB

ON A TRAIN, BUT SCARY. I SIT BACK DOWN. OTHER PASSENGERS SIT BACK DOWN AS WELL.

MUM There's probably a simple explanation.

ME Like what? The train leaves in two minutes. Name one possible thing.

MUM I don't know, he could be getting a paper.

I THINK ABOUT THIS.

ME He's foreign. He probably can't read English.

MUM THINKS ABOUT THIS.

MUM He could be getting a snack.

I THINK ABOUT THIS.

ME What if he's only allowed to eat special foreign food? The station only sells Australian pies and Australian sandwiches and Australian lollies and Australian chewing gum.

MUM THINKS ABOUT THIS.

MUM He could be ringing his family from a public phone because he hasn't got a mobile.

I THINK ABOUT THIS.

ME He's got a briefcase. People who have briefcases always have mobiles.

MUM DOES ONE OF THOSE LOOKS SHE DOES WHEN SHE FORGETS THAT SOMETIMES OTHER PEOPLE ARE RIGHT EVEN WHEN THEY'RE YOUNGER THAN HER.

MUM For goodness sake Ned use your imagination he could be going to the toilet or getting some exercise or having a quick coffee or asking for a timetable or picking up some dry-cleaning or sniffing the flowers on the flower stall or looking for an umbrella he left in the ticket office or buying an MP3 player.

MUM SLUMPS BACK IN HER SEAT, OUT OF BREATH.

ME If you're right, why didn't he take his briefcase?

MUM DOESN'T HAVE AN ANSWER TO THAT. I LOOK AT HER IN TRIUMPH. I'VE WON. THEN I REMEMBER I HAVEN'T WON. WE'RE ON A TRAIN WITH A BOMB. THE TRAIN GIVES A JOLT AND STARTS MOVING.

ME Quick Mum, open the window.

I FLING MYSELF AT THE BRIEFCASE. SOME OF THE OTHER PASSENGERS SCREAM. I SNATCH THE BRIEFCASE OFF THE SEAT. AS I SWING IT TOWARDS THE WINDOW THE CATCH BREAKS BECAUSE OF A MANUFACTURING FAULT AND EVERYTHING TUMBLES OUT ONTO THE FLOOR. BOOKS, TEA BAGS, PENS, TISSUES, PHOTOS, FRUIT, BITS OF PAPER, COUGH LOLLIES.

NO BOMB.

I STARE AT THE STUFF ON THE FLOOR TO MAKE DOUBLE SURE THERE ISN'T A BOMB. THEN I START GRABBING THE THINGS AND PUTTING THEM BACK INTO THE BRIEFCASE. I PICK UP A PHOTO. THE MAN'S IN IT AND A WOMAN AND A GIRL AND A BOY ALL IN FOREIGN CLOTHES. THEN I PICK UP A PIECE OF OLD NEWSPAPER WRAPPED IN CLEAR PLASTIC. I READ THE HEADLINE – *REFUGEE BOAT SINKS, 353 DROWN, MOSTLY WOMEN AND CHILDREN.*

MAN Please, let me.

I LOOK UP. THE MAN IS BACK. HE'S STANDING THERE HOLDING THREE ICE-CREAMS CAREFULLY IN A BUNCH LIKE THEY'RE REALLY PRECIOUS.

MAN One you, one your mother.

FOR A MOMENT I'M NOT SURE WHAT TO DO. I STAND UP. I TAKE TWO OF THE ICE-CREAMS.

ME Um, thank you.

I SIT DOWN NEXT TO MUM AND GIVE HER AN ICE-CREAM. SHE GIVES IT BACK TO ME AND STANDS UP AND GOES OVER TO THE MAN.

MUM That's very kind. You shouldn't have. Thank you.

MUM HELPS THE MAN PUT THE THINGS BACK INTO HIS BRIEFCASE. SHE SEES THE PHOTO AND THE PIECE OF NEWSPAPER. I CAN SEE SHE WANTS TO SAY SOMETHING TO THE MAN BUT SHE CAN'T THINK OF ANYTHING. SHE TOUCHES HIS ARM. HE LOWERS HIS EYES.

MUM SITS BACK DOWN. SO DOES THE MAN. I GIVE MUM HER ICE-CREAM.

THE TRAIN'S GOING FAST NOW. I EAT MY ICE-CREAM. I THINK ABOUT THE THINGS IN THE MAN'S BRIEFCASE. SPECIALLY THE PICTURES OF HIS FAMILY.

I FEEL SAD.

I LOOK AT MUM. SHE LOOKS SAD TOO. SHE'S NOT EATING HER ICE-CREAM.

MUM You have it love.

I EAT HER ICE-CREAM.

WHEN I'VE FINISHED I LOOK OVER AT THE MAN. HE'S NOT EATING HIS ICE-CREAM EITHER. IT'S MELTING. LITTLE TRICKLES ARE RUNNING ONTO HIS HAND. HE DOESN'T NOTICE BECAUSE HIS EYES ARE CLOSED. LITTLE TRICKLES ARE RUNNING DOWN HIS FACE. NOT ICE-CREAM.

HE OPENS HIS EYES. HE HOLDS HIS ICE-CREAM OUT TO ME.

MAN You have please.

I DON'T REALLY FEEL LIKE ANOTHER ONE BUT I TAKE IT AND EAT IT BECAUSE SOMEBODY HAS TO DISPOSE OF IT.

THE MAN CLOSES HIS EYES AGAIN AND HUGS HIS BRIEFCASE TO HIS CHEST. I TRY TO THINK WHAT I CAN GIVE HIM IN RETURN FOR THREE ICE-CREAMS.

ME I spy with my little eye something beginning with B.

THE MAN OPENS HIS EYES. HE LOOKS AT ME AND THINKS FOR A BIT.

MAN Bomb.

SOME OF THE OTHER PASSENGERS LOOK ALARMED AGAIN. THE MAN POINTS OUT THE TRAIN WINDOW. WE'RE STOPPED AT A STATION. I SEE WHAT HE'S POINTING AT.

ME You mean that old car parked over there with rusty doors?

MAN Yes.

ME No.

THE MAN THINKS AGAIN.

MAN Briefcase.

ME Yes.

ME AND THE MAN PLAY I-SPY TILL HE GETS OFF AT PENRITH. HE'S VERY GOOD AT IT, BUT ONLY WITH WORDS STARTING WITH A, B AND C. ME AND MUM WAVE TO HIM ON THE PLATFORM. THEN TO MY SURPRISE MUM STARTS PLAYING I-SPY WITH ME.

MUM I spy with my little eye something beginning with LM.

I LOOK AROUND THE CARRIAGE. I POINT TO A BLOKE UP THE OTHER END WHO'S YELLING INTO HIS PHONE.

ME Loud mobile?

MUM POINTS TO HERSELF.

MUM Lucky mum.

SHE GIVES ME A HUG. WE PLAY I-SPY FOR THE REST OF THE TRIP. I'M GLAD I FORGOT MY MP3.

THE END

Germ Meets Worm

'You need a holiday,' said Aristotle.

'No I don't,' said Blob.

Blob was sweeping so fast, Aristotle felt dizzy just watching his brother's broom.

'Yes you do,' said Aristotle. 'I can spot the signs.'

Blob was the tiredest-looking germ in the whole nostril. His body was flat and fatigue-wrinkled. His ectoplasm was grey. OK, some of the grey was dirt, but most of it was exhaustion.

'I haven't got time for a holiday,' grumbled Blob. He pointed to the vast space around them. 'I've got to sweep out this nostril, wash the nose hairs, clean out the mucus ducts, the smell equipment needs servicing, and if you don't pull your tendril out and get on with that dusting, I'll have to do that too.'

Aristotle sighed.

Or he would have done if nose germs could blow out air in an exasperated way. As they can't, he just stuck out his bottom in an exasperated way.

'Give yourself a break, Blob,' said Aristotle. 'You don't have to do all the housework yourself.'

He pointed to the thousands of other nose germs in the nostril who were busily sweeping and dusting and washing and cleaning and whistling happily.

'Pah,' said Blob. 'They don't do it properly. There's only one germ around here who knows how to keep a human nostril clean and tidy, and that's mmpff . . .'

Blob wasn't able to finish because of the feather duster Aristotle stuffed into his speech duct.

'Listen to me,' said Aristotle. 'We've been slaving in this nostril most of our working lives. Four and a half hours at least. And we've never taken holidays. That means we're owed nearly twenty minutes off.'

Aristotle took the broom away from Blob, who didn't protest because he was busy pulling the feather duster out of his speech duct. And busy realising it was actually made from dust-mite armpit hair. And busy feeling sick.

'So,' said Aristotle, leaning Blob's broom against a pimple. 'Where shall we go for our holiday?'

Down in the stomach, Wilton the tummy worm was having a holiday he didn't need, or want, or like.

It was called his life.

'Please,' he begged the bacteria and enzymes and other stomach microbes hard at work all around him. 'I want to work too. I want to do something useful. I want a job.'

'Give it a rest, you jiffing harpic,' said a microbe foreman up to his waist in melting ice-cream. 'We've been through this a million times. You're a worm. We don't employ worms.' He yelled across the stomach cavity. 'Hey, can we get some digestive juices over here?'

'I'll get them,' said Wilton. 'Let me get them.'

'Stay where you are,' said the foreman. 'The squirties'll do it. It's their job.'

'But I want to help,' said Wilton.

'Surf and ajax,' said the foreman. 'Get it through your thick ectoplasm, you great fat lump. You're a worm. You don't have to work. You're a parasite. Enjoy it.'

Wilton curled up miserably.

He couldn't enjoy feeling bored and useless. All around him the vast tummy was gurgling with happy industry. Millions of lucky microbes leading enjoyable and satisfying lives doing interesting and important work.

Sorting the veggies from the meat.

Making neat piles of fingernail fragments.

Rounding up globules of fat and sending them off to the bloodstream where they belonged.

Wilton felt a familiar tickle in his mid-section.

'Half your luck,' said a cheery voice. 'Wish I had a life of leisure. I'd swap places with you any day.'

Wilton tried to stay calm. He reminded himself

he was very lucky to have a best friend living inside him, even if that best friend was sometimes a bit insensitive about jobs and tickling.

Algy's tiny microbe head appeared from inside one of Wilton's waste ducts.

'It's non-stop housework in here,' said Algy happily. 'Tidying your inside bits, cleaning your walls and floors, keeping all your vital organs neat. Then I turn my back and you've messed them all up again.'

Wilton looked enviously at his tiny friend.

'You're right,' he said. 'And I'm very grateful. But you don't have to do all the housework yourself. I could do some.'

'Don't be a dope,' said Algy gently. 'How are you going to sweep out your own insides? You haven't got any tendrils. How are you going to hold the broom?'

Wilton knew Algy was right.

'That's the real reason those tummy workers won't employ me,' said Wilton. 'If I had tendrils, I bet they'd give me a job.'

Algy shook his head.

'They won't employ you,' he said, 'because you're about a hundred times bigger than them and you won't fit in the tea room.'

Wilton sighed.

Or he would have done if tummy worms could exhale oxygen-related gases in a sad way. As they can't, he just let his bottom sag.

'Come on,' said Algy. 'Don't start feeling sorry for yourself. There must be a job somewhere for an oversized worm. We've just got to find it.'

Up in the nostril, the travel agent went amazed-shaped.

'A twenty-minute holiday?' he said to Aristotle and Blob. 'You are two lucky nose germs. The longest I've ever been away for is three minutes. And two minutes of that was the flights.'

'We've never had a holiday before,' said Aristotle. 'We'd like to go somewhere exotic and restful.'

'I've got just the thing,' said the travel agent. 'How about twenty luxurious minutes lazing by a pool?'

'Sounds good,' said Aristotle. 'Where are we travelling to?'

'Just over there,' said the travel agent, pointing. 'That pool of snot.'

Aristotle saw how many other holidaying germs were already splashing around in it.

He also saw what Blob was doing. Pulling cleaning gear out of his travel bag.

'Disgraceful,' said Blob. 'Look how cloudy that shallow end is. Filter must be clogged. I'll need to get at that with my scrubbing brush.'

'Have you got anywhere else?' said Aristotle hastily to the travel agent. 'Somewhere a bit more exotic and far away?'

'I certainly have,' said the travel agent. 'How

does a luxury golfing holiday sound? Eighteen hole course, all natural skin-pores, and it's way over the other side of the nostril.'

'Pah,' grumbled Blob. 'I've heard about the disgraceful state of the other side of the nostril. If we're going over there I'll have to take my broom.'

'Even more exotic,' said Aristotle to the travel agent. 'And even further away.'

The travel agent had a think.

'Aromatherapy retreat?' he said. 'Nose-hair hang-gliding? Mucus safari?'

'Somewhere,' said Aristotle, 'not in the nostril.'

The travel agent went alarmed-shaped.

'Oi,' yelled the angry digestion foreman. 'Harpic. Put that jiffing gravy down right now.'

Wilton winced and the drop of gravy he'd been trying to balance on his tail rolled off with a plop.

All around the stomach, thousands of bacteria glared at Wilton with that expression tummy workers get when they think you're trying to steal their job.

Algy peered nervously over Wilton's shoulder.

'Accept it, Wriggles,' he said. 'There just isn't a place for you in the digestion industry. Come on, let's go for a paddle in the spleen.'

Wilton didn't want to. All he did these days was paddle in the spleen. He was sick of it.

'There must be something useful I can do,'

he said. 'I can't swim, so that rules out the blood industry. And I haven't got a sense of rhythm, so I'd be hopeless in the heart industry.'

Algy hated seeing his friend so unhappy.

'You're big and strong,' he said to Wilton. 'Maybe in the spleen they'll let you put out the deckchairs and beach umbrellas.'

Wilton wasn't listening.

He had just noticed something very unusual. Two strange microbes were speeding down the stomach wall in a rental saliva bubble.

Wilton stiffened in alarm.

'Nose germs,' he said. 'Look, you can tell, they've got noses. And one of them's armed.'

'It's not a weapon,' said Algy quietly. 'It's a broom.'

'The other one's got a camera,' said Wilton.

'Tourists,' said Algy.

'They could be the advance party for an invasion force,' said Wilton. 'That's what happened when the bottom germs invaded.'

Wilton looked anxiously around the stomach. The tummy workers were all working busily. Some of them were giving the nose germs a glance, but that was all.

'They're leaving it to me to stop the invaders,' said Wilton.

'Are you sure?' said Algy.

'You said it yourself,' replied Wilton. 'I'm big and strong. I was made for this sort of work. Fighting to the death with violent invaders.'

'I didn't say that last bit,' squeaked Algy, hastily retreating into one of Wilton's waste ducts.

'Hold tight,' said Wilton.

'Try not to be too violent,' pleaded Algy. 'I've just tidied all your internal organs.'

'I'll be as violent as I have to,' said Wilton, wriggling towards the nose germs. 'To get the job done.'

Aristotle parked the saliva bubble and peered nervously through the windscreen.

He was beginning to see why the travel agent hadn't wanted to book this trip for them. Why they'd had to tickle him until he'd given in.

The tummy was huge and crowded and noisy and dirty and not in the slightest bit exotic.

'I think we might have made a mistake,' said Aristotle to Blob.

'No we haven't,' said Blob. 'This is definitely the tummy. See, there's the back of the belly button.'

'I mean it doesn't seem like a very good place for a relaxing holiday,' said Aristotle. 'Look at the rough way those tummy germs are flinging that food around.'

'Disgraceful,' said Blob. 'This place needs a complete sweep out from top to bottom.'

He grabbed his broom and started to get out of the bubble.

'Wait,' said Aristotle, grabbing him. 'Stay here. I don't like the look of the locals.'

'They're only tummy germs,' said Blob. 'They're just microbes like us, only messier.'

'I don't mean the tummy germs,' said Aristotle.

With a trembling tendril he pointed at the huge worm wriggling towards them and looming over them in a very determined and possibly violent way.

'Arghhh,' squeaked Blob. 'This wasn't in the brochure.'

Then everything went brown.

It was the biggest lump of chocolate Wilton and Algy had ever seen.

'Wow,' said Algy, peeping out from inside Wilton. 'A lump of chocolate bigger than a worm. Now I've seen everything.'

Wilton tried to stay calm.

The giant brown lump had dropped from the throat tube at the top of the tummy and landed on the saliva bubble with a splat, completely burying the two nose germs.

'That,' said Algy, 'was a really silly place to park.'

Wilton tried to see if the nose germs were all right. Suddenly he was feeling a bit confused about his new job. It seemed a bit unfair to be fighting two nose germs to the death when they were buried in chocolate.

'Come on,' he said to Algy. 'We'd better get them out.'

Wilton started burrowing into the mound of

soggy chocolate, his whole body rippling with the effort.

Algy helped.

'Faster,' said Wilton. 'They're buried alive.'

'I'm only a small microbe,' said Algy. 'I'm eating as fast as I can.'

'Oi,' yelled an angry voice. 'You two jiffing drainos leave that chocolate alone. Pine-o-clean, how many times do I have to tell you?'

Wilton pulled his head out of the chocolate and glared down at the foreman.

'This isn't work,' he said. 'It's a rescue.'

The foreman didn't looked convinced. Wilton drew himself up to his full length. The foreman, noting that Wilton was about a hundred times bigger than him, backed off.

'I'm watching you, ajax,' he muttered to Wilton. 'I don't mind you mucking around with tourists, but if I catch you doing any food processing, I'll be down on you like a tonne of marshmallows.'

That's when Algy had the idea.

He stopped eating the chocolate and stared at Wilton. He even forgot there was more chocolate to eat, that's how amazing the idea was.

'I can't get over how clean and tidy this place is,' said Blob, gazing around inside Wilton. 'I couldn't make this place cleaner and tidier if I tried. Though I probably will try a bit later.'

He took another sip of his chocolate cocktail

and relaxed in his deckchair.

Algy glowed with pride.

Aristotle glowed too, with relief. He settled back on a wonderfully comfortable sofa made from the softest skin cells he'd ever sat on.

At last, he and Blob were having a real break.

What a nice tummy worm and tummy microbe, thought Aristotle. More like holiday resort hosts than vicious killers.

'This is such a great spot for a holiday,' he said gratefully to Algy. 'It's so quiet and peaceful in here. And you've done wonders with the décor.'

Algy glowed even more.

'I couldn't go wrong,' he said modestly. 'Wilton's so roomy and his internal organs were made for the place.'

Wilton listened contentedly to the chatter inside him.

What nice nose germs, he thought. More like polite houseguests than violent invaders.

'Everyone OK in there?' he called. 'Algy, let them play table tennis if they want to. I don't mind, I like the tickly feeling.'

It was the happiest twenty minutes of Aristotle and Blob's whole lives, and they felt like it would never end.

But like all gloriously long holidays, it finally did.

While Algy went off to organise a rental stomach-gas bubble for their return journey to the nose, Aristotle and Blob climbed up onto Wilton's shoulder to thank him. And to let him know they hadn't had anything from the mini-bar.

'We had a wonderful stay,' said Aristotle.

'You are the best holiday destination in the whole world,' said Blob. 'And when we tell our travel agent about you and your very reasonable rates, you're going to be the most booked out.'

Wilton grinned.

Or he would have done if worms had grin muscles. As they don't, he let gentle ripples of contentment run along his whole body so each waste duct was briefly stretched into a little smile.

If all the future guests were as nice as these two nose germs, Wilton couldn't wait.

'You won't mind?' said Aristotle. 'Being booked out all the time?'

'Of course not,' said Wilton happily. 'It's my job.'

Snugglepots And Cuddlepies

Those Cuddlepies are scum.

I'm sorry, I know it's not a nice thing to say. Mum would probably punish me if she heard me. Stop me watching *Australian Idol* for a week or something. Mum believes we should behave with compassion and respect towards other human beings, including Cuddlepies.

But I can't help it.

They are scum.

Wait till I tell you what a bunch of them did today.

I don't know what they were taught at those Cuddlepie Early Learning Centres, but it sure wasn't compassion or respect. Or nice smiles. We did nice smiles in the first week at my Snugglepot Kindy Solutions Centre. It wasn't easy because I was only one and a half, but I did the homework and I passed nice smiles in first term.

OK, I know that's boasting, but I'm proud to be a Snugglepot even after all these years, and Mum reckons it's OK to be proud of yourself if you deserve it.

'Give yourself a pat on the back, Paloma,' Mum said to me a few days ago when I told her I'd been chosen for the year six netball team. She asked me to do the patting myself cause she was delayed in Perth at a meeting and probably wouldn't be home till after midnight.

After we hung up I gave myself a pat.

I could have asked Dad to do it, but he was rushing around getting ready to go to his men's group. He was in a flap because he had to give them a talk on his experiences as a workaholic, so I didn't want to distract him.

I didn't mind. Patting myself on the back is another thing I learned at kindy. They teach it at all the Snugglepot Kindy Solutions Centres around the country, so if you ever see somebody patting themselves on the back, they're probably a Snugglepot.

That bunch of Cuddlepies who attacked me and Cheri today weren't patting themselves on the back.

Or smiling nicely.

I was on my way to school with Cheri and we ducked into Northpoint to check out the lipsticks in Pricerite. Mum reckons I'm too young to wear lipstick, but she's a big supporter of people planning ahead in their lives.

Cheri was sniffing a Dusky Peach tester when I gave her a nudge.

'Cuddlepies,' I whispered.

There were about six of them coming out of Subway. You can spot Cuddlepies a mile off when you know the signs and you've had them in your class since year one.

Tyson Phelps was at the front. He saw us and pointed.

'Check the Snugglepots buying the ugly sticks,' he jeered.

The others all laughed and did that cruel Cuddlepie sneer. Including Gale Bishop who always rubs her tomato sauce on her lips to look sexy when she thinks nobody's looking.

Cheri pretended to ignore them, which was sensible. Cuddlepies can be vicious if you get them worked up.

I wasn't sensible.

'She's not buying, cretin brains, she's just looking,' I said to the Cuddlepies. 'And anyway, she's not a Snugglepot, so rack off.'

Tyson Phelps did another Cuddlepie sneer.

'Don't lie,' he said. 'Why would she hang around a smelly Snugglepot like you if she wasn't one herself?'

Cheri put the lipstick down and turned and faced the Cuddlepies and put her hands on her hips. She's pretty short, but she read somewhere that putting your hands on your hips makes you look bigger and tougher.

'I hang around her because she's my friend,' said Cheri. 'You heard her, rack off.'

When Cheri's defending you, her face goes really pink and she gets asthma and can't breathe properly. But it doesn't stop her. And do you know what's even more amazing? She's not even a Snugglepot. Her parents didn't send her to a Snugglepot Kindy Solutions Centre. They didn't send her anywhere. When she started in year one, she confessed to me that she'd never been to a single Kindy Centre or Long Daycare Playschool or Early Years Speed-growth Camp or anything.

Poor kid.

'Rack off yourself,' replied Tyson Phelps to Cheri.

You can see the sort of wit they teach at those Cuddlepie so-called Early Learning Centres.

I turned my back on the whole lot of them because by this stage Cheri was bending over and wheezing and I had to help her find her puffer in her school bag.

While we searched, I felt cold sloppy things hitting my face.

Tyson and the others were flicking bits of Subway at us. Turkey loaf and salad extender and slices of pickle that really sting if they hit you in the eye.

I haven't been able to get much work done this morning here in class. I've just been sitting here thinking about them doing that.

Only Cuddlepies would attack a sick kid like

Cheri and do it with really vinegary sandwich fillings.

See what I mean about scum?

At 4pm I had my first netball match ever against another school.

It was a very big occasion for me.

And, as it turned out, a very confusing one.

The hall was full of parents. Mum couldn't be there, she's in Cairns at a meeting, and Dad had an appointment at his therapist, but I didn't mind because I had Cheri. She's not allowed to play netball on account of her wheezing, but she's a fantastic supporter as long as she doesn't get too carried away and pass out.

I was on the bench for the first quarter. New team members always are.

Cheri came and sat next to me and we tried to work out which people on the visiting team were Cuddlepies.

I hadn't met any of them before. Their school is about ten suburbs away. But you can spot a Cuddlepie on the netball court a mile off if you know the signs.

Rough play is one.

And sneering at the umpire behind her back.

With this visiting team it was really hard to tell. They played tough but fair. When the umpire blew her whistle against them, they copped it. Some even with nice smiles.

'Amazing,' I whispered to Cheri. 'They must all be Snugglepots.'

Cheri didn't say anything. She'd spent most of the match so far crouched down rummaging in her bag. Probably looking for her spare puffer, I thought, in case the last quarter was a nail biter.

I studied the visiting players more closely.

There was one, their wing defence, skinny with long bleached dreads, who kept glancing over at me and Cheri.

That made me suspicious. Cuddlepies reckon they can spot Snugglepots a mile off too.

'I reckon she's a Cuddlepie,' I muttered to Cheri. 'Plotting some way to get me next quarter when I'm playing.'

Cheri still didn't say anything.

Just looked worried.

So I figured I must be right.

Then the first quarter ended and an amazing thing happened. The Cuddlepie wing defence girl trotted over to us, bold as really bold lipstick.

'G'day Cheri,' she said. 'I thought it was you.'

Cheri gave her the sort of pasty smile she gives adults when she's trying to persuade them she feels better than she really does.

The girl saw me staring and gave me a friendly grin.

'Me and Cheri used to know each other,' she said. 'We went to the same Cuddlepie Early Learning Centre.'

I felt like a netball had just whacked me in the head.

Cheri?

A Cuddlepie?

Cheri was looking like she was having a major attack, eyes wide and mouth open, except she wasn't wheezing.

I grabbed at a wild thought. Perhaps this was all lies. An evil Cuddlepie plot by this other girl to break me and Cheri up. But if it was a lie, why wasn't Cheri denying it?

The girl stared at me with a friendly frown.

'You weren't at our Centre, were you?' she asked.

I shook my head.

'Didn't think so,' she said. 'Which Cuddlepie Centre did you go to?'

Cheri was looking panicked now and that's when I knew the only Cuddlepie lie here today is the one Cheri has been telling me for the last five-and-a-half years.

I glared at them both.

'I went to a Snugglepot Kindy Solutions Centre,' I said.

The girl took a step back. She stared at me like I was a lump of dog poo in a netball uniform.

'Gross,' she said to Cheri. 'Why are you hanging around with a slimy Snugglepot?'

Cheri looked at us both helplessly. I'd never seen her lost for words before, except when she was slipping into unconsciousness.

The girl turned and walked away.

Cheri grabbed me and tried to say something.

I didn't want to hear it.

The umpire blew her whistle for the second quarter and Mrs West our coach came over and told me I was playing goal shooter.

The rest of the match was a blur. I scored some goals and the Cuddlepie wing defence girl fouled me every chance she got and at half time I stayed in the team huddle and we won I think.

I tried to concentrate on the match but my dazed mind just kept thinking the same thought.

My best friend is a Cuddlepot.

I mean Cuddlepie.

See how confused I am?

At the end of the match as I hurried towards the changing room, Cheri came up to me. She looked like she'd been crying.

'I'm sorry,' she mumbled miserably. 'I hated lying to you but I just wanted to be your friend.'

I pushed past her into the changing room and locked myself in a cubicle and I've been here ever since.

Confused.

I should be furious with Cheri for pulling a typical low Cuddlepie stunt and lying to me. That is so typical of them.

But I'm sitting here trying to be angry with her, and I just can't do it.

When I saw how upset she was I wanted to

put my arms round her. That's partly because I'm a Snugglepot and I have compassion and respect towards other human beings, but mostly because she's my best friend.

This is weird.

I'm feeling all warm and loving towards a Cuddlepie.

OK, here's what I reckon has happened. Cheri has spent so much time with me over the past five-and-a-half years that she's turned into a Snugglepot.

Yes, of course, that must be it.

Phew, I'm feeling better already.

Here's what I'm going to do. Go out there right now and give Cheri a hug and say sorry for ignoring her. It might be a bit hard for her at first, discovering she's a Snugglepot, but she's a pretty amazing person so I reckon she'll cope.

Here I go.

Hang on.

Oh, no.

What if it happened the other way round?

Over the past five-and-a-half years I've spent just as much time with Cheri as she has with me.

What if I've turned into a . . . ?

No way. I can't believe I'm even thinking this. It couldn't happen. It's impossible. Me turn into a Cuddlepie? Not a chance.

Except if I'm a Snugglepot and Cheri's a Cuddlepie, why do we care about each other so much?

Of course.

Yes.

I know what's happened.

Why didn't I realise it before?

OK, here I go. I'm on my way to give Cheri a hug and explain the whole thing to her.

I know.

People will laugh.

Specially that Cuddlepie lot. The Snugglepots probably will too.

But me and Cheri won't care because we'll have our friendship. We'll stand side by side and proudly tell the world the truth.

We're not Snugglepots.

Or Cuddlepies.

We're a mixture.

We're Snugglepies.

Or, if Cheri prefers, Cuddlepots.

And anyone who says we're not, they're scum.

Why My Dad Could Be Prime Minister

My dad could be Prime Minister because he's kind to animals and he knows good jokes and he loves Australian food including noodles and he lets the neighbours borrow our whipper snipper and he doesn't snore and he can wiggle his ears and he's modest after he's put a fire out in somebody's house and he gives other people his seat on the bus except if they're hoons and he only cries if a movie is really sad or it's got onions in it and he does his own ironing and he trims his own nose hairs and he can bend metal with his bare hands and he's got heaps of friends and he can lift a telly if it needs rescuing and he knows quite a lot of cartoon voices and he's good at putting band-aids on cut fingers and he gives you a hug after.

But he does have three bad habits he would have to change if he was going to be Prime Minister.

One is, he sometimes gets words wrong.

Like tonight.

Dad was reading the politics part of the paper, which he does a lot, and suddenly he looks at the clock and sees we're still up.

'OK, you kids,' he says. 'Let's have a new law in this house. Let's call it the Bedtime Choices Act.'

Me and Beth and Charlie all cheer. We like the idea of choosing our own bedtime. It means we can finish the Sim city we're working on. But most of all we want to wait up till Mum gets home.

'Agreed?' says Dad.

'Yes,' yell me and Beth and Charlie.

'OK,' says Dad. 'I want you all in bed in three minutes. Which is just enough time to save your game, do your teeth and give me a very big kiss.'

I look at Dad, confused.

He does breathe in a bit of smoke at work sometimes from the burning buildings. Maybe it's affected his brain.

'But,' I stammer. 'You said . . .'

'Bedtime Choices,' grins Dad. 'Your bedtime, my choice.'

Me and Beth and Charlie stare at him.

'Not fair,' wail Beth and Charlie.

I wonder if I should explain to Dad that he's got it wrong. I decide not to. It might take more than three minutes.

'We want to stay up till Mum gets home,' I say quietly.

Dad's face goes serious.

'I know you do, Jack,' he says. 'But she might be home pretty late. Very late, actually. As you know, she's gone to the movies. I'm not sure what time her movie ends.'

A small flicker of worry starts in the bottom of my guts. Like one of those little flames that can grow into a huge fire.

Why doesn't Dad know what time Mum's movie ends? The movie times are on the internet. I bet the Prime Minister always knows what time his wife's movie ends.

Maybe Mum hasn't gone where she told us she was going. To the local movie theatre. Maybe she's gone to that big multiplex, the one on the very busy dangerous road. Maybe I was right when she was saying goodbye earlier and I saw that strange look on her face.

The guilty one.

I wondered then if something was going on and I'm wondering it again now.

'Two and a half minutes,' says Dad.

As I lead Beth and Charlie off to the bathroom I wonder if Dad has got the words 'gone to the movies' wrong just like he got the words 'bedtime choices' wrong.

If he has, that means Mum could be anywhere.

I don't ask Dad about it in case it upsets Beth and Charlie.

That's the thing about having a dad who's a firefighter. Who risks his life every day at work.

Who you can never be totally sure will come home safely.

You grow up to be a kid who worries a lot.

I can't sleep.

The worry flame is getting bigger and my insides are burning.

I get out of bed and creep into the living room. Dad is asleep on the lounge in front of the telly. The clock says 11.47.

Mum still isn't home.

'Dad,' I say, giving him a prod.

He opens his eyes.

'Is Mum in hospital having a serious operation?' I ask.

Dad stares at me. Then he pulls me onto his lap.

'No, mate,' he says. 'She's not.'

I can see he's telling the truth. He's got little crinkles round his eyes. Mum calls them crows feet. Dad calls them heat lines. I call them truth crinkles.

'Is she having a love affair with another bloke?' I ask.

Dad doesn't grin.

Even though it's a very crazy idea, he knows how awful it would be if she was.

'No, Jack,' he says. 'Definitely not.'

He's still telling the truth.

I tell him my last worry. That's the great thing about a dad like him, you can. If I was voting for a

Prime Minister, I'd always vote for one who lets you sit on their lap and tell them your worries.

'Has Mum committed some crime,' I say, 'and she's gone to hand herself in?'

Now Dad does smile. But he's shaking his head and his truth crinkles are still there.

'So Mum really has just gone to the movies?' I say.

Perhaps tonight our local cinema is showing all six *Star Wars* movies back to back.

'She really has,' says Dad.

I stare at him.

Something has happened to his eyes. The truth crinkles have vanished. He's not telling the truth.

This is the second bad habit he'll have to change. He doesn't tell lies much, but you can't tell them at all if you want to be Prime Minister.

I don't have that thought at the time.

I'm too panicked.

Plus, one second after I discover from Dad's face that Mum isn't at the movies, she walks in. Very slowly. Like she's in pain. She looks even more pained when she sees I'm up.

I stare at her, a worry bushfire ripping through me.

Mum's shirt is unbuttoned and underneath it I can see a big bandage round her chest.

The other bad habit Dad will have to change if he's ever Prime Minister is the one where he says he's thinking about other people when he's really thinking about himself.

That's what happened tonight when Mum walked in all bandaged up.

I gasped at the sight of her.

'Love,' says Dad to Mum. 'Are you OK? You look terrible. Tell Jack you're OK.'

What he really means is 'tell me you're OK'.

Dad looks like his insides are ablaze with worry too.

'Relax, both of you,' says Mum. 'I'm fine.'

She doesn't look fine.

'What is it?' I say. 'What happened?'

I try to prepare myself for really bad news. Like she's been shot. Or stabbed. Or had her appendix out.

Mum hesitates. I can see she wishes I was asleep. But I'm not.

'It's just a tattoo,' she says.

My brain must be a bit heat-affected from the burning worry because I don't get it at first.

'A tattoo?' I say.

'That's all,' she says.

Then I do get it. Dad's had a tattoo for years and Mum's always saying how she'd like one.

I wasn't born when Dad got his tattoo, but he's told me how it hurt a lot and went scabby for the first few days.

'Show me,' I say to Mum.

She and Dad look at each other. They know it's

the only way to get me back to bed without a fuss, so Mum shows me.

'Yuk,' I say as Dad unwinds the bandage. Mum's back is red and swollen and definitely starting to go scabby.

Then I see what the tattoo is.

It's me and Beth and Charlie and Mum and Dad. We're all smiling out of the middle of Mum's back with our arms round each other. I think the tattoo artist must have used the photo from when Dad volunteered to fight the bushfires in Gippsland and we all went with him to keep him company in the motel.

'That's great,' I say.

It is.

Tattoos are permanent.

Like families.

Mum's tattoo isn't as action-packed as Dad's, but not many tattoos are. He's got flames shooting up out of the back of his undies and a big squirting hose coiled round his shoulders.

People would be so impressed to have a Prime Minister with a tattoo like that.

Mum works in a deli, which I think is why she didn't make her tattoo about her job. When people saw the ham and salami, they might think the tattoo hadn't healed.

'Why did you say you were going to the movies?' I ask Mum.

She looks a bit embarrassed.

'I was worried I might chicken out,' she says. 'You know, when I got to the tattoo parlour and saw the needles. That's why I asked Dad not to tell you where I was going. If I didn't get it done, I didn't want you kids to think I was a coward.'

'We'd never think that,' I say to her.

It's true, we wouldn't. In the motel in Gippsland Mum pulled a huge splinter out of Dad's armpit with her teeth.

'I knew you wouldn't chicken out,' says Dad, giving her a kiss.

That's another reason why Dad could be Prime Minister. He has total faith in people. You have to when you're sharing a hose and a ladder. Plus he's incredibly gentle at putting a bandage back onto a new tattoo. As he does it, Mum doesn't even wince.

And he's generous.

'I like yours even more than mine,' he says to Mum.

His truth crinkles are there the whole time.

I'm not sure if Dad would ever want to be Prime Minister on account of he loves being a firefighter heaps, but if he does give it a crack one day he'll be really well qualified if he can kick those few little bad habits.

I used to want Dad to be Prime Minister so we wouldn't have to worry about him so much. It's a known fact that very few Prime Ministers have ever perished in fires in other people's houses.

But I don't think I'll be worrying about Dad

quite so much now. If I feel those tummy flames coming on, I'll just ask Mum to take her shirt off so I can have a squiz at her back.

Oh, there is one more thing Dad knows how to do that I reckon would make him a brilliant Prime Minister.

He did it just now.

I'm back in bed and almost off to sleep, and Dad pokes his head round my bedroom door.

'That bull I told you about Mum being at the movies,' he whispers.

'Don't worry about it, Dad,' I murmur.

'No,' he says, 'I want to apologise.'

He doesn't have to because I understand, but he does anyway.

'Sorry,' he says.

I reckon I'd vote for him even if he wasn't my dad.

So Unjust

Samantha loved reading stories.

The part of each story she liked best was the twist at the end. That funny and unexpected moment when everything is suddenly OK and the main character ends up delighted and relieved and a bit stunned all at the same time.

'Yes,' chuckled Samantha as she read how the puzzled owner of the giggling limping parrot discovered that the parrot's previous owner had been very ticklish, specially near his wooden leg.

'Good one,' laughed Samantha when the forgetful boy who swallowed his iPod found his memory was improving.

'Brilliant,' she chortled when the airport terminal that had always been jealous of the planes got blown up and discovered it could fly too.

Samantha loved those twists.

But each time she read one, sprawled on her

bedroom floor, a tiny part of her always ended up feeling sad.

The truth was, much as she loved her shelf of neatly-arranged books packed with twist-enriched stories, they weren't quite enough.

What Samantha wanted more than anything was a twist or two in her own life.

Nothing huge like discovering Mum and Dad, who both loved Mars Bars, were Martians. Or having her teacher Ms Quigly, who could whistle through her teeth, fall in love with her dentist and not be able to stop whistling the ring tone of the dentist's dead wife's mobile. Or saying 'to die for' a lot and then actually dying.

Nothing that big. Just a few small fun twists that would make life more interesting.

But they never happened.

Samantha's life was twistless.

Then one Saturday morning she read a story and understood why.

It wasn't the best story she'd ever read, and the twist was a bit ordinary. It was about a boy who swallowed a tea bag and then had to do a parachute jump. The boy was terrified he'd land in a tree and hang there jiggling and never be rescued. So he swallowed some coffee beans, ones that had been ground because that's where he wanted to land. But when he jumped out of the plane his parachute didn't open, so he quickly swallowed another tea bag and his fall was broken by the shade cloth over the staff BBQ area of a teapot factory.

Wow, thought Samantha. So that's how it works. You have to make twists happen.

For the rest of that day, Samantha worked hard to make twists happen in her own life.

Instead of trying to have a conversation with Dad, which she did every Saturday morning, and instead of getting frustrated while Dad read his paper and only replied in grunts, which he did every Saturday morning, Samantha went down to the shopping centre and juggled half-litre milk cartons outside Officeworks.

She hoped that a newspaper photographer would notice her. And that her photo would be in the paper the following Saturday morning. And that Dad would see it just as he was in the middle of not paying her very much attention.

That, she was pretty sure, would be a twist.

But unfortunately the photographer from the local paper was doing his first parachute jump that day and wasn't around.

Passers-by were impressed, though. They'd never seen a girl juggling half-litre milk cartons before. They thought Samantha was busking, and dropped money at her feet, over $150 in total. But Samantha knew that didn't count as a twist because she'd put the plastic bucket there herself.

After lunch, while Mum was sewing, which she did every Saturday afternoon, Samantha asked if Mum would teach her to sew, which she did every Saturday afternoon, and Mum, as usual, said not until Samantha was older because the sewing machine was a very expensive one, and dangerous.

So Samantha went back down to the shops and spent her busking money on a chainsaw.

She hid it under her bed and spent a happy few hours looking forward to next Saturday. At which time, when Mum said that the sewing machine was dangerous, Samantha planned to show her the chainsaw and say, 'No, Mum, this is dangerous.'

It would be a satisfying moment, but it still wouldn't be a twist because Dad's birthday was the week after and he'd been saying he wanted a chainsaw for ages.

Samantha sighed. It was Saturday evening now and she still hadn't made a twist happen.

Mum and Dad were watching TV, which they did every Saturday night, and only replying with vague murmurs when she spoke to them.

Samantha thought about going next door and strangling the elderly couple who lived there, Mr and Mrs Kemp.

That would be a twist, because Mum and Dad were watching Midsomer Murders.

But she didn't. Strangling elderly neighbours wasn't a good thing to do, even though they were grouchy and threw pill bottles at her when she went into their garden to get her ball.

Samantha decided to call it a day.

'Night, Mum,' she said. 'Night, Dad.'

They both murmured something vague.

Samantha got into bed and re-read the story about the boy and the tea bag. Had she missed something? Some important clue about how to make twists happen? She didn't think so.

As her eyelids got heavy, she had a hopeful thought. That even as she was closing the book, a local parachutist, making his or her first night jump, would lose control of the parachute and crash through the roof of the house and dent Mum's sewing machine and Mum would be sad she hadn't let Samantha have a go while it still worked.

But nothing like that happened.

Samantha slid the book under her pillow and her last thought before she drifted off was that perhaps she would never find a way to make a twist happen.

Unless, she thought dreamily, an author who's looking for a story idea with a twist at the end finds out about me. And is fascinated by a girl who loves twists in stories but never has them in her own life.

Now that would be a twist, thought Samantha, if I ended up in a story myself.

PIZZA CAKE

Saving Ms Fosdyke

Dad was flabbergasted when I told him the news.

He nearly dropped the plate he was washing up. He stared at me, water dripping off his elbows.

'Fifty million?' he said. 'Your school is selling Ms Fosdyke to West Chirnside Primary for fifty million dollars?'

I nodded sadly.

'That's crazy,' said Dad. 'They could get heaps more for a teacher like her. The primary school near the library just paid over seventy million for a year-four teacher with half her experience.'

Mum nodded as she took the plate from him and dried it.

'And that was a bargain,' she said. 'Last week the high school paid a hundred million dollars for a maths teacher.'

'Crazy,' said Dad. 'Giving away a top teacher like

Ms Fosdyke for fifty million. You don't even get a good soccer player for that these days.'

I agreed. It was crazy.

And it was all my fault.

'Emmy, love, don't chew your pen,' said Mum. 'Those pens cost nearly a dollar each. Have you finished your homework?'

'Almost,' I said. 'I'm doing my creative writing task. I'm making up a story about some teachers who are badly paid and overworked and don't get much respect.'

Mum frowned.

'Sounds a bit far-fetched,' she said.

'It's a fantasy story,' I said. 'Ms Fosdyke encourages us to use our imagination.'

Dad wiped his hands and picked up my exercise book and read a couple of sentences. He frowned and put the exercise book down again.

'Even fantasy stories need to be a little bit believable, Emmy,' he said. 'You can't just write totally impossible crazy stuff.'

Mum sat down next to me at the kitchen table and put her arm round me.

'You must be feeling sad,' she said. 'About Ms Fosdyke being transferred.'

I nodded.

Mum and Dad both looked sympathetic.

Suddenly I knew I had to risk it and tell them. So they'd see why it was so important that Ms Fosdyke didn't leave.

'Ms Fosdyke thinks that one day . . .'

I hesitated for a sec. Was this going to sound dopey?

'. . . that one day I could be a teacher.'

Mum and Dad just stared at me. They were both flabbergasted.

'A teacher?' said Mum.

'Are you sure?' said Dad.

I nodded.

'Oh love,' said Mum. 'That might be pushing it a bit. Why don't you lower your sights just a little. What about being a doctor? Or a lawyer?'

'I want to be a teacher,' I said quietly. 'I want to help people's minds blossom like Ms Fosdyke does.'

Mum sighed.

'Emmy,' she said. 'Only the smartest, cleverest, most brilliant people get to be teachers. You know that. It's good to be ambitious, but it's not good to set yourself up for disappointment.'

'Airline pilot,' said Dad. 'Why not give that a go? That's more sensible, eh?'

I didn't reply.

Mum and Dad meant well, but the trouble was they didn't really believe in me. Not really. Not like Ms Fosdyke.

That's why I had to stop her going.

The next day I asked Dad to drop me off early at school.

He said he would, but halfway there the ute got

a puncture and by the time he'd fixed it he was late for his first job, which was a leaky toilet, so I had to walk the rest of the way.

When I got to school, the bell had gone. In the playground, the volunteer parents were lining everyone up in class rows.

I ducked down behind the only car in the staff carpark. Ms Fosdyke's Lamborghini. She always came in early to do her marking. That was one of the ways she was different to the other teachers. She reckoned teachers should do their own marking and not just get big law firms to do it.

I crept into school without anyone seeing me.

As I hurried down the corridor, all the staffrooms were quiet. I wasn't surprised. Most of the other teachers didn't come in till ten. Eleven if they felt like a lie-in. But I knew Ms Fosdyke would be in her staffroom.

I tapped on her door.

I could hear voices inside. The radio probably. Ms Fosdyke often listened to the radio while she did her marking so she could find out what was happening in the world and let us kids know. She also went overseas in the school holidays, but you couldn't see everything in only four trips a year, not even when you had your own plane.

The door opened.

'Hello, Emmy,' said Ms Fosdyke, staring at me, surprised, but in a nice way. 'Is everything OK?'

She looked amazing. She was wearing a knitted

silk and cashmere dress with real gold thread at the neck and cuffs, tastefully matched with a Hermes scarf with her own initials on it.

I know about this stuff because Mum works in a drycleaners.

'Everything's not OK, is it Emmy?' said Ms Fosdyke gently.

'Please don't go,' I said. '6F needs you. You're worth more than fifty million dollars to us.'

Ms Fosdyke sighed. Not in an impatient way, in a concerned way.

'Come in,' she said. 'Let's have a talk.'

I followed Ms Fosdyke into her staffroom.

'Have a seat,' she said.

I sat down on a soft white leather lounge, hoping I didn't have any tap grease on the back of my skirt from Dad's ute.

'Would you like a juice?' asked Ms Fosdyke. 'I've got apple, cranberry, mango, watermelon, mandarin, peach, pineapple or lychee.'

'No thanks,' I said.

'Donut?' she said.

Normally I'd have said yes, specially as Ms Fosdyke had her own Krispy Kreme display case, but I was feeling a bit overwhelmed by actually being in a teacher's own private staffroom.

Except, now I looked around, I saw that Ms Fosdyke's staffroom wasn't quite as huge as I'd thought it would be. She didn't have a jacuzzi or a round bed or a disco floor, not like some teachers.

And her TV wasn't much bigger than ours at home. The paintings on her wall were better, though. She had one that we had, the waterlily one by that French bloke. But hers were done with real paint rather than just printed.

'Emmy,' said Ms Fosdyke, sitting next to me on the lounge. 'It doesn't have to change anything, me leaving. You'll still study hard and go to university, and eventually you'll be a really good teacher, I know you will.'

I mumbled something about how I couldn't do it without her.

'You can,' said Ms Fosdyke. 'I used to be just like you. I used to look at teachers and think, how could I ever do that job, the most important and prestigious and highest-paid and hard-to-get job in the world?'

'Exactly,' I said.

'Get real, my dad used to say,' sighed Ms Fosdyke. 'Be a brain surgeon.'

'Really?' I said.

Ms Fosdyke nodded.

'But I wanted to teach,' she said. 'So I made myself have courage.'

Before I could ask her how, the toilet in her ensuite bathroom flushed and a man came out. He was much older than Ms Fosdyke and wearing a business suit. I wondered if he was an uncle of hers. One who'd encouraged her to be teacher. And to say thank you, she let him use her private bathroom.

'Emmy,' said Ms Fosdyke, 'this is Joe Greely, my agent.'

I knew what an agent was. A sort of business manager. You have to have one when you earn as much as a teacher does.

'That name rings an unpleasant bell,' said Mr Greely, frowning at me. 'Emily. It was you who put this whole West Chirnside idea into Debra's head, right?'

'It's Emmy,' I said in a small voice.

But he was right, it was me who told Ms Fosdyke about West Chirnside Primary and how they didn't have enough teachers because they couldn't afford them, and how my cousin's year-three class was being taught by the school caretaker.

Now I wished I hadn't. I should have guessed that a kind and wonderful teacher like Ms Fosdyke wouldn't be able to control herself when she heard about a school where a whole year-three class was only learning about door-hinge oil and leaf-blowing. And that she'd offer herself to the poor school, even though they couldn't really afford her.

It was all my fault. If I'd kept quiet, Ms Fosdyke wouldn't be leaving us.

'Don't blame Emmy for this, Joe,' said Ms Fosdyke. 'It's my decision.'

Mr Greely helped himself to a drink that didn't look like juice from Ms Fosdyke's cocktail bar, and a donut. He kept giving me looks and I could tell he did blame me.

I decided that if I was ever a teacher I'd insist on having a much lower wage than normal so I wouldn't need an agent.

Except I knew I probably wouldn't ever be a teacher, so it didn't matter.

'Fifty million,' said Mr Greely to Ms Fosdyke with a scowl. 'Creyton College would have coughed up a hundred and twenty million for you, even though you're stubborn and pig-headed.'

'We've been through this,' said Ms Fosdyke, sounding almost as annoyed as she did when she lent the year-six science club her very own electron microscope and they dropped it. 'I'm a teacher. I'm not doing this job for the money. I go where children need me.'

I was about to point out to Ms Fosdyke that the children at our school needed her too, but Mr Greely butted in.

'West Chirnside haven't even got the full fifty,' he said.

'I don't care,' said Ms Fosdyke. 'Do you know how many cake stalls and fetes a school fundraising committee has to put on to raise fifty million dollars?'

She paused.

'How much have they got?' she asked.

'Forty-seven million, six hundred and thirty-two thousand, nine hundred and twenty-eight dollars,' said Mr Greely grumpily. 'So that's even less of a fee I get.'

'You do OK,' said Ms Fosdyke. 'Anyway, some

things are more important than a measly two and a half million. Right now I'd rather you were concerned about a little girl who's feeling very sad.'

Ms Fosdyke turned back to me, and for a few moments her shoulders slumped.

Then she gave my arm a gentle squeeze, stood up, and tossed her head so her fantastic haircut flopped perfectly into place.

I know about this stuff because my auntie works in a dog-trimming parlour.

'I'm sorry, Emmy,' said Ms Fosdyke. 'I've loved being at this school, but I've given West Chirnside my word.'

She sighed and poured herself a juice.

Suddenly I realised what was happening.

Ms Fosdyke was feeling sad too. And trapped. She'd made West Chirnside Primary a promise, but now she was about to leave us, she didn't want to go. And was wishing somebody could get her out of it.

I stood up.

'Thanks for the talk, Ms Fosdyke,' I said. 'I should be off to class now.'

I needed to get there as quickly as possible.

To start planning how to save Ms Fosdyke.

Ms Fosdyke was a bit late getting to class.

The volunteer warm-up parent was starting to look anxious. He'd done all his warm-up things twice, and was just starting us on our times tables for the third time when Ms Fosdyke arrived.

'Sorry,' said Ms Fosdyke after the applause and cheering had died down. 'It's turning into a bit of a morning.'

I didn't mind, because the extra time had given me a chance to work out exactly what we were going to do to save Ms Fosdyke.

My plan was to wait until the volunteer warm-up parent left, then get all the biggest kids in the class to lie down against the door and barricade it shut. Then I'd ring the TV news and tell them we were holding Ms Fosdyke hostage, but in a good way. And when they asked what our demands were, I'd tell them we only had one. That West Chirnside Primary School spend their forty-seven and a bit million dollars on a different teacher.

The volunteer warm-up parent said goodbye and left.

Which was a bit sudden. I wasn't ready. I didn't have the phone number for the TV news, and I hadn't explained my plan to the rest of the class.

I waited till Ms Fosdyke started the lesson, which was a group conversation about personal choices in life. Then I got my phone out and googled under the desk and found the TV news number.

I sent a text to all the other kids explaining my plan. Trouble was, they were all enjoying being part of the conversation so much, they didn't notice.

I decided I'd have to start the plan on my own and explain it as I went along. I knew I wasn't big enough to barricade the door without help, but once I was lying there, the others would get the idea and join in.

I stood up.

And saw something weird through the classroom window.

A TV news cameraman was outside in the corridor with some other TV news people. Which was amazing because I hadn't even rung them yet.

Ms Fosdyke saw me standing up. Then she saw the TV news people in the corridor. Mr Greely was with them.

'I'm sorry,' Ms Fosdyke said to us. 'Looks like we're going to have a bit of an interruption. I'm guessing it's my agent's idea. He's probably thinking that if I'm going to a poor underprivileged school, I might as well get some publicity for it.'

She gave Mr Greely a glare, and I could see she wasn't happy.

I wasn't either. Once this was on the news, and the nation was saying what a saint Ms Fosdyke was, she'd have to keep her word to West Chirnside. I wondered if I should fling myself against the door and try to keep the TV news crew out.

Before I could, they came in.

One of them introduced himself as the director and asked me to sit down and told the class not to wave at the camera.

Another one, who you could tell was a reporter because she was reporting, explained to the camera what an unusual teacher Ms Fosdyke was. Then she interviewed Mr Greely, who agreed that Ms Fosdyke was a very unusual teacher, and said that her generosity was priceless. He also said that after Ms Fosdyke finished her two-year contract with West Chirnside, she'd be available for transfer to another school for a hundred and fifty million dollars.

The director asked Ms Fosdyke if they could film some scenes in the classroom that would show viewers what an unusual teacher she was.

'Sure,' said Ms Fosdyke. 'I'm feeling a bit tired, so I'm going to ask Emmy to take the class for a while.'

I was sitting down, but I almost fell over.

'Me?' I croaked.

Ms Fosdyke smiled and beckoned me out the front.

Everybody was looking at me.

I went and stood in front of the class. The TV news people switched on a couple more lights and out of the corner of my eye I could see the camera staring at me.

The class was staring at me too, stunned.

'What do you want me to do?' I whispered to Ms Fosdyke.

'Up to you,' she said. 'You're the teacher.'

I was on the news that night.

They didn't show all my lesson, because it went for nearly twenty minutes and that wouldn't have left time for several wars and a new polar bear cub at the zoo.

But they had nearly thirty seconds of it, enough to show how brilliant 6F were at getting over their camera nerves and coming up with some great ideas in the thought experiment I did with them.

We were brainstorming about teachers, and what the world would be like if they were overworked and underpaid and didn't get much respect.

Garth Webster, who was usually one of the shyest in the class, said a really good thing about how teachers wouldn't be able to give the best of themselves if they had to worry about their car repair bills and their blood pressure and their social lives. I reckon Garth might be a TV host one day.

After the segment finished, I glanced at Mum and Dad.

They were both staring at me, mouths open.

'You were amazing,' said Mum.

'Jeez,' said Dad. 'I think we're gunna be better off in our old age than we thought.'

I knew that was just his way of letting me know how proud he was.

'Don't choose a mansion yet,' I said. 'If I do get to be a teacher, I'm probably going to be working in a fairly poor school.'

Mum and Dad didn't look like they were too upset by that.

Not as upset as they were by the sudden thought Mum had.

'We should have recorded that segment,' Mum wailed.

I didn't mind we hadn't, because I knew I'd never forget it.

Specially the last shot of Ms Fosdyke smiling, her kind eyes shining and her expertly-whitened teeth gleaming. I know about that stuff because Dad's best friend is a tiler.

On the screen you couldn't see who she was smiling at.

She was smiling at me.

Thanks, Ms Fosdyke.

Whatever they pay you in the future, you're worth every cent.

Pizza Cake

The changing room looks like a battlefield.

Not one of those battlefields you see in old war photos.

A cricket battlefield.

Glenn can hardly bear to look. He forces himself to. This is his team and they're in pain. Most of them are either slumped on the benches groaning, or lying on the floor thinking about groaning.

It'll be his turn in about ten minutes.

'That bowler should be banned,' mutters Daisy Taylor, one of the openers. She's holding a damp bunched-up towel to her forehead.

'There should be a law against people in year six bowling that fast,' says Stefano Priori, batsman number three, hugging his bruised arm. 'Bowling that fast isn't natural. I reckon that kid's mum gives him steroids. And I bet he's got one of those exercise machines from daytime TV.'

The rest of the Dudley Park Primary School team murmur their agreement from the floor.

Outside on the oval there's another explosion of cheering. Glenn sighs. More delight from the St Catherine's Primary School parents and players. Another wicket down. And probably another Dudley Park batsman down too.

Only numbers eight, nine and ten to go, thinks Glenn nervously. And then it's my turn.

'Come on, Dougal,' he says. 'You're number eight.'

Dougal McCoy stands up, his pads only half-buckled, flaps across the changing room and locks himself in the toilet.

'Dougal,' groans Glenn. 'You can't do that now.'

Mr Leung comes in with his arm round Desiree Walsh's shoulders. Desiree, number seven, is limping. And crying.

'She'll be OK,' says Mr Leung. 'She fell on her wicket.'

'I was pushed,' sobs Desiree. 'By the ball.'

Glenn gives Desiree a sympathetic look and a damp bunched-up towel.

Easy for teachers to talk about being OK, thinks Glenn. Teachers don't have cricket balls hurtling towards them at four hundred kilometres an hour.

'Mr Leung,' he says out loud. 'I think we should declare.'

Mr Leung stares at Glenn, speechless for a second. But only a second.

'Dudley Primary does not declare,' says Mr

Leung. 'Specially not at six for thirteen.'

Glenn wants to remind Mr Leung that cricket is meant to be fun rather than life-threatening. But Mr Leung is already asking who's batting next.

There's a silence.

Dougal's plaintive voice comes from behind the toilet door.

'I've got the squirts.'

Mr Leung frowns.

'Somebody has to go in next,' he says.

He looks around the changing room. So does Glenn.

Ralph Watson (number nine) is hiding behind the swimming floaties. Mia Katsiannis (number ten) is pretending she's already batted and has been knocked unconscious.

'I'll bat next,' says Glenn.

He starts buckling his pads on.

If somebody has to go in, he thinks grimly, it might as well be me. At least I've got something the others haven't.

Mr Leung gives him a not-very-encouraging look. Glenn knows what Mr Leung is thinking. Glenn Gershwin, number eleven, worst batsman in the team. Won't even last one ball.

'Go on then,' says Mr Leung. 'Get it over with.'

As Glenn leaves the changing room, he sees the team are all watching him. A couple (numbers nine and ten) are giving him grateful looks. Most of the others are staring at him as if he's mad.

‘Just try and get your bat behind the ball,’ says Mr Leung.

Thank you Mr Leung, thinks Glenn as he heads towards the smirking St Catherine’s parents and players. I wouldn’t have thought of that.

Glenn takes his time walking to the middle of the oval, partly to give his hands a chance to stop shaking and partly so he can finish chewing.

He reaches the wicket, swallows, takes guard with his bat, and squints down the pitch at the bowler.

Who is big.

Very big.

Stefano’s right, thinks Glenn. That kid’s mum is giving him something. Steroids, vitamins, organic beef, something.

The bowler takes a very long run-up.

Glenn takes a very deep breath.

He tells himself to remember Grandad.

Be brave, he thinks. Don’t step back. Don’t try to get out of the way of the ball.

The ball hurtles out of the bowler’s hand. Sally Pung (number six) turns away at the other end as if she can’t bear to look.

Glenn takes a step forward. The ball thunders into the centre of his bat. Shock waves shudder up his arms.

The ball rolls along the pitch back towards the bowler, who looks stunned that Glenn isn’t on the ground, bleeding.

Cheers erupt from the Dudley Park parents.

Glenn starts breathing again.

That wasn't so bad.

The next ball is even faster. Glenn takes a bigger step forward. The ball snicks off the edge of the bat. Glenn closes his eyes, waiting for delighted yells from the fielders after he's been caught. But the only delighted yells come from the Dudley parents.

Glenn turns and sees the ball rolling over the boundary line.

Four runs.

The bowler is glaring so hard his eyebrows look like they're joined. He turns and walks back for an even longer run-up.

Glenn smiles to himself. Thanks to Grandad, this isn't so hard after all.

'Pizza cake,' he whispers to himself.

After the match, as Glenn is walking home, Dougal catches him up.

'You were amazing,' says Dougal. 'Seventeen not out. Top scorer. Amazing.'

Dougal is bouncing with excitement, despite the lump on his forehead.

Glenn glances at Dougal's shining eyes, concerned. He hopes it's just enthusiasm rather than concussion.

'You were amazing too,' says Glenn. 'Mine were mostly lucky runs. Your four runs were great.'

'They weren't really runs,' says Dougal. 'They're called leg byes when the ball bounces off your head and goes to the boundary.'

'They're still runs,' says Glenn. 'We wouldn't have won without them.'

'We wouldn't have won without your amazing fielding,' says Dougal. 'Nine catches. How brave were you, fielding so close to their batsmen.'

'It's called silly point,' says Glenn, starting to feel a bit embarrassed by Dougal's praise.

'I'd call it fearless point,' says Dougal. 'You totally messed with their minds, standing less than a metre away from them.'

Glenn doesn't say anything.

He wants to change the subject before Dougal starts asking how he manages to be so brave. But before he can, Dougal's face drops.

'I wish I was as brave as you,' says Dougal.

'You were very brave,' says Glenn. 'After you dropped those four catches, you didn't cry or go home or anything. You stayed on the pitch and stopped the ball several times with your body.'

'I was trying to duck,' mutters Dougal, rubbing his ribs. 'I wasn't as brave as you.'

'Hey, it's the weekend tomorrow,' says Glenn, changing the subject. 'Doing anything good?'

Dougal looks even gloomier.

'Tomorrow morning,' he says, 'I've got to do the scariest thing in my life.'

Glenn looks at him.

He wonders what the scariest thing in Dougal's life could be. Going round to the big bowler's place and demanding money for medical treatment?

Probably not.

'My nan died on Tuesday,' says Dougal. 'Her funeral's tomorrow morning. I've got to stand up in front of everybody in a big church and talk about her.'

'That's tough,' says Glenn. 'It's hard to get words out when you're feeling really sad.'

'It's not the sad words that's worrying me,' says Dougal. 'It's the huge crowd I have to say them to.'

Glenn nods. He understands about public speaking. He had to introduce a visiting author on stage once in front of the whole school, and it was the scariest experience of his life.

Or it would have been without his secret weapon.

'I loved Nan and I want to do a good job,' Dougal is saying. 'But hundreds of people will be looking at me and I'll probably panic and I won't be able to speak and if they start laughing I might try to run outside but I'll probably pick the wrong door and get wedged behind the christening font and they'll have to get the fire brigade to rescue me and I'll be on the national news and everyone at school will be laughing too.'

Dougal stops and holds onto a fence for a moment. Glenn isn't sure if Dougal is out of breath or dizzy with fear. Probably both.

Poor bloke.

For a moment Glenn is tempted to tell Dougal his secret. The secret of being brave. But what if Dougal thinks it's stupid? What if he laughs or scoffs? And what if, after that, the secret doesn't work any more?

What then?

'I'll never be as brave as you,' says Dougal sadly. 'When you were fielding at fearless point, you weren't wearing extra padding or anything. You were completely unprotected.'

'Not completely,' says Glenn. 'I did have some protection.'

What am I doing? he thinks. I'm telling Dougal my secret.

'The plastic thing over your goolies?' says Dougal. 'That doesn't count. Everyone has that. I had two on when I was batting.'

Glenn shakes his head.

'My protection was in my back pocket,' he says.

Dougal stares at him for a moment, puzzled.

'Bandaids?' says Dougal.

Glenn shakes his head again.

Tell him, he says to himself. Dougal's your friend. He needs your help.

'Pizza,' says Glenn.

Dougal stares at the old photo of Grandad, amazed.

'Your grandfather climbed into that castle with his bare hands?' he says. 'While Nazis were shooting at him? And when he got inside he took them all prisoner? On his own?'

Glenn nods.

'Amazing,' says Dougal.

'Keep your voice down,' whispers Glenn. 'For some reason Mum doesn't like me looking at Grandad's photo album.'

He glances at his bedroom door. It's tightly shut, so with a bit of luck no noise is leaking out.

Dougal turns the page in the album.

'Wow,' he whispers. 'Is that a Nazi tank?'

Glenn nods again.

'Grandad invented a way of capturing tanks by jumping onto them from trees,' he says. 'It was so successful, all the resistance fighters in Czechoslovakia started using it.'

Dougal's eyes are shining as he stares at the faded photo.

'Your grandad was a war hero,' he says.

'Yes,' says Glenn quietly. 'He was.'

'No wonder you're so brave,' says Dougal. 'When you were little, he probably gave you bravery lessons.'

'Sort of,' says Glenn.

Dougal turns to the next page and stares again.

'Is that your grandad up that mountain?' he says.

'When he first came to Australia after the war,' says Glenn, 'he went to work on a big dam in the Snowy Mountains. But because he was so brave, he spent a fair bit of time rescuing mountain climbers.'

'That looks like a goat he's carrying on his back,' says Dougal.

'And goats,' says Glenn.

Dougal turns the page. His eyes go even wider. Glen sees that Dougal has found the photo of Grandad swimming through rough seas towards a damaged passenger boat with a rope in his mouth.

'He was a volunteer in the State Emergency Service all his life,' says Glenn. 'Well, not quite all his life. They made him resign when he was seventy-six.'

'I wish I had somebody that brave in my family,' says Dougal wistfully. He frowns. 'Except I don't understand, what's all this got to do with pizza?'

'When Grandad was very old,' says Glenn, 'me and him used to look at his photos together. I used to ask him how he did all these incredibly brave things. He used to just shrug and say pizza cake.'

'Huh?' says Dougal.

'I couldn't ever get him to explain exactly what he meant,' says Glenn. 'But after he died, I worked it out.'

'Pizza cake?' says Dougal.

'Pizza cake,' says Glenn.

'What's pizza cake?' says Dougal.

'Glenn, my man,' says Rick.

Glenn waits as usual while Rick wipes the flour off his hands, glances at the pizza oven to make sure nothing's burning, and gives him a high-five.

'You're early,' says Rick.

Then he sees Dougal and hesitates.

'It's OK,' says Glenn. 'Dougal's in on the secret.'

Rick looks surprised, then shrugs.

'Your call,' he says. 'You know my motto. What happens in the pizza shop stays in the pizza shop. I'm a pizza guy, not a social worker. Or a dentist. Your friends and your teeth are your business.'

While he's talking he grabs several lumps of pizza dough, twirls them till they're flat, and lays them out on the pizza board.

'What do you fancy?' he says.

'Same as last week, please,' says Glenn. 'Marshmallows, Maltesers, Mars Bars, strawberry jam and peanut butter. And on top, jelly snakes, licorice bullets, sour sucks, chocolate sultanas, dried pineapple and sugar frosties.'

'You're the boss,' says Rick.

Glenn hands Rick the usual supermarket bag. Rick pulls out the ingredients and starts putting them onto the pizza bases.

'Wow,' breathes Dougal. 'Amazing.'

'It's an art,' says Glenn.

'Not many people realise that,' says Rick.

When the pizza bases are covered, Rick stacks them one on top of the other, adds the jelly snakes, licorice bullets, sour sucks, chocolate sultanas, dried apricots and sugar frosties, and then the final ingredient.

'Is that cheese?' says Dougal doubtfully.

'Unsalted,' says Rick. 'It's delicious. Trust us.'

He puts the pizza cake into the oven.

'Eight minutes,' he says. 'Have a seat.'

While Glenn and Dougal wait, and Rick serves other customers, Dougal bombards Glenn with questions. Glenn doesn't mind. He was expecting it.

'How can you afford one of those every week?' says Dougal.

'Pocket money,' says Glenn. 'Plus I do weekend jobs for rellies.'

'And you just carry it around with you?' says Dougal. 'Doesn't it go mouldy?'

'Sugar's a preservative,' says Glenn. 'After the pizza cake's cooled, we cut it into slices and wrap them in plastic. I always have a slice with me in case I need it.'

'And,' says Dougal, 'when you want to be brave you just eat some?'

Glenn nods.

'Amazing,' says Dougal. 'How does it actually work, scientifically?'

This is the question Glenn was hoping Dougal wouldn't ask.

'I don't actually know, scientifically,' says Glenn. 'I just know it works. It used to work for Grandad and it works for me.'

'Such as yesterday at cricket,' says Dougal.

'Any time I need to be brave,' says Glenn. 'Like last weekend at a family barbie when I knew aunties would be kissing me after they'd been eating garlic. And the week before that when I had to go up onto the school roof to get my bag. Or when I have to go to the dentist. Or my cousin's school musical. Or change our neighbour's baby's nappy.'

Glenn pauses for breath. Dougal is starting to look more hopeful than Glenn has seen him look for ages.

'Remember when they made me introduce the visiting author in assembly?' says Glenn. 'I had some pizza cake just before I went on stage and I was fine.'

'I remember,' says Dougal. 'We couldn't believe you did it. So it works with public speaking too?'

'Definitely,' says Glenn. 'Have a few bites before you go to your gran's funeral tomorrow morning and you'll be fine.'

Dougal stares at the pizza oven, eyes shining.

'Thank you,' he says to Glenn. 'You've saved my life.'

Glenn opens his eyes.

He blinks a few times. He's in bed and it's morning. He can tell it's morning because Mum is standing in his doorway telling him to get up.

'It's Saturday,' mumbles Glenn.

'I know it's Saturday,' says Mum. 'That's why I want you to tidy your room. So I can vacuum.'

Glenn groans.

Mum starts picking things up off his floor.

Go away, Mum, pleads Glenn silently. I don't need reminding how to tidy a room.

'I'll do it,' he mumbles.

Mum stops picking things up.

But not, Glenn sees, because of what he just said. Because she's staring at something in her hand.

Grandad's photo album.

'Glenn,' sighs Mum. 'You know I don't like you looking at this.'

'I know,' says Glenn. 'Sorry. But they're only photos.'

'They're more than photos,' says Mum. 'They're the silly trophies of a reckless man who caused a lot of worry to the people who loved him.'

Glenn hates it when Mum talks about Grandad like this. He was a brave hero. And her dad.

'All my childhood it was the same,' says Mum. 'He used to come home battered and bruised, one crazy escapade after another. Every time he left the house, we thought we'd never see him again.'

'Didn't you think he was brave?' says Glenn.

'We thought he was selfish,' says Mum. 'We begged him not to go off on any more rescues. But every time all he'd say was, piece of cake.'

Glenn stares at Mum.

She's never said this before.

'You mean pizza cake,' he says.

Mum looks at him, puzzled.

'Pizza cake?' she says. 'No, he used to say piece of cake. It's a stupid expression that means something's as easy as eating a piece of cake. Which, when it involves mountains or storms at sea, it's not.'

Glenn sits up in bed.

Cold panic is starting to churn his insides.

'You didn't hear it properly,' he says to Mum. 'What Grandad used to say was pizza cake.'

Mum gives a bitter laugh.

'I lived with him for about twenty years longer than you did,' she says. 'Trust me, it was piece of cake.'

'No,' says Glenn. 'Pizza cake.'

Mum rolls her eyes. She calls out to Dad, who is shambling towards the bathroom.

'What was it my father used to say each time he went off to try to get killed?'

Dad pauses and hitches up his pyjama trousers.

'Something about taking the biscuit?' he says. 'No, hang on, piece of cake.'

'Thank you,' says Mum.

She turns triumphantly to Glenn.

But Glenn isn't arguing any more. He's flopped back into bed, sick with panic. He's trying not to think about how his life has just fallen apart.

The stupid risks he's taken.

Unprotected.

The rest of his life, scarily ahead of him.

Totally unprotected.

Glenn struggles out of bed. He can't let himself think these thoughts. Not yet.

First he has to get to the church and warn Dougal.

Dougal was right. St Catherine's is a big church.

Very big.

Glenn recognises it as soon as he sprints out

of the side street. It's the church where they had Grandad's funeral.

Glenn crouches on the front steps, gasping for breath after running all the way from home. Once his breathing gets quieter, he creeps closer to the big doors and listens.

He can't hear sounds of laughter. Or jeering. And there's no fire engine out the front. It's not too late. He's in time to warn Dougal.

Glenn opens the door a crack.

The church is full of people. Hundreds. Glenn closes the door.

OK, he says to himself. This is going to be scary, walking in among all those strangers and finding Dougal and getting him out of there before he makes a fool of himself. It's going to be one of the scariest things I've ever done. Specially if Dougal is angry with me for being wrong about pizza cake. What if he loses it and gets violent? And chases me through the wrong door and I get wedged behind the christening font and they have to get the fire brigade to rescue me and I'm on the national news and everyone at school laughs at me for the rest of my life?

Glenn pulls himself together.

Time for a quick couple of mouthfuls.

He reaches into his pocket.

And remembers.

For a second he wants to run. To the nearest bed and hide under the covers. Forever.

But he can't.

He has to warn Dougal.

Glenn pushes open the door and goes in.

Too late. The minister's voice is booming around the huge church, introducing Dougal. A proud grandson who wants to say a few words about his beloved nan. Dougal is standing up. He's walking to the front of the church. He turns and faces the congregation.

Glenn waves frantically at him.

I'm too far up the back, thinks Glenn anxiously. He'll never see me.

But Dougal does.

He squints at Glenn, gives him a little wave, a quick thumbs up and pats the pocket of his funeral trousers. Then he squares his shoulders and starts speaking in a loud and fairly confident voice.

'It's a miracle my nan fits in there,' says Dougal, pointing to the coffin behind him. 'Cause her heart is bigger than . . . than . . .'

Oh no, thinks Glenn, 'here we go.'

'. . . than a cricket oval,' says Dougal.

A gentle wave of fond laughter ripples around the church.

Dougal beams.

Glenn watches anxiously.

'I want to tell you some of the things her big heart did for us all,' says Dougal, sounding more confident with every word.

Of course he's confident, thinks Glenn. He

doesn't know yet. He still thinks the pizza cake is helping him.

Glenn wonders how to break the news.

But he stays silent, partly because he's scared to butt in, and partly because he's slowly realising something.

The pizza cake *is* helping Dougal. It's helping him because he believes it will.

Just because I can't ever be brave again, thinks Glenn, that's no reason Dougal can't. He can get his own pizza cake each week and have a fearless life. As long as I don't tell him.

Glenn slips quietly out of the church.

He reaches the street, and heads towards his place. Then he stops. He turns round and walks in the opposite direction towards the cemetery.

It's months since he's visited Grandad's grave.

This feels like a good time to do it.

The cemetery is quite big, and Glenn gets a bit lost for a while, but he finds the grave at last.

'Hello, Grandad,' he says, standing in front of the marble slab. 'You probably think I'm a bit of a dope. But thanks anyway. The pizza cake helped me a lot, even though you probably haven't got a clue what it is.'

To fill Grandad in, Glenn lists the times pizza cake helped him be brave. The garlic aunties and the school roof and the pooey nappies, everything.

By the time Glenn has finished, he's starving.

He remembers why. He sprinted out of the house without any breakfast, and now he's weak with hunger.

He goes through his pockets. Nothing. Just a piece of pizza cake left over from yesterday.

Glenn sits on the end of Grandad's grave and eats it. Now that it's just cake, it's actually a bit too sweet. But when you haven't had breakfast it's better than nothing.

While he chews, Glenn has a thought.

All those brave things Grandad did, he did them on his own.

Without pizza cake.

How?

Glenn stares at the shiny black marble of Grandad's headstone.

Maybe, he thinks, when you've done something a few times, it gets a bit easier. Grandad spent his whole life being brave, which gave him plenty of experience at it.

Glenn realises he can see his own reflection in the headstone.

Me too, he thinks. I've had a fair bit of experience of being brave too.

'Look who it isn't,' says a loud sneering voice.

Startled, Glenn looks up. Looming over him is a tough-looking boy he vaguely recognises.

Oh no.

It's the big bowler from yesterday.

Glenn stands up.

'What are you doing here?' says the boy with a threatening scowl. 'This is our cemetery.'

'How can it be your cemetery?' says Glenn.

'My dead uncle's buried here,' says the boy. 'He died in a karate accident. But not before he taught me everything he knew.'

The boy takes a couple of steps closer to Glenn. Now he's standing very close.

Suddenly Glenn understands. The church down the street. And the school next to it. St Catherine's.

'You're dead meat,' says the boy. 'You might have fluked a win against us at cricket, but it was a big mistake coming over here for a gloat.'

Glenn struggles to keep his voice from wobbling.

'I'm not gloating,' he says. 'I'm visiting my dead grandad. He died in a hang-gliding accident. But not before he taught me everything he knew.'

The boy hesitates. Then he scowls again.

'Smarty pants, eh?' he says. 'This the old codger's grave here, is it? Good, I need a leak and all this marble looks exactly like a bathroom to me.'

He starts to unzip his fly.

Glenn takes a step forward and stares directly up into the boy's eyes.

'Remember yesterday,' he says, 'when I wasn't scared of your bowling? That's because I'm fearless. You've probably never tangled with a fearless person before, have you?'

Feeling sick, he waits for this to sink in, his eyes not leaving the boy's.

After what seems to Glenn like several years, the boy looks away. And zips his pants back up.

'Not wasting good pee here,' growls the boy. 'We've got a lemon tree at home needs it.'

He stamps away.

Suddenly Glenn's legs don't feel completely fearless any more. He sits back down on the corner of Grandad's grave and takes a few moments to recover. He catches sight of his own reflection again in the shiny marble.

There's a grin on his face.

He's never felt like this before.

Trembling, but really good.

He gives Grandad a thumbs up.

Then, once his legs start working again, Glenn heads back towards the church to meet Dougal after the service.

On the way he thinks about the big bowler and hears himself say something he's never said before. He says it very quietly. So quietly he's not completely sure it's him saying it, but he's pretty sure it is.

'Piece of cake.'

Charles The Second

My name is Charles Rennie Mackintosh and I wish it wasn't.

I'm nervy enough as it is. The last thing I need is a name everyone thinks is hilarious.

Well, not everyone. Mostly just the kids in my class.

'Look, it's Charles Rennie Mackintosh,' they say several times a day. 'Could that be the legendary early-twentieth-century Scottish furniture design genius?'

Everyone sniggers because they know what's coming next.

'Oh no,' they say. 'Our mistake. It's just farty-pants.'

They're right, I'm not the legendary early-twentieth-century Scottish furniture design genius. I was born in Australia but now we live in London. I'm in year seven. I don't even do woodwork.

And I am a bit of a farty-pants.

I've tried every type of diet to stop it. Meat-free, wheat-free, dairy-free, sugar-free, spice-free, fruit-and-veggie-free, bubble-gum-free. I even tried food-free for a few days. That didn't work either. I just got so weak that when I did one I almost fell over.

Mum says it's because I'm so nervy. The doctor says my digestive process is a victim of stress. The kids at school say I let one out so often I should have an exhaust pipe.

They're right, but I wish they weren't so cruel and unkind about it.

Specially as it's their fault.

Nobody thought my name was hilarious till our new art teacher, Mr Pugh, arrived. At the start of his first lesson he noticed my name on the class list.

'Amazing,' he said, looking around the class. 'Charles Rennie Mackintosh, where are you?'

I put my hand up.

'That's wonderful,' said Mr Pugh, beaming at me. 'You must be named after the legendary early-twentieth-century Scottish furniture design genius.'

I looked at him, puzzled and confused. I'd never even heard of the other Charles Rennie Mackintosh. None of us had.

'No, sir,' I said. 'I'm named after a singer and a dead dog and my dad, sir.'

I explained that Ray Charles is Dad's favourite singer and Rennie was a dog Mum had when she was a kid in Adelaide and Mackintosh is Dad's family name even though we're not Scottish.

Mr Pugh looked a bit puzzled and confused.

Then he spent the rest of the lesson telling us about the other Charles Rennie Mackintosh, who as well as designing furniture also designed plumbing, curtains, pottery, jewellery, rooms, oil paintings, clocks, buildings and cutlery.

Mr Pugh went online and put photos on the whiteboard of Charles Rennie Mackintosh's own house, which is on display in an art gallery in Glasgow. Not the photos, the actual house.

You couldn't see why they'd bother. It was a bit boring. The rooms were all decorated the same, mostly white. And there were little pieces of blue glass stuck in the middle of the doors and bed-heads and kitchen cupboards. It looked a bit mental. I felt sort of embarrassed for both us Charles Rennie Mackintoshes.

Then it happened.

'Your house sucks, Mackintosh' muttered somebody behind me. 'It looks like a very old iBook.'

Everyone laughed.

I'd never had a whole class laughing at me before.

I went so tense my tummy hurt and before I knew it I'd let one out. A loud one. Which had never happened to me in public before.

Everyone laughed again.

Which made it happen again.

Mr Pugh hardly even noticed. He just told us all to be quiet and carried on showing us pictures of Charles Rennie Mackintosh's very weird furniture. Including very tall chairs with bits of wood missing from their backs on purpose.

'Look,' somebody whispered. 'His chairs have got air holes.'

I glanced around the room. The class were grinning at each other and sniggering at me.

I could see exactly what they were thinking.

Farty-pants chairs.

I don't get the school bus anymore.

It's too stressful with everyone putting on those fake Scottish accents. I'd rather walk. It's only another half hour.

Anyway, Mum's got me on a high-fibre diet at the moment, which means I have to eat these sorghum pellets straight after school and I'd rather do it in private.

Yuk, they taste horrible.

'Charles Rennie Mackintosh,' says a voice behind me. 'Slow down, yeah?'

I turn.

A girl in my class is hurrying towards me. Her name's Jane something. She's hardly ever spoken to me before.

'Alright?' she says.

'I'm in a rush,' I mutter, hurrying away.

She's probably on a dare. A mockery dare.

I glance up and down the street to see if any of the others are hiding in hedges or front gardens.

They don't seem to be.

'I know how you feel, Chas,' she says, catching up and walking next to me.

I give her a look. I doubt she does know, seeing as she hasn't got the same name as a legendary early-twentieth-century Scottish furniture design genius and, to the best of my knowledge, she's never let one off in class.

'I've got a suss name too,' she says. 'Jane Austen, innit.'

I shrug.

'What's so bad about that?' I say.

'Jane Austen,' she says. 'You know.'

I don't know. I've never heard of Jane Austen.

'Story writer,' says Jane. 'Centuries ago. You want classic novels and literature and stuff, she's the business. Mr Bailey says she's well legendary.'

Mr Bailey, our English teacher, is obviously keeping this to himself because he hasn't said anything to the rest of us. I wish Mr Pugh was more like him.

'People gunna get the goss on her one day,' says Jane. 'When they do, I'm knackered.'

She's right. Knowing the kids in our class, she will be.

'Why did your parents call you that?' I say.

'It was my gran in Jamaica,' she says. 'When I was born, my mum was missing Gran so much she let her choose my name. Not clever, eh?'

I shake my head sympathetically.

My parents weren't clever either, it turns out. The thought makes my tummy hurt.

Jane Austen sniffs and wrinkles her nose.

'Was that you?' she says.

'Sorry,' I say, fanning the air behind me. 'What'll you do if people find out about your name?'

'Dunno,' she says. 'They'll probably start dissing me about historic prose styles and satirical subtexts and that.'

I nod. They probably will if they know what those things are. Which I don't. I'm impressed. I've never met a kid before who can talk like Mr Bailey.

'Listen,' says Jane. 'Wanna do a deal? If I look out for you now, will you look out for me if I get sprung?'

I think about this.

'OK,' I say.

She doesn't tell me how she's going to look out for me. Just gives me a thumbs up and heads off.

I feel myself grinning.

There probably isn't anything she can do to help. But it feels good, having Jane Austen watching my back.

By the time I get home I'm exhausted. Sorghum pellets just don't give you the energy for long-distance walking.

'I'm home, Mum,' I yell. 'I'm going up for a snooze.'

I stop at the bottom of the stairs.

Something smells strange. Like wet paint.

'Come in here, Charlie,' calls Mum from the living room.

I go down the hall. But I don't go into the living room straight away. Instead I stare at the door. This morning when I went to school it was just wood. Now it's got little pieces of glass in it, arranged in a pattern. Light is coming through the bits of glass, making them glow.

They're blue.

I think I've seen bits of glass like that somewhere before.

'In here, Charlie,' calls Dad.

That's unusual. They must both have finished work early. Usually they only do that when I have a medical appointment.

I go into the living room. And almost fall over with shock.

Our carpet has gone. So has our wallpaper. The armchairs, dining chairs and TV have gone too.

Everything's white. The whole room. Walls and floorboards. And white armchairs that I've never seen before, weird-shaped ones. Our dining table used to be light brown, but now it's white. Around it are white dining chairs, really tall ones, with bits of wood missing from their backs.

I stare at them.

I know where I've seen chairs like that before.

'What do you think?' says Mum.

She and Dad are standing by the fireplace,

grinning. They've got old clothes on and they're both covered in white paint splotches.

I look around the room again.

I'm gobsmacked. I can't even find the words to tell Mum and Dad how gobsmacked I am.

'We've been planning this for a while,' says Mum. 'Since we found out who Charles Rennie Mackintosh was, and realised we'd put you right in it.'

I don't know what to say.

'That's why I've been spending so much time in the shed,' says Dad.

I've been wondering. I hoped he was inventing underpants that filtered smells, but I thought he was probably just watching football on his very old iBook.

'When we saw how beautiful Charles Rennie Mackintosh's designs are,' says Mum, 'we wanted to show you. So you'll feel better about your name.'

'Thanks,' I say quietly.

I mean it.

I notice a big book on the dining table. On the cover is a photo of Charles Rennie Mackintosh's white living room, like the pictures Mr Pugh showed us.

The book is called *Charles Rennie Mackintosh, Architect, Artist, Icon.* I don't know what an icon is, but I can see he was quite a bit better at it than Mum and Dad.

His living room paint was more of a soft glowing

yellowy-white with no brush hairs stuck in it. His rugs and curtains had beautiful delicate patterns with no paint splotches. And his furniture didn't have a single nail showing.

But I don't care, because what Mum and Dad have done is a very loving thing, plus it must have cost a packet.

'Do you like it?' says Mum.

I nod and give them both a hug.

I wonder if the first Charles Rennie Mackintosh had great parents too.

'Read it?' says Jane Austen, looking suspicious. 'Why?'

I glance around to make sure nobody can see us here behind the bike shelter. I push the library book into her hands.

'So you'll feel better about your name,' I say.

She stares at the book.

'*Pride And Prejudice*,' she says. 'I don't even know what that means, do I?'

'Just give it a try,' I say. 'I've read the intro. It's quite interesting.'

Jane has a sudden thought.

She stares at me, horrified.

'Did you get this from the school library?' she says.

I nod.

'That's it,' she says. 'I'm knackered, innit.'

I know what she's worried about.

'Relax,' I say. 'It's the only Jane Austen book in

the whole library. It hasn't been borrowed for about eight years. Nobody else here has read it. Your secret's safe.'

She looks doubtful.

'I'm not much of a reader,' she mutters. 'I'm well slow.'

'Give it a try,' I say. 'I read a book last night about Charles Rennie Mackintosh, and I'm feeling a bit better already.'

I don't say anything about Mum and Dad redecorating the living room. Jane's mum might not be able to do that. The local council probably won't let you put eighteenth-century Tudor beams in a modern house.

Jane is staring at the book.

'I'll think about it,' she says. 'Ta, anyway.'

In English I let out a big one.

I don't mean to. I never do. They just creep up and then, whoosh, too late.

Everyone sniggers.

We're doing verbs. To teach. To learn. To snigger. Those sorts of words. That's probably what caused it. The stress of knowing exactly what people will mutter if I do one.

They're starting now.

'To woof.'

'To blatt.'

'To fluff.'

'That's enough,' says Mr Bailey in a weary voice

without turning round from the board.

'To fumigate.'

Bang.

There's a sound from the back of the room like a gunshot.

We all turn round.

Jane is sitting at her desk, her hands on the book I gave her. She must have just slammed it down.

She glares at the other kids.

'It is a truth universally acknowledged,' she says, 'that a bunch of idiots who spout the bleeding obvious must be in want of a brain.'

We all stare at her.

We look at Mr Bailey.

Mr Bailey is staring at her too.

Then he grins.

'Well said, Jane,' he chuckles. 'Very well said.'

After Jane looked out for me in class like that, the least I can do is invite her and her mum round to our place for tea.

I explain to Mum and Dad it will have to be Saturday because Jane's mum works late at the video store during the week.

'Jane Austen?' Mum says. 'Like the writer?'

I nod.

'Better have cucumber sandwiches with our chips then,' says Mum with a grin. 'Like they did in the eighteenth century.'

'Good idea,' I say.

Mum sees I'm not joking.

I look forward to it all week.

It's only now I'm realising how it could all turn into a disaster. If Mrs Austen thinks our living room is stupid, and laughs, and I feel embarrassed for Mum and Dad, and my digestive system becomes a victim of stress and . . . I don't want to think about it.

Jane and her mum both blink as they step into our living room.

'Blimey,' says Jane.

'Very striking,' says Mrs Austen.

'It's well white,' says Jane. 'Whitest room I've ever seen. Including most toilets.'

'Jane,' whispers her mum. 'Manners.'

'I'm just saying,' says Jane. 'A truth universally acknowledged, innit.'

I concentrate on keeping my tummy calm.

Dad takes Jane and Mrs Austen's coats.

'Please,' says Mum. 'Sit down.'

We all sit on the white chairs.

I can guess what Mrs Austen is thinking. White chairs aren't very practical. We'll go through gallons of stain remover. I wonder why the Charles Rennie Mackintosh book didn't mention anything about stain remover.

'Nice chairs,' says Mrs Austen.

'Thanks,' says Mum. 'White's our favourite colour.'

She stops and stares awkwardly at Jane and Mrs Austen.

My tummy gives a lurch.

Dad jumps in.

'Cup of tea?' he says.

'Yes please,' says Mrs Austen. 'Oh, before I forget, I made this for you.'

She reaches into her bag and pulls out something and half unwraps it. She hands it to Mum. It's a big round sausage nestling in greaseproof paper.

'Thank you,' says Mum, taking it doubtfully.

'It's a haggis,' says Mrs Austen. 'But you'd know that, being Scottish.'

Mum and Dad glance at each other.

They don't say anything.

'I tell you what's funny,' says Mrs Austen. 'That haggis has almost exactly the same ingredients as an old Jamaican recipe my mother uses.'

'How about that,' says Dad.

'Alas,' says Jane. 'How we humans strive to keep each other at a distance, only for coincidence to undo all our, like, labours.'

While Mum and Dad get busy in the kitchen, I ask Jane how she's going with *Pride And Prejudice*.

'Don't ask,' says Mrs Austen.

'She's a well slow writer to read,' says Jane. 'But her movies are fit. I been watching them all. *Pride And Prejudice* and *Sense And Sensibility* and *Persuasion* and all them. That Jane Austen rocks.'

I give Jane a grin and she gives me one back.

We talk about the eighteenth century for a while, specially how elegantly they used to speak, and then we talk about the early twentieth century, specially how elegantly they used to make furniture, and then Mum and Dad bring in the chips and the cucumber sandwiches and the haggis.

While Mum serves, I feel a high-pressure system building up in my insides. I've never eaten haggis before, and I'm always worried with new food that my exhaust pipe's going to get a serious work-out.

'What's in this?' I say, getting a lump of haggis on my fork.

'The usual,' says Mrs Austen. 'Oats, onions and spices.'

'Mmmm,' says Mum. 'Sounds yummy.'

'And minced sheep's heart,' says Mrs Austen. 'And chopped up lungs and things.'

'I think I'll start with a cucumber sandwich,' says Mum.

Dad does too.

I can't. I've already got a lump of minced sheep's innards on my fork.

Jane and her mum are watching me.

I put it in my mouth and chew.

'How often we fear the strange,' says Jane through a mouthful of chips, 'and find fear itself the only fearful part of it, innit.'

She's right.

Haggis tastes really nice. Nutty, meaty, spicy and sheepy all at once.

I love it.

And an amazing thing's happening. My high-pressure system's going away. I eat some more. My insides relax some more. I keep eating. Not a peep, not a whistle.

'Thanks for bringing this,' I say to Mrs Austen.

She gives my hand a squeeze.

'Thought you might like it,' she says. 'What with your name and all.'

She smiles and I notice that her eyes are as blue as the glass in the living-room door. I remember something I read once about the Caribbean, which is where Jamaica is. They have a type of ancient magic there called voodoo, which can kill but it can also heal.

I know I shouldn't be nosy, but I can't stop myself.

'What does your mother do in Jamaica?' I say to Mrs Austen, trying to sound casual. 'Does she have a job or, you know, hobby?'

'Before she retired, she was a lecturer at Kingston University,' says Mrs Austen.

'Really?' says Mum. 'What did she teach?'

'English literature,' says Mrs Austen.

I glance at Jane, who grins and rolls her eyes.

'So I was never gunna get Kylie, was I?' she says. 'Know what I mean?'

'I think Jane Austen's a beautiful name,' says Mum.

'Ta,' says Jane, putting some chips into a cucumber sandwich.

Mrs Austen is still smiling, and looking at me.

'Charles Rennie Mackintosh,' she says. 'That's a nice name too.'

I smile back and have another mouthful of haggis.

I wonder if Jane Austen wrote a book about a person who was universally in need of a friend and got one and ended up much less of a farty-pants.

I'll have to ask her.

Secret Diary Of A Dad

Sunday, 3 January

Not a good day.

This morning the kids said to me, 'Dad, why are you kneeling on the floor with your head in the fridge? Have you got a headache?'

I explained I hadn't, I was just telling the plastic salad containers about my school days.

Maddy and Dylan stared at me.

Nine-year-olds and seven-year-olds can be a bit slow sometimes.

'It's one of my New Year resolutions,' I explained, showing them the list I'd made. 'See? Number four.'

'*Spend more time talking to the kids*,' read Maddy.

I took the list back.

'Does it say kids?' I said, peering at it. 'I could have sworn it said lids.'

The kids sighed. So did the lids of the plastic salad containers.

'Pity you haven't kept the first New Year resolution on your list,' said Dylan.

'I have,' I said, showing them the brochure for the package tour I've just booked to the Antarctic. 'See? *Find new glaciers.*'

The kids sighed again. 'Dad,' they groaned, pointing to the list, 'it says *Find new glasses.*'

I squinted at the blurry writing. A chill crept up my spine and not just because I'd left the fridge door open.

'Oh dear,' I said. 'Now I'm feeling a bit worried about New Year resolutions two and three.'

The kids studied the list and found number two.

'*Polish the car*,' they read. 'What's wrong with that?'

I took them outside and pointed up to the roof of the house.

'There's no car up there,' said the kids.

Then they saw the shiny cat.

The cat slid off the roof, leaving a trail of wax polish on the tiles. The kids caught it, glared at me and we went inside.

'Number three can't be worse than that,' said Maddy.

I could feel a headache coming on, so I put my head in the fridge again.

The kids read out number three.

'*Get more sleep*. What's so bad about that?'

I closed my eyes, laid my head down next to the lettuce and waited for them to hear the sounds of baaing coming from the living room.

Wednesday, 6 January

I'm feeling very proud today.

Actually, the feeling started a couple of days ago, when I found my glasses and built my first ever piece of furniture. OK, it wasn't perfect, but I did it without help and I was proud of myself. I could feel my chest swelling almost as much as the finger I'd hit with the hammer.

'Well?' I said to the kids when they came to look. 'What do you think?'

I held my breath as they ran their hands over the four sturdy legs, the finely stitched upholstery and the skilfully hung mirrored door.

'Funny-looking bookshelves,' they said.

My chest deflated. They were right. Who was I kidding? I've always been a hopeless handyman.

'Do-it-yourself furniture,' I said bitterly. 'If there's anyone who can actually build this stuff I'd like to know their secret.'

The kids looked at the empty boxes strewn around the room.

'Perhaps, Dad,' said Maddy gently, 'it involves assembling the bookcase, the couch, the coffee table and the bathroom cabinet as four separate items.'

Kids can be know-it-alls sometimes, specially when they're right.

'It was the stupid instructions,' I said. 'They were impossible to understand. Look at that diagram. I broke a screwdriver trying to follow that.'

The kids sighed.

'That's the furniture shop logo,' said Dylan.

I realised what my problem was. I didn't speak the language of do-it-yourself.

I went to my local language school and enrolled.

'Which language would you like to learn?' said the receptionist. 'French? Spanish? Japanese?'

'Furniture Assembly,' I said.

The language teacher tried hard, but by the end of the day I still couldn't translate the phrase '*Slot base-support bracket A into side-panel rib B.*' I couldn't even say it.

'I'm sorry,' said the teacher. 'I can't do any more for you.'

I looked at him pleadingly. 'Not even put my bookshelves together?'

He shook his head.

At home, I stared gloomily at the assembly instruction booklet for the stupid bookshelves. Why could I make other complicated things like sandwiches and hot chocolate with marshmallows, but not a piece of furniture?

Well, no point brooding. Give up and move on.

I stuffed the instruction booklet into the row of books on the bookshelf and turned away.

Hang on.

I turned back.

The bookshelves were built. With base-support brackets slotted into side-panel ribs and everything.

'We did it while you were at the language school,' said Maddy.

'It was actually quite easy,' said Dylan.

I stared at them, amazed. I gave them both a big hug.

Incredible. My own kids can build furniture.

I am so proud.

Tuesday, 12 January

Today on holiday I finally got a chance to take the kids somewhere I've wanted to take them for a long time.

'If you think the green mould down the back of the fridge is amazing,' I said to them, 'wait till you see a rainforest.'

'Mum,' said Maddy, 'are you sure you don't want to come with us?'

'No thanks, my loves,' said Anne, settling down on the motel verandah with a book. 'Have a good time.'

In the car I could see the kids were puzzled how anyone could prefer reading a first-aid book to visiting nature.

I didn't blame them. I didn't get it either. If I had, I would have turned the car round. Instead, I parked it in the rainforest carpark.

'OK,' I whispered to the kids as we crept into the awesome green cathedral of trees and ferns. 'I want you to remember this is a very fragile place. Be gentle and respectful and don't touch anything. Let's just stand absolutely still for a moment and listen to the sound of nature in harmony. Let's appreciate the delicate balance of a beautiful forest unspoiled by the destructive ways of man.'

'I wouldn't stand absolutely still if I was you, Dad,' said Maddy. 'A millipede the size of a comb has just run up your leg.'

I took her advice. I didn't stand still. I ran around in circles beating at my trousers with bracken and rubbing my bottom against several species of tree fern.

'You said we weren't allowed to touch anything,' said Dylan. 'You told us the rainforest is a fragile and delicate ecosystem and touching one leaf could muck it all up.'

'It is,' I said as I whacked at my upper thighs with a cedar log. 'And it could. Which is why I'm trying very hard not to touch any leaves.'

It wasn't easy.

I rolled around on the ground for a while, then reached inside my shirt, rummaged a bit, and pulled out a stag beetle the size of a telephone.

'Don't hurt it,' said the kids. 'And don't wave it around your head like that. You'll give it an upset tummy.'

The beetle finally released my arm from between its mandibles and scuttled away. Weak with relief, I tried to stand up. Something gave way underneath me.

'Dad,' said Dylan, 'do you think you should be sitting in that scorpions' nest?'

I didn't answer. I didn't want to disturb the big scorpion on my tongue.

'Also, Dad,' said Maddy, 'that's a rare stinkhorn fungus you're squashing. That foul-smelling slime is meant to be for the insects, not you.'

I spat the scorpion out and staggered to my feet.

'OK,' I said. 'Let's all calm down. Let's remember we're guests here in this idyllic paradise.'

I reached down to pick up my camera. It wasn't there. A large spider had just eaten it. The spider took a step towards me. It wanted my binoculars.

'Run,' I yelled to the kids.

We ran, crashing through the lush undergrowth. Leeches the size of drinking straws leapt up at us. Fruit-sucking moths the size of fruit swooped down on us. Green pythons the size of green pythons (the big ones) stuck their tongues out at us.

'Wow,' said the kids. 'You didn't tell us rainforests were this exciting.'

Exhausted, dripping with sweat and the rather unpleasant substance that double-eyed fig-parrots exude from their bottoms, I collapsed onto a large moss-covered rock.

The rock moved. It was a giant tree frog looking for a tree that could support its weight.

'Arghhh,' I yelled. 'Please, don't hurt us, we're a protected species.'

We ran again. I led the way, sinking into swamps, struggling with giant ferns, wrestling my way past orchids that kept giving me karate kicks.

The kids stayed on the walking track.

Finally we reached the carpark.

I hugged the car with relief for a while, then took a deep breath and turned to the kids.

'Well,' I said, 'there you have it. The tropical rainforest, nature's most precious gift to the planet.'

'And,' said Maddy, 'her most threatened one.'

Dylan nodded in agreement.

'You're right,' I said. 'Even as we stand here, watching my ankles being nibbled by Herbert River ringtail possums, rainforests all over the world are being burned, chopped, mulched and bulldozed.'

The kids looked at me.

'We agree those things are awful, Dad,' said Maddy. 'But they're definitely not the biggest threat to rainforests.'

I didn't understand what she meant.

The kids opened the car and made me sit inside it with a book. Then they went back into the rainforest without me.

Saturday, 16 January

Normally we all feel a bit down in the dumps at the end of a holiday, but not today. We're all very excited.

We've just got our first dog.

She arrived this morning. I think I was even more excited than the kids. The confusion. The noise. The joyful howls (the dog). The puddles on the carpet (me).

'Don't worry,' I said. 'It's only tea. Come on, we've got a dog to look after.'

I'd read all the dog-care manuals, so I knew exactly what to do first.

Give her a feed.

'Better let us do that, Dad,' said the kids, taking the bowl. 'Better safe than sorry.'

I was indignant. The dog was indignant.

'Why?' I demanded.

'Because,' whispered Maddy so the dog wouldn't hear, 'you're hopeless with pets.'

I was deeply hurt.

'That goldfish,' I retorted, 'died of a bad cold.'

The kids looked at me sternly.

'It died,' said Dylan, 'because of what you fed it.'

I was even more indignant.

'The box had pictures of fish on it,' I said. 'How was I to know it was cat food?'

The kids looked sad. The dog looked nervous.

I took her for a walk round the block.

'We'll do that,' called the kids, running to catch up. 'Better safe than sorry.'

I boiled with indignation. The dog tried to hand them the lead.

'You're not being fair,' I said. 'I've never had a single accident taking a dog for a walk round the block. Or a fruit bat. Or a blue-tongue lizard.'

'That's right,' said Dylan sadly. 'Just a mouse. What on earth possessed you to throw that stick and tell our mouse to fetch it?'

'With a hungry cat on the loose,' said Maddy. 'Whose dinner you'd just fed to the goldfish.'

Before I could answer, I realised I was holding an empty lead.

The dog had disappeared.

We found her up a tree, trembling with fear.

The kids managed to coax her down, but only after I'd made a promise. That when I enrol the dog in training and obedience classes, I'll enrol as well. Ten weeks for the dog, twelve for me.

Sunday, 17 January

I try to be a good dad, but there are some skills I just don't have. Like watching TV while I'm being stared at. Specially by a dog with a lead in her mouth and two kids with cricket bats in theirs.

'Dad,' said the kids, 'you promised you'd take us to the park.'

'Wmpf,' agreed the dog.

'Please don't talk with your mouths full,' I said. 'I promised we'd go after I've finished watching *The Bill*.'

'But Dad,' they wailed, 'we thought you meant one episode on telly, not two hundred and eighty-seven episodes on DVD.'

I sighed.

'Please,' I said. 'I'm trying to concentrate.'

I turned back to episode fifteen. Or was it sixteen? This was criminal.

'We'll go after I've finished watching *The Bill*,' I said firmly, 'and nothing you can say will make me change my mind.'

'Suit yourself,' said the kids. 'But if you don't get any exercise, you'll die.'

It was pouring with rain in the park, but I didn't care because I took a brilliant diving catch.

'Howzat!' I yelled through the mud.

The umpire shook her head.

'Wmpf,' she said, licking her bottom.

On the way home I decided there must be a way to combine telly and exercise and mud-free nostrils.

That night I experimented.

'Who wants a lolly?' I asked, tossing one up and swinging my table-tennis bat.

It was a big success with the kids. They're such quick learners. When I told them they could have dinner in front of the TV, they just sat there with their mouths open so I could lob the rissoles in with a squash racket and whack the peas in with a golf club.

'Let him, Mum,' they squealed happily. 'It's exercise.'

My dear wife rolled her eyes in that loving way of hers. And later in the evening, when I tried to feed the dog and sliced my shot with the pool cue and put a can of dog food through the TV screen in the middle of episode nineteen of *The Bill*, she smiled approvingly.

Thursday, 21 January

Our new goldfish arrived yesterday. And our new telly. We all sat down and watched the news.

There was a report about how most men let their wives buy their clothes because they have no idea about fashion.

The family were looking at me and nodding. Which was unfair.

'I spilt sauce on my shirt at lunch,' I said. 'That's the only reason I'm wearing this green garbage bag.'

Today I decided to show them I do know about fashion. So I went shopping and bought myself a shirt. A very fashionable colourful bright one.

'Absolutely you, sir,' said the menswear assistant, putting on a second pair of sunglasses.

I squinted at my reflection. I looked like I'd just staggered out of an explosion in a paint factory.

'Are you sure?' I said.

'Computer screens have got millions of colours, right?' said the assistant. 'Well, this shirt's got even more millions. Definitely suits you, sir. The greens match your complexion.'

I wore it home. Cars swerved, buses ran into each other, and a light plane made a forced landing dragged down by the temporarily blinded birds clinging to its wings.

Not really. As if one shirt could cause a reaction like that.

Except at our place.

When I walked in, the whole family dived for cover, including the dog.

'Dad,' winced the kids, shielding their eyes

with thick metal baking trays. 'Take it off. All the neighbours are closing their curtains.'

Patiently I explained why I needed to leave the shirt on. I was going to their school tonight for a parent–teacher meeting, and I was worried the teachers would lose interest and start chatting among themselves.

'Bright colours grab people's attention,' I said. 'Look at fire engines, and The Wiggles.'

'Dad,' sighed the kids, shielding the goldfish's eyes with lolly wrappers. 'When our teachers cop an eyeful of that shirt, they won't be giving you attention, they'll be giving you detention.'

'Rubbish,' I said. 'Teachers are tough, specially around the eyeballs.'

I was right. At school tonight I had the teachers' attention from the moment I walked in.

'So,' I said to Dylan's class teacher. 'How's Dylan going with maths?'

She just kept staring at the shirt. Her lips were moving, and for a second I thought she was answering my question, but she wasn't.

'One million,' she was murmuring. 'Two million, three million . . .'

Saturday, 23 January

The judge looked at me sternly. 'Today,' he said, 'you have been charged with one of the most serious crimes ever to be tried in this courtroom. How do you plead?'

The public gallery was packed and the jury was staring at me accusingly. My mouth felt like a sandpit in the Simpson Desert.

'Not guilty,' I croaked. 'I'm innocent. I didn't do it. Honest.'

The prosecutor was on her feet. 'I put it to you,' she said, 'that on the fourteenth of November last, at bedtime, you read your children *The Twits* by Roald Dahl and that you wilfully and intentionally left out the bit about the wormy spaghetti because you didn't want to miss the start of the footy on telly.'

'Not true,' I cried. 'It wasn't footy, it was netball.'

The jury stared at me without blinking. Stuffed toys can be very stern.

I put my head in my hands.

'All right,' I moaned, 'I admit it. I couldn't bear to read all of *The Twits* again. I'd read it 127 times in the past year.'

My son took the witness stand.

'That wasn't the worst example,' he said to the prosecutor. 'In July, Dad read us *War And Peace* and all we got was, Once upon a time there was a war, and then there was peace, the end.'

'I couldn't stand it again,' I moaned. 'Not for the eleventh time.'

'And was that,' said the prosecutor to her brother, 'the same week he read us *Ode To A Nightingale* by the very famous English poet John Keats?'

Dylan looked at her sadly. 'He said it was Keats,

but we just didn't think that, Tweet tweet OK kids time to settle down now *The Bill*'s started, sounded much like a classic poem.'

It was a long trial.

I was found guilty.

While the main witness for the prosecution returned to his judge's chair and put his fluffy toilet-seat-cover wig back on, I looked pleadingly at the jury for mercy.

Nothing.

The jury foreman, who'd taken her prosecutor's dressing gown off, explained to me that the jury was pushing for a long sentence, except for one of the fluffy pink teddies, who wanted death.

Fortunately the judge didn't agree.

He sentenced me to nineteen years hard labour.

I knew what that meant. Nineteen years hard labour each night before bedtime.

I groaned and reached for *The Twits*.

Sunday, 24 January

I've always encouraged the kids to stand up for what they know is right, and I'm pleased to say I think I've succeeded.

Take today for example.

'We want you to promise,' the kids said to me this morning, 'to look after our polluted planet and not make any more unnecessary trips in the car.'

'I promise,' I said.

They opened the boot and let me out.

'Because let's face it, Dad,' said Maddy, 'you are very lazy when it comes to walking.'

'Not any more,' I protested. 'This week I did the supermarket shopping on foot.'

'Only partly,' said Dylan. 'You got exhausted between Frozen Foods and Breakfast Cereals and hitched a ride on someone's trolley.'

Kids, they don't miss anything.

'OK,' I said. 'But on Friday I went to the dentist on foot.'

'Part of the way,' said Maddy. 'We had to carry you the last fifty metres, as usual.'

I gave a sigh. Which turned into a gasp when the kids said they wanted us to do our trip to the museum today by public transport.

'By leaving the car at home and taking the train,' said Maddy, 'we'll be reducing our consumption of scarce fossil fuels and our emission of harmful gases.'

I think that's what she said. I'd locked myself in the car after the word 'train'.

'It's not a long drive,' I mouthed through the windscreen. 'Just a couple of litres of unleaded.'

Using hand signals and the karaoke amplifier, the kids reminded me about our previous car trip into the city. After driving there (2.3 litres), we'd looked for a parking spot (19.7 litres). Failing to find one, we'd parked on the footpath (8.6 litres – it was a high kerb). We'd returned from the museum to find a parking ticket on the car (5.2 litres attending court to dispute the fine, 164 litres getting the car back from Bundaberg after it was stolen from outside the courtroom).

The kids had made their point.

We were on the platform in plenty of time for the 12.15 train to the city. So were lots of other families with environmentally stubborn kids like mine.

A metallic voice crackled above us.

'The 12.15 train to the city is running eighty-seven minutes late due to running into the back of the 11.47 which was running thirty-one minutes late due to the driver being late to work due to the trains running late.'

I took a deep breath.

Boy, it's not easy treating our planet with care and respect. I still haven't forgotten the fiasco with our new solar hot-water system. I mean, where in the owner's manual does it say, Don't put block-out cream on the solar panels?

On the platform the kids made a pensioner squeeze up on a bench so I could sit down.

'Try and relax, Dad,' they said. 'Getting angry and breathing heavily increases your carbon output and contributes to global warming.'

The 11.28 arrived soon after one o'clock and we travelled into town.

At the museum there was an old train on display. I asked the staff if it could be returned to service, possibly at 12.15 each day. They explained it was too old. They said they were, however, expecting a newer train which had been donated last year but which was running thirty-seven weeks late.

When we arrived at the city station for the trip home, the platform was packed. The train arrived on time. Applause broke out. The kids told me to stop as I was the only one doing it.

'See?' they said. 'Public transport isn't so bad.'

Then we noticed that the train had only half the usual number of carriages.

'We always run smaller trains on the weekend,' said a railway employee as he disappeared under the surging mob.

We were packed in like sardines in a really small bit of ocean.

The kids didn't mind, but I was thin-lipped the entire trip home. I tried not to be, but I had someone's umbrella hooked into one corner of my mouth and someone else's two-year-old hooked into the other.

We managed to struggle off the train three stops past ours. We made it back to the station carpark before midnight. The car had been stolen.

I'm writing this while I wait for the train to Bundaberg.

It's running thirty-eight minutes late.

Luckily the kids aren't here to check my breathing.

Can't Complain

As soon as the waiter put Petal's plate on the table in front of her, Petal knew that breakfast was going to turn ugly.

The mushrooms were sliced.

Piffle, thought Petal.

It wasn't fair. The eggs were perfect, the bacon was brilliant, the sausage was dandy and the tomato was tops. You could see why this was Mum and Dad's favourite cafe.

It was just the mushrooms.

Petal glanced at Mum and Dad. Maybe she could eat the mushrooms very quickly, before Mum and Dad noticed them. It was possible. Dad was busy on his phone, complaining to a clothing manufacturer that the label on his underpants was too scratchy. Mum was on her phone too, texting a complaint to the neighbours about their squeaky garage door.

Petal grabbed her fork.

Too late.

'Those mushrooms are sliced,' said Mum, frowning. 'You asked for them not sliced.'

'It doesn't matter,' said Petal. 'Honest.'

'The waiter asked if you wanted them sliced or not sliced,' said Mum. 'And you said not sliced.'

'I just said that because he asked,' said Petal. 'I don't mind, really.'

Dad put his phone down.

'I'll send them back,' he said.

'No,' said Mum. 'I think Petal should do it.'

Dad thought about this and nodded.

'Mum's right,' he said to Petal. 'You should send them back.'

Petal sighed.

Coming to a cafe for a cooked breakfast was meant to be a school holiday treat, but this wasn't feeling like a treat any more.

'Please,' said Petal. 'It's OK. I like mushrooms sliced or not sliced. I don't mind how they're done.'

Mum sighed. So did Dad.

'Petal,' said Mum. 'You've got to stop this ridiculous everything's-OK-in-the-world attitude. Everything's not OK, and the world won't improve until more people speak up. You've got to start complaining more, Petal.'

Petal wanted to complain now.

She wanted to complain to Mum and Dad that they were making her life a misery with their non-stop complaining. She wanted to tell them that the world would be much more OK if it wasn't full of people getting cross and arguing and fighting. And complaining about mushrooms.

But she didn't.

Mum and Dad always won arguments. And then complained about how Petal wasn't very good at arguing.

The waiter came over nervously with Mum and Dad's breakfasts.

'Two fried eggs,' he said as he put Dad's plate down. 'Free-range, no salt, yolks up, cooked for one minute forty seconds in grape seed oil not butter.'

Dad peered suspiciously at his plate.

The waiter put Mum's plate down.

'Herb omelette, one and a half eggs,' he said. 'Thirty-five grams of cheese, five grams of parsley, no chives, no dill. With linseed and buckwheat toast, medium rare.'

'That's not five grams of parsley,' said Mum.

The waiter looked like a man hearing exactly the bad news he was dreading.

'It must have been a bit damp when the chef weighed it,' he said. 'Here, I brought extra just in case.'

Petal wanted to crawl under the table and stuff French loaves in her ears. Instead she watched as the waiter held out a small plastic container of chopped parsley and Mum took a pinch.

'Hang on,' said Dad. 'What's that plastic container made of?'

The waiter looked at Dad in alarm.

'Plastic,' he said.

Dad took the container and turned it over. Chopped parsley fell onto the table. People at other tables were watching. Petal tried to look like she was only with Mum and Dad because she'd been kidnapped and taken out for a cooked breakfast against her will.

'See that recycling number?' said Dad to the waiter, pointing to the bottom of the container. 'Number seven. That means the plastic's made with polyethyldextrose hexachloride, which latest studies show gets into food and builds up in the human body.'

Particularly in the human brain, thought Petal, looking at Dad wearily.

'It's just a plastic pot,' stammered the waiter. 'We use them all the time.'

'Do the health inspectors know you use them?' said Mum.

'I'm sure they do,' said the waiter miserably. 'They've been here four times this year, remember? After you complained to them about the chipped plate, the squeaky chairs, the size of our salt grains and the taste of our tap water.'

'Well if they know about this,' said Dad, handing the container back to the waiter, 'and if they haven't done anything, it's a disgrace. When we've finished our meal, I'm going over to the council offices to complain.'

Petal sighed.

Breakfast at home would have been so much simpler. Except Mum had a complaint in to Kelloggs. Something about their rice bubbles making too much noise.

'How's your meal?' said the waiter to Petal.

'Lovely, thanks,' said Petal. 'I really like the mushrooms.'

After breakfast, Petal followed Mum and Dad over to the council offices.

'Can I wait outside?' she said.

'No,' said Mum. 'This is part of your education. We want you to grow up to be an assertive consumer and a citizen who stands up for her rights.'

What about my right to a quiet life, thought Petal as she followed them in. And everyone's right to a peaceful world.

'Is there anything else we need to complain about while we're here?' said Dad.

Mum had a ponder.

'Noisy leaf blowers in their parks,' she said.

'Good thinking,' said Dad.

Good grief, thought Petal. We'll be here all day.

Soon Mum and Dad were in an argument with the council officer at the service counter. Petal tried to find a spot behind Mum and Dad where they'd think she was hearing everything, but where she wouldn't have to listen to them.

'. . . chemically-impregnated parsley,' she heard Dad say to the man.

Petal took a step back. Two more steps and she'd be behind the ornamental fountain in the council foyer. Then she wouldn't have to watch them either.

'Petal,' said Mum. 'Pay attention.'

Wearily, Petal took half a step closer.

'... United Nations declaration of human rights,' she heard Dad say.

Then Petal noticed two other people in the foyer, sitting on a bench. A woman in a big dark-coloured Arabic dress. It looked a bit like a dress Mum had bought online and then complained that the website had got the sizes wrong.

The woman's head was covered by a scarf, but her face was uncovered and Petal could see she was crying.

A girl was with her. The girl looked about the same age as Petal, and her hair was covered too. She was trying to comfort the woman.

Petal went over.

'Excuse me,' she said to them. 'Are you alright?'

The woman shook her head.

'Thank you,' she said. 'But is no good.'

She sobbed some more.

Petal looked at the girl, who was hugging the woman. She looked close to tears herself.

'Can I get someone to help you?' said Petal.

The girl scowled.

'They won't help,' she said.

She held out a printed piece of paper. Petal saw the words *Camera Parking Infringement Notice*.

'One hundred and seventeen dollars,' said the girl. 'For something we didn't do.'

Petal saw that next to *Offence* was written *Stopped in a loading zone.*

'With council cameras you can ask for photos,' said Petal. 'They have to give you a photo to prove you did it.'

Mum and Dad had asked the council for photos heaps of times. They'd done it last week to prove that parking near the bottle shop made your car extra dirty because everyone braked heavily when they saw the specials of the week and sprayed out extra brake-lining dust.

'We've got photos,' said the girl.

She held out another sheet of paper.

Printed on it were fuzzy black-and-white images of a battered old car in a loading zone parking space.

'Is that your car?' Petal asked the girl.

The girl nodded.

'Is not justice,' sobbed the woman.

Petal wasn't sure what to say next. The photos showed their car was in a loading zone, which Petal knew was just for trucks and utes. They didn't have a leg to stand on as Dad said recently in the chicken shop when he was complaining that the drumsticks were too fatty.

'It was that day last month with very heavy rain,' said the girl.

Petal remembered the day. A massive storm had swept across the city. Lashing rain and huge hailstones that piled up in drifts. Nobody had seen anything like it in summer before. It just happened without any warning. Afterwards Mum complained to the TV weather people.

'We drove through a flood,' said the girl.

Petal remembered the flood. She and Mum and Dad had driven through it near the supermarket. Dad complained to the Roads And Traffic Authority about their drains not being big enough. Or their phone complaints call centre.

'We couldn't see the road properly,' said the girl. 'So we pulled over. The rain was so heavy, at first we didn't see we were in a loading zone. As soon as we realised, we drove away. We were there for one minute and a half, but the camera saw us.'

Petal peered at the photos. One showed the car driving into the loading zone. It had a time on it. *15:42:16*. The next photo showed the car driving off. The time on that was *15:43:45*.

Frowning with effort, Petal did the calculation. And kept frowning as she realised the girl was right.

One minute twenty-nine seconds.

A hundred and seventeen dollars.

In blinding rain.

'Have you told this to the council?' said Petal.

The woman and the girl both nodded.

'They said if we don't pay, we must go to court,' said the girl. 'We can't afford to pay. My mother works cleaning offices at night and her wages are really low.'

Petal stared at the photos again.

A quiet life was one thing, but this wasn't fair.

'Petal,' called Mum crossly.

Petal glanced over. Dad was showing something on his phone to the man at the counter. A list of chemicals found in plastic, probably. Or in parsley.

'What are you doing, Petal?' said Mum. 'I want you over here listening to this.'

Petal turned back to the girl and pointed to the pieces of paper.

'Can I show my parents?' she said. 'I think they might be able to help. They're very good at complaining.'

The girl and her mother looked at each other. They both nodded to Petal. The girl handed over the sheets of paper.

'Thank you,' said the girl's mother.

Petal went back to the counter.

'. . . if the council wants to use leaf blowers,' Dad was saying to the man, 'ratepayers should be issued with earplugs.'

'Mum,' whispered Petal. 'Those people over there need help. They're victims of a heartless council camera. Can you and Dad complain for them?'

Mum looked at the papers Petal was holding.

She sighed.

'Petal,' she said. 'This is exactly what we've been trying to get through to you. If you don't learn to stand up for yourself, you'll be a victim all your life. Like those people.'

'But will you help them?' said Petal.

Mum sighed again.

'Helping them wouldn't really be helping them,' she said. 'How are they going to learn to stand up for themselves if other people do all their complaining for them?'

Petal tried to point out that the girl and her mother had already complained, but Mum wasn't listening.

'It's the same with you, Petal,' said Mum. 'You have to stop hiding behind other people. You have to start standing up for what you believe in.'

Alright, thought Petal grimly. I will.

She stepped over to the counter.

Dad was in the middle of telling the council officer some statistics about leaf-blower-related hearing loss.

'Excuse me, Dad,' said Petal.

Dad stopped, surprised.

Petal looked sternly at the council officer.

'I want to complain,' she said. 'People shouldn't be fined for taking refuge in a storm.'

The council officer looked at Petal.

He glanced at the papers she was holding.

'Roads And Traffic Act, paragraph one seven nine, subsection three,' he said. 'Passenger vehicle stopped in loading zone. Their appeal has been rejected.'

'That's not fair,' said Petal. 'There was hail up to people's knees. It was on the news.'

'Roads And Traffic Act, paragraph one seven nine, subsection three,' said the man again.

Petal showed the man the times on the photos, and how smoke was coming out of the car's exhaust pipe in all of them.

'They were only there for one minute twenty-nine seconds,' she said. 'Look, they didn't even turn their engine off.'

'Roads And Traffic Act, paragraph one seven nine,' said the man. 'Subsection three.'

Petal was about to thump her fist down on the counter, but before she could, Dad stepped in.

'Hey,' he said to the man. 'Give her a break. It's her first time.'

The man didn't look impressed.

Before Petal could say anything else, she was steered away from the counter. Mum was holding one arm, Dad the other.

They were both gazing at her in delight.

'That was wonderful,' said Mum.

'Well done, love,' said Dad.

'But he wouldn't listen,' said Petal.

'Don't worry,' said Mum. 'It happens a lot. You'll get used to it. But it was a very good start. We're proud of you.'

Petal didn't feel proud of herself.

'Pop over and give the lady her documents back,' said Dad. 'We're almost finished here. I just need to have another word to this bloke about airborne particles near bottle shops.'

Petal went back over to the girl and her mother. They were both looking hopeful.

'How'd you go?' said the girl.

Petal started to say not very well. But something in their faces stopped her.

'I haven't finished yet,' she said to the girl. 'But you'd better get your mum home. Things could turn a bit ugly here.'

When Petal came out of the toilet, Mum and Dad were still arguing with the man at the counter.

'... and what's more,' Dad was saying, 'brake dust gets spread even further by leaf blowers.'

Petal walked carefully to the centre of the foyer and climbed up onto the ornamental fountain. She climbed carefully because she didn't want the toilet rolls under her t-shirt to fall out.

Once she was up there and had found her balance, she faced the counter.

'Attention council officers,' she said in her loudest voice. 'I have toilet rolls taped to my body.'

This wasn't completely true because she didn't have any sticky tape, but she carried on, hoping her bluff would work.

'If you don't give in to my demands,' she said, 'my mum and dad will take photos of me on their phones and email them to the media. Everyone will see them and wonder why a person would stick six toilet rolls up their t-shirt in public. They'll think, if people have to do that to get this council to listen to them, this council must be really slack.'

Petal paused for breath.

She glanced at Mum and Dad. They were looking a bit slack themselves. Around the mouth. Petal hoped the council gave in to her demands, because Mum and Dad didn't look like they'd be taking many photos. Not if they stayed in shock like that.

'Here are my demands,' said Petal loudly. 'One, nobody gets fined for spending less than two minutes in a loading zone in bad weather. Two, all the council's cameras get painted a bright colour so we can see where they are. Three, people who pay office cleaners really low wages are not allowed to use the library. Four –'

But Petal didn't get to deliver her fourth demand because Mum and Dad grabbed her and yanked her off the fountain and hurried her towards the door.

'Are you crazy?' muttered Mum, pulling a toilet roll from under Petal's t-shirt. 'What if people thought this was a bomb?'

'I'd have blown my nose on it to show them it wasn't,' said Petal. 'But they noticed me, which is the most important thing when you're complaining, right?'

Mum and Dad didn't say anything.

They grabbed the rest of the toilet rolls, left them in a pile just inside the door, and hurried Petal out into the street.

Dad kept glancing nervously over his shoulder to see if they were being followed.

'That was a good start,' said Petal. 'But we need to do more. I promised the lady and her daughter I would.'

She felt in her pocket to make sure she still had their phone number.

'I think it'd be safer if you just write a letter to the local paper,' said Dad.

'I'm planning to,' said Petal. 'But first let's go to the hardware store and get some chains and padlocks, and chain ourselves to a loading zone sign.'

Mum and Dad glanced at each other with worried faces as they hurried Petal towards the car.

Petal wondered if they were going off the idea of complaining. That would be a shame, because she was just getting a taste for it.

After all, thought Petal. They did show me how to do it, so they really can't complain.

Draclia

Corey woke up suddenly.

It was dark. At first he wasn't sure where he was. In his ear a squeaky voice was hissing something about blood.

Corey tensed. He could just make out a shadowy figure looming over him, pressing him into the pillow. A figure with big staring eyes and white teeth.

Corey didn't panic.

He waited till he could see better.

Yes, it was just as he'd feared. He was being pinned to the bed by a five-year-old boy in dinosaur pyjamas clutching a plastic truck.

'Will,' groaned Corey. 'You're kneeling on my neck.'

'It's got her,' squeaked Will. 'In the front yard. A vampire's got Shelley and it's eating her blood.'

Corey closed his eyes. Maybe he was still asleep.

Maybe if he tried really hard, he could go back to his dream about the ice-cream cake Mum and Dad got him last week for his birthday. Three delicious flavours in the shape of a footy stadium.

'If you don't wake up,' said Will, 'I'll tell Mum how you stayed in bed and let a vampire get Shelley while she was supposed to be babysitting us.'

Corey groaned again.

He got up. He didn't have any choice. Will was dragging him by his bottom lip.

They stumbled to the window.

Will wrestled open the curtain. Corey helped him. Will pointed down into the front yard.

'See?'

Corey squinted. Mostly he could just see shadows. Then the moonlight went brighter and he saw Shelley leaning against the side of the carport.

Somebody was with her. Another teenager.

Corey shuddered. It was a fairly yukky sight. Shelley had her arms wrapped around the teenager, and the teenager's mouth was on her neck.

'I think it's Draclia,' whispered Will, his breath hot in Corey's ear.

Corey sighed.

'The word is Dracula,' he said. 'And that's not Dracula down there, it's Jarrod Bennet.'

Will didn't look convinced.

'Jarrod Bennet's in high school with Shelley,' said Corey. 'His younger sister Brianna goes to our school.'

Will thought about this.

'Does Brianna know her brother's a vampire who bites people on the neck?' asked Will.

Corey sat down wearily on his bed.

'Jarrod is Shelley's boyfriend,' he said. 'They've been going out for nearly a week.'

Corey tried to explain to Will that Shelley and Jarrod were just kissing. And that because Shelley was very tall for her age, Jarrod couldn't reach her lips, not even on tiptoe, and so he had to make do with her neck.

Will still didn't look convinced.

Corey realised it was all probably a bit technical for a five-year-old.

'I saw it on telly,' said Will. 'Vampires don't care if they're short cause they've got big teeth.'

Corey sighed again.

You couldn't really blame a little kid. Not in a world gone vampire mad. There had hardly been a day in Will's young life without a new vampire movie being released or a new vampire romance book being published or a new vampire TV show being launched or a new vampire burger being advertised on the car radio.

Little kids noticed things like that.

It had been the same for Corey when he was small and the world had been dinosaur mad. For a few weeks when he was five, Corey had seriously suspected there were dinosaurs trapped in the ice under the frozen peas in Coles.

Corey made Will sit next to him on the bed.

'Vampires are just stories,' he said to Will.

His little brother shook his head. He jumped up onto Corey's lap. Corey could smell something weird on Will's breath.

'Vampires live among us,' muttered Will darkly. 'Shelley told me.'

Thanks Shelley, thought Corey. I hope I'm that thoughtful and considerate when I'm fifteen.

'Why does your breath pong?' he said as he lifted Will down.

'It's garlic butter,' said Will. 'I went downstairs and had some. To stop Jarrod Bennet biting me.'

Corey looked at the clock.

Ten past ten. Mum and Dad probably wouldn't be back from book club till eleven.

Corey needed sleep now. Desperately.

But he knew there was only one way he was going to get it.

'OK,' he said to Will. 'Come on. I'll prove to you that vampires are just stories.'

Shelley's room was full of vampires.

But, as Corey carefully pointed out to Will, none of them were real.

Shelley had about a hundred vampire romance story books and DVDs on her shelves. Plus posters of hunky heart-throb teenage vampire guys, and plastic models of them, and a *Twilight* bedcover.

'See,' said Corey. 'Vampires are just pretend.'

'Mum's got heaps of gardening books,' said Will, 'and gardening's real.'

Corey took a deep breath.

'Look,' he said, 'even if there was such a thing as vampires, which there isn't, Shelley wouldn't go out with one. She can be a bit bossy at times, but she's not stupid.'

'She would so go out with one,' said Will. 'She told me. She likes vampire boyfriends. All her friends do.'

Corey stared at the *Twilight* bedcover.

It's all that movie's fault, he thought bitterly. I wish I had the phone numbers of the people who made up that movie and all those books. I'd make them come round and stay up half the night arguing with Will, so I could get some sleep.

'Anyway,' said Will, 'Draclia makes you be his girlfriend. I saw it on a cartoon.'

Corey opened his mouth to remind Will that (a) information from cartoons isn't that reliable and (b) the word is Dracula.

Before he could, Shelley burst into the room.

'What are you doing in here?' she said, glaring at them.

'Um,' said Corey. 'We couldn't sleep.'

'Out,' said Shelley.

'We've come to save you,' said Will. 'From Draclia.'

Shelley rolled her eyes angrily and gave Corey a 'grow up' look. Which Corey felt was very unfair as he was grown up, almost. Will was the little kid with the dopey ideas.

'I was just trying to explain something to Will,' said Corey. 'He's got some dopey idea about Jarrod. Of course it's completely –'

Corey didn't finish. Shelley grabbed the front of his pyjama top and twisted it so tight he could hardly breathe.

'Stay away from Jarrod,' she hissed, eyes blazing. 'If you do anything to upset him, you're dead meat, both of you.'

Even though his brain was struggling for oxygen, and he was concerned about Will who looked close to tears, Corey was still able to work out almost instantly why Shelley was being so emotional.

It was her height.

Teenage boys didn't like teenage girls who were taller than them, not as girlfriends. Shelley had said that tearfully to Mum a million times.

But now, at last, she'd found one who didn't mind. So of course she didn't want him driven away by a loony five-year-old vampire hunter and a not-very-good-babysitter brother.

Corey could understand that.

The thing he couldn't understand, now Shelley had pulled him even closer for a glare and he could see her skin in more detail, was why she had blood smeared on her neck.

'Corey, wake up. Corey, wake up. Wake up, Corey.'

Corey woke up.

Will's face was touching his. It was sticky. Corey

could smell milk and cornflakes and truck plastic and just a hint of garlic.

'Draclia's in the kitchen,' whispered Will urgently.

Corey closed his eyes. The early morning sunlight was hurting his head. So was Will's voice. For a moment he wondered if Will was a vampire. A sleep vampire who took all your sleep.

'In *our* kitchen,' said Will, even more urgently.

'Go and keep him busy,' mumbled Corey. 'Show him your truck. Don't let him leave. And don't say anything about vampires. I'll be down soon.'

'OK,' said Will, and hurried off.

Corey was tempted to go back to sleep. But he didn't. He had to fix this once and for all. Put Will's mind at rest. So life could go back to normal.

In the shower Corey made a list in his mind of all the things he knew about vampires.

1. They hate sunlight.
2. They hate having wooden stakes stuck in them.
3. They hate garlic.
4. Sometimes they can turn into bats.

Right, thought Corey as he went down to the kitchen. I must be able to use at least one of these to prove to Will that Jarrod Bennet is not a vampire.

Mum and Dad and Will were at the kitchen table.

Nobody else was.

'Where's Shelley?' asked Corey casually. 'And, um, Jarrod?'

'Don't know,' said Dad. 'They were here a moment ago, then they just sort of vanished.'

'Shelley wouldn't let me show Draclia my truck,' said Will bitterly.

Corey sighed. Will was glaring at the chair Jarrod must have been sitting in. Which was empty now except for a cricket bat.

A cricket bat?

Corey stared at the bat, mind racing.

Could vampires turn into that sort of bat?

He shook the thought away and told himself to stop being silly. This wasn't helping anyone.

'I think they've gone to the mall,' said Mum.

'Strange one, that Jarrod,' said Dad. 'I asked him if he wanted to watch me play in the over-forties cricket, but he wasn't interested.'

'Yes he was, love,' said Mum. 'But he's got very sensitive skin. He doesn't like being in the sun.'

Corey told his imagination to calm down. Lots of people had sensitive skin. Babies, for example.

Could babies be vampires?

Corey took a deep breath. This sort of wild thinking wasn't getting him anywhere. Next he'd be wondering if goldfish could be vampires.

What I have to do, thought Corey, is be more scientific.

'Got any plans today, Corey?' said Mum.

'Um,' said Corey. 'I'm going to Brianna Bennet's house to do a scientific experiment. I can take Will if you like. I think he'll be interested.'

'Yes,' shrieked Will. 'I love scientific speriments. I'm a vampire for scientific speriments.'

'The Bennets live next to the cemetery, right?' said Dad.

Corey nodded.

'Go the long way round the block,' said Mum. 'So you don't have to cross any roads.'

Corey nodded again.

He was only half listening.

Mostly he was wondering if Mum had any garlic butter left.

'Why don't we just ring the bell?' said Will.

Corey dragged Will back down into the bushes.

'Because,' whispered Corey, 'we can't just stand at the front door and say, hello Mrs Bennet, we've come to hide a lump of garlic butter in Jarrod's bed to prove he's not a vampire, and, by the way, could you let us know if he starts foaming at the mouth or writhing around on the floor or not being able to concentrate on his homework.'

'Why can't we?' said Will.

Corey took a deep breath.

He decided to keep it simple.

'Because,' he said, 'it's more fun to climb in through Jarrod's bedroom window.'

'Yes,' shrieked Will, or would have done if he hadn't been muffled by the hand Corey slapped over his mouth.

Luckily the Bennets' house was single storey,

and Jarrod's room was easy to spot. Shelley had been telling everyone for days that Jarrod had black curtains.

What Shelley hadn't told anyone, Corey discovered, was that Jarrod also had a really sharp flyscreen that cut your finger when you pulled it off the window.

'Ow,' said Corey, sucking his finger.

'Don't let it bleed,' said Will. 'If Jarrod smells your blood he'll go into a frenzy and want to marry you.'

Corey didn't think there was a huge chance of that happening.

He concentrated on sliding Jarrod's window open as quietly as he could, then helping Will climb through. It took a while because Will had his school backpack on, which got wedged in the window.

Corey muttered some cross things very quietly and pushed as hard as he could. Suddenly Will and the backpack tumbled forward onto Jarrod's bed. Corey climbed through after him.

'Why did you bring your backpack?' he whispered, helping Will off the bed. 'You don't need your truck for vampire hunting.'

'It's not my truck,' said Will indignantly. 'It's a stake.'

Corey stared at him.

'A stake for vampire hunting,' said Will. 'If you jab a stake into a vampire, they –'

'I know,' said Corey hurriedly.

He was shocked that Will even knew about this, let alone was planning to do it. And where had he got the stake anyway?

Corey slid the backpack off Will's back.

Best if I look after it, he thought. That's all we need now, a five-year-old running riot with a piece of sharp wood.

Then Corey saw something and froze.

Blood was dripping from the bottom of the backpack onto Jarrod's floor.

Corey stared, horrified.

Had the stake already been used?

Frantically he fumbled with the backpack zip, jerked it open and pulled out what was inside.

A torn plastic bag with raw meat in it.

'I told you,' said Will. 'It's a steak. I got it from the fridge at home. If you jab a steak into a vampire it distracts them and –'

'Not a steak,' said Corey weakly. 'A stake.'

'That's right,' said Will. 'A steak.'

'Jarrod, is that you?' called a grown-up voice outside the door.

Corey froze again. He gave Will a pleading look to make him stay still. He tried to stay completely still himself. Which wasn't easy because he had blood trickling along his arm.

The door opened.

Mrs Bennet put her head in and stared, surprised.

'Hello,' she said.

'Hello,' said Corey weakly.

Mrs Bennet stared at him some more.

'You're Shelley's brother, right?' she said.

Corey nodded. He could see she was looking at the dripping steak in his hand.

He tried to work out how he was going to explain to Mrs Bennet (1) why he and Will were in her son's bedroom doing a vampire hunt, and (2) why they were doing it in such a stupid way.

'Oh, silly me,' said Mrs Bennet, suddenly smiling. 'Of course. Jarrod must have invited you over for a bite.'

Will gave a terrified squeak.

Corey swallowed nervously.

'Your mum needn't have bothered with this,' said Mrs Bennet warmly, taking the meat from Corey. 'My husband always gets too much steak for our barbecues. Come on through, lunch is nearly ready. Brianna and the others will be pleased to see you.'

Dazed, Corey grabbed Will's hand as Mrs Bennet steered them out to the back patio.

'Look who's here,' said Mrs Bennet to the people sitting around the table.

Everyone turned and stared at Corey and Will.

Mr Bennet and Brianna looked surprised, but pleased as well.

Jarrod just looked surprised.

Shelley looked cross.

'They even brought their own meat,' said Mrs Bennet.

Nobody else said anything. They were all looking a bit puzzled and lost for words.

Corey decided he should say something.

'And our own garlic butter,' he said.

At first it was quite a tense barbecue.

Particularly for Will. Corey could see he was extremely tense, glancing nervously at Jarrod. Shelley looked very tense too, glancing nervously at Corey and Will.

Corey decided to help everyone relax.

'Vampires,' he said. 'You can't get away from them these days, can you?'

Everyone looked a bit startled at first.

Corey had to hold Will's hand tight under the table to keep him there.

But soon everyone was talking about their favourite vampire movies and TV shows and books. Even Shelley started to relax.

Corey chose his moment.

'Sorry we broke into your room, Jarrod,' he said.

'My room?' said Jarrod, looking surprised again.

'Will wanted to get to know you better,' said Corey. 'Now you're one of the family. Lucky your bed was there to break our fall. And lucky it's a strong bed. With strong bedsprings. In your bed.'

He hoped he'd said it enough for Will to get the message.

'That bed needs to be strong,' said Mrs Bennet. 'The number of hours Jarrod sleeps.'

Thank you, said Corey silently.

'Twelve hours a night, if they let him,' said Brianna.

Thank you as well, said Corey silently again.

'Easy to see Jarrod's not a vampire,' he said out loud.

Everyone looked at Corey.

Corey realised he hadn't explained enough.

'Vampires don't need beds,' he said. 'They don't sleep. Not ever. Not even on long trips in the back of cars.'

Everyone laughed. Including Shelley. And when Corey glanced across at Will, he was grinning too.

Corey felt light-headed with relief.

Problem solved. Except for one little nagging thing. The blood he'd seen on Shelley's neck. If Jarrod wasn't a vampire, how did it get there?

Corey wondered if Shelley had cooked dinner yesterday evening and maybe had tucked the meat under her chin so she'd have both hands free to chop onions.

It was possible, except last night they'd had fish and chips.

'OK, time to eat,' said Mrs Bennet. 'Jarrod, get rid of that revolting gum, please.'

Jarrod stuck something on the edge of his plate.

Red bubblegum.

Corey stared at it.

Of course. The red smears on Shelley's neck. It wasn't blood, it was bubble-gum juice.

Corey felt happier than he had for ages. Happy

that Shelley had managed to find a boyfriend at last. Happy that Jarrod's family were so nice and friendly and mortal. Happy that with a bit of luck Will would stop carrying on like an insomniac Transylvanian innkeeper and let him get some sleep.

Then Mr Bennet brought the steaks over from the barbecue.

Corey stared.

They were barely cooked. The outsides were sort of scorched, but the insides were still red.

'We always have our steak rare,' said Mr Bennet. 'Hope you like it that way.'

Mrs Bennet plonked a steak on Corey's plate.

'There you go,' she said. 'Folk who climb in through windows have to keep their strength up.'

Corey felt faint.

He hadn't even cut his steak yet, and a puddle of blood was trickling out of it. What could he do? Everyone thought he and Will had come to lunch. You couldn't come to lunch and not eat the lunch.

Corey cut off a small piece of steak. He tried not to look at the blood. He put the piece of steak into his mouth and hoped he wouldn't throw up.

He didn't.

The steak was delicious.

He had another piece.

This was incredible. It looked revolting but tasted fantastic. The mixture of crisp burnt outside and tender juicy inside was the best thing he'd ever tasted that wasn't in the shape of a footy stadium.

Corey had more.

Then he remembered Will. He turned to his brother.

Will was eating even faster than Corey. His eyes were shining as he chewed. He grinned at Corey, lips red and gleaming.

Corey grinned back.

He looked around the table. Everyone was eating as enthusiastically as Will.

'Good, eh?' said Mr Bennet.

Everyone nodded, mouths full.

Corey put another big tender dripping chunk of meat into his mouth and chewed happily.

Then he had another little nagging thought and stopped.

Was this how it all began? The taste for blood. Centuries ago. Before anyone had ever bitten anyone else in the neck. Was the first vampire just someone who'd been to a really good barbecue?

Corey smiled to himself.

Don't be silly.

But he hesitated.

Then he reached over to the garlic butter and cut off a dollop and smeared it over the rest of his steak before he put the next big chunk into his mouth.

Just in case.

Tickled Onions

I hate doing this, but every morning I have to.

The other kids call it Clyde Craddock's mental moment.

As soon as I arrive at school, I hurry over to the garbage bins behind the canteen. First I check the bins for leftover bread from yesterday, because by 8.45 in the morning I'm always starving.

There's usually a slice or two. I wipe off the soggy lettuce or coffee powder or pencil sharpenings and gobble it down.

Then, meal finished, I get busy with the other thing I have to do.

I pull the plastic bag out of my pocket, careful not to spill what's inside it. Cold porridge, maybe, with stewed apple and sun-dried tomatoes. Or a sour plum and choko yoghurt pancake. Or goat sausages with pig-liver marmalade. Or whatever else we had for breakfast at our place.

I always feel guilty as I dump my breakfast in the bin, because I know it was cooked with love. Mum and Dad are the most loving parents in the world. They're just not that good at cooking.

Or listening.

After I've dumped my breakfast, I take my lunch box from my school bag, open the lid carefully, try not to breathe in the revolting smell, and dump my lunch too.

Today's smell is even worse than usual.

It's partly the salami-mousse sandwich, which is one of Mum's favourites. But mostly it's the tickled onions.

That's what Dad calls them, and I suppose he's allowed to because he invented them. They're like regular pickled onions except for the rose petals and chilli powder and fermented fish paste.

Into the garbage they go.

Some of the kids from my class are watching me and giggling.

'Mental,' I hear a couple of them whisper as usual.

I sigh as usual.

I don't really mind. Not that much. I'm used to it. I've been doing this since year one and we're in year six now.

But I live in hope that one day I'll hear the other kids whisper something else. Something like, 'Poor Clyde, it must be really hard for him, having parents whose hobby is amateur cooking.'

I'd really like that.

Oh well, at least my morning routine isn't as bad as Hamish Hodge's. At least I don't have to actually eat this muck. Not like poor Hamish.

Here he comes now, with Rick, Jock, Mick, Jack and Vic.

I hate this. They're twisting Hamish's arms even further up his back than they usually do.

I wish they'd grow up. Most of us year sixes are in the footy club or the movie club or the phone club. But Rick, Jock, Mick, Jack and Vic had to be different. They had to start a club called Overweight Watchers. A whole club just to make fun of overweight people.

'Hodge Podge coming through,' the club members are chanting like they do every morning. 'Starving fat boy hasn't eaten for ten minutes. Needs to see what's on the breakfast menu.'

This is usually when I turn away.

It's not just the horrible sight of Hamish having his head forced into a bin. It's the look he usually gives me before it happens. A look that says, 'If only you'd eat your breakfast, I wouldn't have to.'

But today I'm not turning away.

I'm taking a couple of steps towards Rick, Jock, Mick, Jack and Vic.

'Hey,' I say. 'Lay off him.'

What's going on? Hunger must be scrambling my brain and giving me the powerful desire to spend a couple of weeks in hospital hooked up to a drip.

Rick, Jock, Mick, Jack and Vic are glaring at me. They're all big, specially Vic who does weightlifting as part of her netball training.

I'm quite tall, but I don't have much meat on my bones. It's not really surprising, seeing as I live on one meal a day from the bins, plus whatever sandwiches I can get from people for doing their homework.

'Creepy Craddock's being a hero,' says Jock, narrowing his eyes at me. 'Risking his neck for Hodge Podge. I didn't know you two were friends.'

Hamish Hodge is looking at me as well, eyes wide and confused because we're not friends. Other expressions twitch onto his plump face. He's hoping I'll save him. He's also worrying I'll make things worse.

I started this, so I have to finish it. Dad says it's important to finish what you start, though he's usually talking about food.

'Yeah, me and Hamish are good friends,' I say to Jock. 'I'm going to his place for dinner tonight.'

I hadn't planned to say that, but now I have, it sounds like quite a good idea.

Rick, Jock, Mick, Jack and Vic are looking surprised.

So is Hamish.

Then all the others smirk.

'I'd like to see that,' says Vic. 'A loony who chucks his food in the bin having dinner with a fatso who can't stop eating.'

They all have a big laugh.

Until Jock stops and gets serious.

'And why exactly should we lay off Hodge Podge?' he says, sticking his face close to mine. 'Is it cause you're gunna make us?'

Jock's breath smells of bacon. I feel faint with hunger. But I manage to remember what I need to say.

I look Jock right in the eyes.

'PD project,' I say.

Jock frowns. Rick, Mick, Jack and Vic glance at each other. Slowly they realise what I mean.

Yesterday Ms Dunphy set a really difficult Personal Development project. It's on Empathy. Four hundred words on Other People's Feelings, by next Tuesday.

'If you let Hamish go,' I say to Rick, Jock, Mick, Jack and Vic, 'I'll help you with it.'

Jock thinks about this.

'If we let the fat boy go,' he says, 'we're not giving you sandwiches as well.'

'Deal,' I say.

The Overweight Watchers club members look at each other, nod, scowl at me, scowl at Hamish, and wander away.

Hamish is panting with relief.

'Thanks,' he says. 'I thought I was going to have to eat those stinky horrible onions again.'

He remembers where the onions come from.

'Sorry,' he says.

'That's OK,' I say. 'You can make it up to me with a delicious meal tonight.'

Hamish stares at me, alarmed.

'Were you serious about coming to dinner?' he says.

'Of course,' I say. 'I don't joke about food. Food is the most important thing in my life. I haven't had a decent meal since I was four.'

While we walk to his place after school, Hamish tells me a bit about himself. We've never really had a chance to talk much. He's only been at the school eight months and he's spent a lot of that time with his head in a bin.

'I wasn't always porky,' he says. 'I used to be almost as skinny as you.'

'What happened?' I say.

I heard somewhere that thyroid glands, whatever they are, can sometimes make people fat. Probably depends how they're cooked.

'My mum died,' says Hamish.

I give him a sympathetic look. It's moments like this you realise food isn't the most important thing.

Not quite.

'My dad's in charge of meals now,' says Hamish gloomily. 'He likes huge meals. Every day.'

This sounds promising.

'What's for tea tonight?' I say.

'Dunno,' says Hamish. 'Could be anything.'

I smile.

Anything, sure, but I'm pretty confident it won't be seafood sausages with pig-liver marmalade.

Hamish's house is nice. Bit like ours, but tidier.

As we come in, a man's voice calls out.

'Nearly finished, Hamie. Get yourself a snack.'

We go into the kitchen. Hamish explains that his dad is a freelance journalist who works at home. I nod, but I'm not fully paying attention. I've just noticed something that's making me feel nervous.

There's no food in the kitchen.

In our kitchen there are jars and packets stacked everywhere, and stuff hanging up all over the place. Chillies and herbs and bits of dried goat. It's all yuk, but there's heaps of it.

Here, nothing.

Hamish opens the fridge and takes out a bottle of water.

I peek in while the door's open. I see some old fruit, half a packet of cheese and a jar of vegemite.

Where are the huge meals?

'Hi there, Hamie,' says Hamish's dad behind us. 'Who's this?'

Hamish's dad is exactly the same shape as Hamish. Not blubbery or anything, but happily plump. I'd like to be that shape.

'Clyde's my best friend at school,' says Hamish.

I try to look as though I am. Which isn't that hard because I don't think Hamish has got any other friends.

'Can Clyde eat with us tonight?' Hamish says to his dad.

Mr Hodge looks me up and down.

'Looks like he needs to,' he chuckles. 'We're going to a steakhouse. That OK with you, Clyde?'

I nod so hard I get giddy.

'Right-oh then,' says Mr Hodge. 'Let's give your folks a call.'

I can't believe it.

This steakhouse menu is amazing.

Most of the steaks are half a kilo at least. And this place obviously hasn't even heard of pig-liver marmalade.

The only thing I'm a bit worried about is the prices. I don't want to send Mr Hodge broke.

Mr Hodge looks up from his menu.

'OK, boys,' he says. 'What are you having? Anything you like.'

I glance uncertainly across the table at Hamish.

'It's OK,' says Hamish quietly. 'The magazine's paying.'

I'm not sure what he means.

'My dad does restaurant reviews,' explains Hamish. 'Two a week for a magazine, plus five for their website.'

'Seven restaurants a week,' says Mr Hodge. He grins. 'Lucky there are seven dinnertimes a week. And lucky I've got a hungry son to help me.'

'Yeah,' says Hamish miserably. 'Very lucky.'

'I'm also writing a book,' says Mr Hodge. '*One Thousand And One Restaurants You Must Visit Before You Diet*.'

Hamish rolls his eyes.

'Only joking,' says Mr Hodge. 'Now, what do you like the look of?'

'Um,' I say, trying not to speak too fast, 'can I have the eight hundred and fifty gram Ridiculously Rotund Rump, please?'

'You sure can,' says Mr Hodge. 'I'm having the Ludicrously Large Lamb Fillet, so, Hamie, would you mind having the Colossal Kilo T-Bone so you can tell me what it's like?'

Hamish nods unhappily. I can see he's wondering how much plumper he'll be in the morning. And whether Rick, Jock, Nick, Jack and Vic will notice.

Hamish's dad is studying the menu again.

'Right,' says Mr Hodge. 'We need to have a starter each, two if you can manage it. And lots of side serves. Fries, onion rings, wedges, nachos. OK?'

Hamish doesn't say anything, so I answer for us both.

'OK,' I say, grinning.

'Thanks for last night,' says Hamish the next morning.

I look up from the garbage bin, where I'm dumping a bag of scrambled eggs. The smell of the sardines and the raspberry vinegar in the eggs is making my eyes water, so I can't see Hamish, but

I assume he's being sarcastic. It must be awful, not enjoying eating in restaurants.

My eyes clear and, to my surprise, Hamish is looking grateful.

I'm glad. I'm feeling grateful too.

'Thank you,' I say to Hamish. 'It was the best meal of my life.'

'Dunno how you did it,' says Hamish, 'eating all the side serves and three desserts and half my T-bone as well as your steak, but thanks.'

'My pleasure,' I say, opening my lunchbox and tossing a dried-goat-and-curdled-whey sourdough sandwich into the bin.

A shadow falls over us.

Five shadows, actually.

Before Rick, Jock, Mick, Jack and Vic can get started on Hamish, I reach into my bag and pull out a sheet of paper.

'I've done you some project notes,' I say. 'Just some basic stuff about other people's feelings, what they are, how they work, how to spot them, stuff like that.'

I hold the sheet of paper out to them. Rick, Jock, Mick, Jack and Vic huddle around and peer at it.

'I'll do some more tomorrow,' I say.

The weight-mocking club glare at me. They glare at Hamish. They're probably feeling a bit stressed at the sight of Hamish with his head not in a bin. But Jock snatches the sheet of paper and they leave.

Hamish is looking at me. I can see there's

something he wants to say. I assume it's another thank you, but it turns out to be something slightly different.

'Clyde,' he says. 'Do you want to have dinner with us again tonight?'

'Good word, "yummy", very good,' says Mr Hodge, opening his notebook on the restaurant table and jotting my word down. 'I don't use that word enough. What about the roast chicken? How would you describe that?'

I think of a different word because I figure that's what a journalist would want.

'Delish,' I say.

'Good,' says Mr Hodge, writing again. 'What about you, Hamie?'

'I didn't have any chicken, Dad,' says Hamish.

'No problem,' says Mr Hodge. 'The lamb chops?'

'I didn't have any of those either,' says Hamish.

I did, the lamb chops were yummy, but now I'm struggling to come up with a new word.

'Lambent,' I say.

I don't know what that means, but Mr Hodges smiles and writes it down.

I describe the fish as 'crunchiferous', the veggies as 'snaporific' and the apple tart as 'crustulant'.

'Good on you, Clyde,' says Mr Hodge. 'You're the perfect professional dining companion. And well done, Hamie, for making such a spot-on best friend.'

'You're welcome,' says Hamish quietly.

Mr Hodge looks at me.

'If I have a word with your parents,' he says, 'would you like to eat with us every night?'

I hesitate for a moment. Only because I'm a bit worried about our dog, Garnish. Usually I take him for a walk each evening so I can slip him my dinner. He's missed out for the last two nights. All he's had is the regular dog food Mum gives him. But now I think about it, he's probably better off. Look how much happier Hamish is now he doesn't have to eat so much.

'Thank you,' I say to Mr Hodge. 'I'd like that heaps.'

'Right-oh,' says Mr Hodge. 'I'll call your folks later. Now I need to check out the washroom. A restaurant reviewer's work is never done.'

After his dad has gone, Hamish gives a big sigh.

'Don't worry,' I say. 'I don't have to eat with you every night. Not every single night. You can have your dad to yourself sometimes.'

I already have a plan. If I bring a couple of my plastic bags with me when I do eat with Hamish and his dad, I can stock up for the nights I don't.

'It's not that,' says Hamish. 'I really like having you here. I'm very grateful for how much of my food you eat. I've lost two kilos in the last two days.'

I'm puzzled. Hamish looks like he's about to cry.

'I just hate having a dad who's a restaurant reviewer,' says Hamish. 'I just wish we could eat at home. Normal meals like a normal family.'

I stare at Hamish. I can't believe what I'm hearing. Hamish is like a lottery winner who wishes he hadn't bought the ticket.

'We've been doing this for so long,' says Hamish, 'I think my dad's forgotten what a normal meal at home is.'

Hamish hesitates. He has that look people get when there's something they want to ask but they're not sure how. Even before he spits it out, I guess what it is.

Oh no.

'Clyde,' says Hamish, 'will you invite me and my dad to your place for dinner one night? So he can see how normal people do it. So when I ask him to give up his job he'll understand.'

I open my mouth to tell Hamish what a really bad idea that is. How only an idiot would ask a dad to give up the best job in the world. And how dinner at my place is about as far from normal as you can get without going into outer space and eating radioactive broccoli.

But I don't say it.

Maybe it's Hamish's miserable face, or maybe it's Ms Dunphy's Other People's Feelings project, but suddenly I'm putting myself in Hamish's shoes.

No normal meals.

No mum.

Body shape a whole club has been formed to mock.

Only one friend in the whole world.

And even though the chicken and fish and lamb in my tummy have turned themselves into an anxiety burger, I invite Hamish and his dad to dinner at our place.

'Come in,' says Mum with a big smile a couple of nights later. 'You must be Hamish.'

I introduce Hamish and Mr Hodge to Mum and Dad and Garnish.

We all go into the lounge.

'Peanut?' says Dad, once we're all sitting down.

My tummy goes tense. But it's OK, Mum and Dad are sticking to what they promised. No home-roasted peanuts with curried prawn paste and fermented kelp. Just normal ones with salt out of a supermarket packet.

'Thanks,' says Mr Hodge, taking a handful.

This is going well so far. Mr Hodge likes normal peanuts. If we can give him a whole normal meal, Hamish might get his wish.

I try to concentrate on how good that will be for Hamish. I try not to think about all the restaurant meals I'm going to miss out on.

Hamish loves the peanuts. Well, peanut. He only takes one.

'Chip?' says Dad.

I go tense again, but it's still OK. They're normal chips out of a crinkly packet. Normal flavour, not even a hint of intestine.

It's amazing. I gave up trying to make Mum and

Dad listen to me years ago. But yesterday, when I explained to them why tonight had to be normal, they actually heard me. I don't know how I did it. Maybe when you're trying to help a friend in desperate need, you get more determined.

I'll have to suggest that to Ms Dunphy as an idea for a project.

Anyway, Mum and Dad are doing really well.

We're having a nice normal evening.

So far.

'Let's eat,' says Mum.

OK, that's not so normal. I don't think hostesses normally herd guests towards the dinner table only four minutes after they arrive. I think Mum must be feeling a bit stressed by the effort of serving a normal meal.

We go into the kitchen. Our dining table has been in the kitchen for years. Mum and Dad like to have it close to the stove because a lot of what they cook congeals very quickly.

I glance anxiously around the kitchen. It looks fairly normal. Everything's been packed away in cupboards, or under our beds. Except for the dried goat strips, which are hanging in my wardrobe.

'Hope you like roast lamb, Charles,' says Mum to Mr Hodge.

'I do, thanks,' he says.

He looks like he's enjoying himself. He's not quite as enthusiastic as when he's reading a restaurant menu, but he looks pretty happy.

Hamish is starting to glow with happiness.

Mum takes dinner out of the oven. It's exactly what she said. Normal roast lamb. No stuffing, no crust, no bone marrow sauce with pickled fungus.

Dad carves. With a normal knife.

Mum puts the veggies on the table. Roast spuds. Peas. Carrots. Orange ones. Normal shape. No honey mixed in with them. Or bees.

I have a moment of anxiety about the gravy. But it's OK. It's out of a packet.

'Mmmm,' says Mr Hodge. 'That looks amazing.'

I grin at Hamish. He grins back.

We're both about to have the best meal of our lives.

Then I notice that the thing Mr Hodge is staring at, the thing he just said was amazing, isn't the lamb. Or the veggies.

He's looking up at the shelf over the fridge. At the one thing, I now see, that me and Mum and Dad forgot to pack away.

A jar of tickled onions.

'What unusual onions,' says Mr Hodge.

I'm not surprised he says that. You don't often see onions that have turned purple.

Mr Hodge gets up and goes over to the shelf.

'May I?' he says.

Mum and Dad don't say anything. Are they feeling panicked like me? I haven't got a clue what their thoughts are right now, or their feelings, and I've done a project on the subject.

Mr Hodge lifts the jar down, unscrews the lid, takes out a tickled onion, and puts it into his mouth.

Hamish is looking worried too.

I try to calm down. I tell myself that one unusual food item doesn't stop a meal from being normal.

'Incredible,' says Mr Hodge when he's finished crunching the tickled onion. 'Fermented fish paste, right? And chilli. And rose petals. Where did you get these delicious onions?'

Mum and Dad look at each other.

I can see exactly what they're feeling now. Even Rick, Jock, Mick, Jack and Vic could spot this much pride.

'We made them,' said Mum.

'Amazing,' says Mr Hodge.

'We're quite keen amateur cooks,' says Dad.

He opens the fridge and before I can stop anyone, Mr Hodge is tasting pig-liver marmalade and jellied goat-curd tarts and a whole lot of other stuff, with Garnish panting hopefully at his feet.

Mr Hodge looks like he's having the best night of his life.

'What is this incredibly delicious thing I'm eating now?' he says.

'Salami mousse,' says Mum.

Mr Hodge sits back down at the table, deep in thought. He thinks for quite a while. I wonder if he's thinking about why on earth anyone would make mousse out of salami.

Probably not.

I wonder if he's thinking about whether he can come here for dinner every night, which would mean giving up reviewing restaurants and making Hamish eat three meals at a time.

I hope so.

Then Mr Hodge speaks, gazing at Mum and Dad, his eyes shining.

'Stephanie,' he says. 'Neil. Have you ever thought of opening a restaurant?'

There's a stunned silence.

Except for the soft sound of Hamish's sob.

'Come on boys, your tucker's on the table.'

Me and Hamish don't need to be told twice. We dump our ping-pong bats and dash to the dinner table.

Yum. Veggie soup.

Mrs Walsh is the best housekeeper in the world and she makes the best veggie soup in the world. Her secret is she puts bits of grilled steak in it.

Hamish tucks in. Since Mum and Dad and Mr Hodge opened their restaurant, and Mr Hodge hired Mrs Walsh to take care of his house, Hamish looks forward to dinner at home every night.

So do I. Hamish always invites me.

'Dad's here,' says Hamish happily as a car door slams.

Each evening Mr Hodge comes home from the restaurant for an hour to have dinner with Hamish.

That's only fair, because Mum and Dad have breakfast with me each morning. They don't need to be at Tickled Onions, which is what their restaurant is called, until the first deliveries arrive at ten. Though sometimes the pig livers are delivered earlier.

'Is that veggie soup?' says Mr Hodge, joining us at the table. 'Delish. I'll have a large serve, thanks Mrs Walsh. It's soup, so it's not fattening.'

We all grin.

Mr Hodge has trimmed down a bit since he became a waiter. He reckons he walks twenty kilometres on a typical night in the restaurant. Twenty-five if lots of customers ask for extra pig-liver marmalade.

Hamish reckons he and his dad and me will all be the same shape soon.

It's possible, though modern science reckons body shape is partly the result of body chemistry, as I explained to Rick, Jock, Mick, Jack and Vic in the Personal Development project notes I gave them this morning.

The project is on Violence. My notes explained that violence is sometimes the result of body chemistry too, and that sometimes violent people have to change their diet. I included a recipe for sour plum and choko yoghurt pancakes.

At first Rick, Jock, Mick, Jack and Vic didn't want the notes.

They were more interested in having what was in

my lunch box. I think they could smell Mrs Walsh's pickled onions. But I was hanging on to those.

Mrs Walsh makes them the normal way, and they're delicious.

Stationery Is Never Stationary

'Come on, both of you,' said Mum. 'We'll be late. Jack, switch that game off and get your shoes on. If we don't leave soon, it won't be worth going.'

It's never worth going, thought Jack gloomily. Big family get-togethers should be banned.

While he tied his shoes, Jack imagined a world without Christmas, Easter, birthdays, engagements, weddings, babies, anniversaries, funerals, public holidays, exam results, holiday videos, new houses, overseas trips, footy grand finals and hearing about people's operations.

Heaven.

Because that would be a world where big families wouldn't have any reason to get together. And innocent dads wouldn't feel like losers just because of their jobs.

'Amazing,' said Dad, still on the couch gazing at

his laptop. 'There's a company in Japan that makes teflon-coated staples.'

'Archie,' Mum said to him, her voice loud with exasperation. 'We'll be late.'

'Do we have to go?' said Jack to Mum, like he always did.

'Yes,' said Mum, like she always did. 'Uncle Pete wants us all to see his new home entertainment set-up. Plus it's Aunty Sue's birthday tomorrow, my cousin Niall's just back from Venezuela, Aunty Anthea wants us to meet her new boyfriend and we have to talk about where we're going to have Christmas. Archie, if you don't switch that computer off, I'll brain you with it.'

In the car on the way there, Jack felt miserable like he always did when he and Mum and Dad got together with the rest of the family.

Then he made a vow.

This time he'd try even harder. This time he'd do it. This time he'd make the rest of the family respect Dad's job.

In the driver's seat, Dad turned to Mum.

'You know what this means,' he said.

'What?' said Mum.

'That crowd in Japan must have a staple remover that can handle teflon,' said Dad.

'Concentrate on the road,' said Mum.

Jack concentrated on being determined and hopeful.

He was ten now and he was sure he could do it.

Simple, really.

All he had to do was make Uncle Pete and the others understand that working in a stationery shop was one of the most important jobs in the world.

Uncle Pete opened the front door, his big suntanned face beaming.

'The slack mob have arrived,' he called over his shoulder.

'We're only a few minutes late,' said Mum.

'Doesn't matter,' said Uncle Pete. 'We're just glad you're here. We've run out of paperclips.'

Uncle Pete clearly thought this was hilarious.

Jack thought about taking Uncle Pete to Japan, so Uncle Pete could discover the advantages of teflon-coated staples. In particular how they're less painful when someone staples your mouth shut.

He decided not to.

Give me half an hour, said Jack silently to Uncle Pete, and you'll be gazing at Dad with new respect.

Dad was gazing at Uncle Pete with a nervous smile. Mum was rolling her eyes.

'Thought you top barristers were meant to be witty and original,' she said, kissing Uncle Pete on the cheek.

'I don't do original on weekends,' said Uncle Pete. 'This lot can't afford it. I save it for the people who pay me six grand a day. Probably the same with you, eh, Archie. You probably don't bring your best manila folders home on weekends.'

'Not often,' said Dad. 'Though actually these days the best folders are made from hot-milled cellulose.'

The rest of the family were around the pool. They raised their glasses to Mum and Dad and Jack.

'Rob's just telling us about the hospital he's building in Africa,' said Uncle Pete.

'I'm not actually building it myself,' said Uncle Rob modestly. 'Just arranging the finance.'

Jack waited patiently while Uncle Rob spent the next ten minutes telling them exactly how. Finally he finished. Before Jack could get started with what he wanted to say, Aunty Anthea butted in.

'Rakesh is a digital microchip designer,' she said, giving her new boyfriend a squeeze. 'He's just had a fantastic breakthrough. He's invented a microchip that can be inserted into bananas on trees, and when each banana gets ripe, it sends a text to the farmer.'

Everyone murmured in an impressed way.

Rakesh shrugged modestly.

Jack opened his mouth to say his piece, but Uncle Pete spoke first.

'What about mangoes?' he said to Rakesh. 'I love mangoes.'

'I'm working on that,' said Rakesh.

Everyone murmured again, in an even more impressed way.

'The plum industry in Venezuela's been having a few problems,' said Mum's cousin Niall before Jack could get a word in. 'That's why I was over there. Helping them eradicate the sap-sucking fruit moth. We did it with genetic modification. Quite easy really, but don't tell that to the Nobel Prize committee.'

'South American fruit industry,' said Aunty Sue, snapping her fingers. 'Didn't you have something to do with that, Pete?'

Say no, begged Jack silently.

Uncle Pete shrugged even more modestly than Rakesh had.

'Just helped out a few of the growers,' he said. 'Twenty thousand indigenous Impala people from the northern rainforests. They were being victimized by an oil company who wanted them off their land.'

'How terrible,' said Mum.

'Oil company was burning their homes,' said Uncle Pete. 'Plus it wouldn't accept their supermarket discount coupons at petrol stations. I got it all sorted out for them in the International Court of Justice.'

Everyone murmured in a glad sort of way.

Except Jack. He was starting to feel weak and defeated, like he always did at big family get-togethers.

It was happening again.

He couldn't even get a word in.

'Saw you interviewing the prime minister on telly,' said Aunty Sue to Mum. 'Good job.'

Mum shrugged modestly.

At least when Mum looks modest, thought Jack, she means it.

'What about you,' said Mum to Aunty Sue. 'Heard around the traps they want you to run that new university in Singapore.'

Aunty Sue gave a wry smile.

'Can't see it happening,' she said. 'They want me to stay on as Vice-Chancellor of the uni here as well. I'd be flying up and down every second day.'

'Come on,' said Aunty Anthea. 'Get real. I'm the chairman of Qantas. I can get you discount fares.'

Everyone laughed fondly.

Except Jack, who felt like pushing everyone into the pool.

'What about you, Archie?' said Uncle Pete to Dad. 'What's new for you at work?'

Jack had been dreading this. He felt sick.

Dad thought for a moment, chewing his lip. Then his face brightened.

'There's a very interesting range of non-toxic highlighters that's just come in,' he said. 'Oh, and we've finally found some price labels that don't leave sticky marks on the pens.'

There was a long silence.

Jack watched in agony as the others just looked at Dad.

It was now or never.

'Dad saved several hundred lives last week,' said Jack.

Everybody looked at Jack, surprised. And puzzled. And clearly not believing him.

Specially Dad.

'It's true,' said Jack. 'Don't be modest, Dad. Tell them how many notebooks you sold last week.'

Still puzzled, Dad had a think.

'Ten maybe,' he said. 'And quite a few post-its.'

'There you go,' said Jack. 'Imagine how many disasters would've happened if those people hadn't been able to write themselves notes. *Remember to turn the gas off.* There's a few houses blown up for a start. *Feed the dog.* Pets can turn really nasty when their blood-sugar level drops. *Don't leave the chainsaw where the kids can play with it.* See what I mean?'

Jack looked around at the staring family members.

They didn't seem to see what he meant.

'Sticky tape,' he said desperately. 'Imagine what would happen if people's glasses snapped while they were driving and they didn't have sticky tape. Carnage on the roads.'

Uncle Pete and the others were starting to frown and glance at Mum and Dad.

Jack kept going.

'Pens with sparkly ink,' he said. 'They can prevent wars. If the leaders of two countries are having a border dispute, a birthday card signed in sparkly ink can make all the difference.'

Mum put her arm on Jack's shoulder.

'That's enough, love,' she said. 'It's a good point, but you've made it.'

Jack could see from everyone's faces that he hadn't made it very well.

Even Dad didn't look convinced.

'Bit of advice, Jack,' said Uncle Pete. 'From the legal world. You're talking about things that haven't happened. People don't care about things that haven't happened.'

Aunty Sue and the others nodded.

Jack went into the house.

You're wrong, Uncle Pete, he thought. People can care a lot about things that haven't happened. For example, there's an important thing that hasn't happened right now. Nobody's patting Dad on the back and saying 'Wow, Archie, we hadn't realised how important and interesting your job is.' That definitely hasn't happened.

Jack glanced out the window, just to make sure.

Nope, not happening.

'Wow, Pete,' said Aunty Anthea. 'We hadn't realised how expensive and impressive your new home entertainment set-up is.'

The rest of the family murmured in agreement.

Uncle Pete grinned proudly.

Jack, who'd followed the family down the steps, had to admit it was impressive. A room specially excavated under Uncle Pete's house with a massive

TV screen and a pile of high-tech equipment and about sixteen speakers.

'If you're going to do something,' said Pete, 'you might as well do it properly. I mean, Archie, you wouldn't sell a ring-binder with only one ring, would you?'

Dad shook his head.

Jack saw him struggling to think of something to say, like he always did. Jack felt a pang in his tummy, like he always did.

'Hope you've increased your home contents insurance,' said Mum to Uncle Pete. 'You must have spent a packet in here.'

'Only about a hundred and twenty grand,' said Uncle Pete. 'And I don't have to worry about burglars because this baby's got a state-of-the-art security system.'

He picked up the biggest and most expensive-looking remote Jack had ever seen, and pressed one of the buttons. With an expensive-sounding clunk, a metal door slid shut across the doorway they'd come through.

'Impressive,' said Aunty Anthea's new boyfriend Rakesh. 'Controlled by an 87659SLK Quad, I bet. Very fine chip.'

'I told them I wanted the best,' said Uncle Pete.

As he said this, several more clunks, much louder, came from above their heads.

'What was that?' said Aunty Sue, looking alarmed.

Jack saw that Uncle Pete was looking alarmed too. But only for a moment. Then he grinned.

'Must be the soil settling,' he said. 'The builders cracked a pool pipe when they were excavating down here and it started leaking this week, so I got them to dig under the pool and fix it.'

'They were terrified,' said Aunty Sue. 'Pete said he'd have them in the International Court Of Justice if they weren't finished by Friday.'

Uncle Pete rolled his eyes.

'Not the International Court,' he said. 'Just the High Court.'

Jack was about to comment that the sticky tape Dad sold could have fixed the problem, when he noticed water running down the wall behind Uncle Pete. It was trickling in through the ventilation grilles.

'Excuse me, Uncle Pete,' he said, pointing.

But Uncle Pete didn't hear. He was busy talking to the others.

'The walls are packed with clay specially imported from Bolivia,' said Uncle Pete. 'Bolivian clay is brilliant for keeping noise out. Absolutely no sound gets through it.'

'I was able to advise Pete about that,' said Niall. 'My work with the acoustic properties of Bolivian clay in Third World concert halls won me a Guns 'N' Roses Foundation Research Fellowship.'

The others murmured in an impressed way.

'My research methodology was quite simple,'

said Niall. 'I didn't have a shower for three weeks in Bolivia and discovered I couldn't hear my noisy neighbours due to the build-up of clay in my ears.'

The others murmured in an even more impressed way. Then Mum noticed something.

'Pete,' she said. 'Why is the floor wet?'

'It's because of that water running down the wall,' said Jack.

Uncle Pete turned, and his eyes went wide. Water was coming in through the ventilation grilles even faster now.

'Jeez,' said Uncle Pete. 'That shouldn't be happening.'

Other family members murmured in agreement.

'Quick,' said Uncle Pete. 'Turn all this gear off.'

He and Uncle Rob dashed around, switching all the equipment off.

By the time they'd finished, water was gushing in. It was up to Jack's ankles.

'Everybody out,' said Uncle Pete.

He stabbed a button on the remote. The door stayed closed. He pushed several more buttons. The door didn't open. He pounded all the buttons. Nothing.

'That's the one problem with the 87659SLK Quad,' said Rakesh. 'Doesn't work if it gets damp.'

Uncle Pete sloshed over to the door and dried as much of it as he could with his shirt tail. He wiped the remote as well. Then he pressed all the buttons again. And again. And again.

The door still didn't move.

The water was nearly up to their knees.

'Don't panic,' said Mum to Jack. It'll start draining away in a sec.'

'No, it won't,' said Uncle Pete. 'This room is completely sealed. I didn't want any humidity warping my turntable.'

'I'll ring for help,' said Aunty Anthea, fumbling with her phone. 'What's the number for the State Emergency Service?'

'Don't bother,' said Niall. 'Bolivian clay totally blocks phone signals. It's got tiny particles of mica in it. The CIA use it in all their buildings.'

The family members all stared at Uncle Pete.

'I had to use it,' protested Uncle Pete. 'Phone signals can affect blu-ray picture quality.'

'Why's the air in here starting to smell stale?' said Uncle Rob.

Aunty Sue sniffed.

'Shouldn't be,' she said. 'It's air-conditioned.'

'I put in a three-phase industrial-quality air-management system with anti-static pollen filters,' said Uncle Pete.

He waded over to the only ventilation grille that didn't have water gushing out of it, reached up and held his hand in front of it.

'Poop,' he said. 'The water must have shorted the air-con motors.'

Aunty Sue gave a sob.

The water was over their knees.

And Jack's waist. He looked frantically around the room. No windows. No more doors. Not even a fire escape.

'We'll have to dig our way out,' said Uncle Rob. 'I've seen it done. The workers at the hospital in Africa had to do it when they were building the staff squash court and some scaffolding collapsed. Most of them survived.'

'They only had to dig through low density African clay,' said Niall. 'Bolivian clay goes hard as steel when it gets wet.'

'We're trapped,' sobbed Aunty Sue. 'We're all going to suffocate.'

'Calm down, woman,' said Uncle Pete. 'There's enough air in here for hours. We'll drown long before the air runs out.'

Everyone sloshed over to the door and started clawing at it. And kicking it. And trying to smash through it with items of electrical equipment. They kept trying until all Uncle Pete's speakers were floating around them in fragments.

The door didn't budge.

Mum screamed.

Jack knew why. The water was over her waist, and nearly up his chin.

'Jack,' yelled Mum. 'Hang on to something. Pick him up somebody.'

Dad grabbed Jack and lifted him up. Jack hadn't realised Dad was so strong. Though now he thought about it, the stationery shop didn't have a forklift, so Dad must get a lot of exercise carrying all the boxes by hand.

'A chair,' said Aunty Sue. 'Get him a chair.'

The adults splashed around for ages until somebody found a chair under the water. Dad carefully helped Jack stand on it.

The water was only up to Jack's waist now.

But it was up to everyone else's chest.

Then the lights went out.

There was quite a lot of shouting and screaming. After a while, Mum yelled at everyone to be quiet, and after another while, they were. Mostly because, as Jack saw in the faint light from Aunty Anthea's phone, which she was holding over her head, the water was up to their chins.

'There must be another way of getting that door open,' spluttered Uncle Rob. 'A mechanical override.'

'There is,' gasped Uncle Pete. 'But it needs a tiny allen key, and the builders lost it.'

Aunty Sue started crying again.

Then Jack had an idea.

'Dad,' he said. 'Have you got a paperclip?'

Dad frowned as he thought about this.

'Paperclip,' he said. 'Paperclip . . .'

Then his face brightened.

'Yes,' he said. 'One of the new Ezyglide Anti-statics. I brought it home to show Mum.'

He rummaged around under the water, and Jack guessed he was going through his pockets.

'Please,' murmured Aunty Anthea desperately. 'Please find it.'

Dad raised his hand out of the water.

He was holding a paperclip.

'Thank God,' sobbed Aunty Sue, and then gurgled as her mouth filled with water.

Jack watched Dad move slowly towards the door, paperclip held high.

Dad reached the door, took a big breath of air and ducked under the surface of the water.

Jack stood on tiptoe to keep the water away from his mouth and counted the seconds.

Forty.

Fifty.

Sixty and still Dad hadn't come back up.

Jack prayed that correction fluid got spilled a lot in stationery shops. The stuff that gave off pongy fumes. Which meant Dad would have had lots of practice holding his breath.

Seventy.

So he wouldn't drown.

Eighty seconds.

Suddenly there was a clunk and a gurgle and a loud sucking sound, and the door started to slide open.

The water level dropped immediately, and the family members screamed and cheered and spluttered and sobbed.

Then the water level stopped going down.

Jack saw why. Outside the door, the steep concrete

steps going up to the garden were preventing the rest of the water from flowing away.

But it didn't matter. The door was open now and daylight was coming in, and fresh air, and the distant sound above them of an automatic pool cleaner sucking itself dry in an empty pool.

And there was Dad, head and shoulders out of the water, staring at the paperclip in his hand with relief and gratitude.

Dad wasn't the only one doing that.

The whole family was gazing at the paperclip that way. And at Dad. And not just with relief and gratitude. With awe and admiration and respect as well.

Jack grinned, careful to keep his mouth closed because with so much panic somebody was bound to have done a wee in the water.

OK, he said to himself as he swam over to Mum and Dad. I admit it. Big family get-togethers aren't so bad after all.

Big Mistake

It all started with bosoms.

When me and Imelda were babies, Mum used to breastfeed us. I loved those meals. I loved them even more than I love spicy sausage pizza now.

Until Imelda spoiled everything.

Even nine years later I can still remember what happened. Me sucking away happily on Mum's left side as usual. Imelda doing the same on the other side. Until suddenly Imelda stopped sucking and glared at me across Mum's valley.

'Donald's bosom is bigger than mine,' she wailed.

Mum didn't know what Imelda's wail meant, of course. But I understood. And Imelda was completely wrong. No way was the bosom in my mouth bigger than the one in hers.

'No, it's not,' I wailed. 'Hers is bigger.'

I'd never compared Mum's bosoms before, but now that Imelda had introduced the topic I could clearly see that my bosom was actually smaller than Imelda's bosom.

'Not fair,' I wailed. 'Hers is much bigger.'

'Rubbish,' wailed Imelda. 'His is.'

Mum didn't have a clue what we were on about. But she could see we weren't happy, so she burped us and checked our nappies for recent visitors and tickled us under our chins and got us sucking again.

Imelda didn't make any more wild accusations that day. Or that year. But every mealtime as she sucked grumpily and glared at me from her side, I could see what she was thinking.

His is bigger.

I glared back.

I was thinking the opposite.

Hers is bigger.

When you're a twin it's very important that the other twin doesn't get more than you. You probably have to be a twin to understand how important that is. How very, very important.

I knew it wasn't going to end with bosoms.

It didn't.

On our first birthday Dad made us a cake in the shape of Thomas the Tank Engine. Me and Imelda both loved Thomas, so we were very happy.

At first.

All our aunties and uncles and grandparents were there and they helped us blow out the candles. We had one candle each. Exactly the same size. I checked and Imelda did too.

Mum cut the cake and gave us half a Fat Controller each.

Imelda's face went red with distress. She pointed at my plate and said her first word.

'Bigger.'

Mum had cut the Fat Controller so we each had one side of his body, including half his bottom. Imelda was saying that my Fat Controller buttock was bigger than her Fat Controller buttock.

Which was rubbish. Hers was bigger.

I pointed at Imelda's plate and said my first two words.

'Bigger buttock.'

We both burst into tears.

All the grown-ups tried to make our birthday happy again. Mum offered us exactly half a coal truck each instead, then realised that one of the coal truck's eyebrows was bigger than the other. Auntie Pauline explained how most people in real life don't have perfectly matching buttocks, and pointed to Uncle John's as an example. Dad got a bowl of icing and a brush and painted some extra underpants on the Fat Controller's buttocks to try and disguise their size, but me and Imelda saw through that.

Poor Mum and Dad.

Every birthday it was the same.

When we were five, me and Imelda both asked for exactly the same birthday present. A tape measure. Mum and Dad gave us one each.

Identical tape measures.

Or so they thought.

Imelda measured my tape measure with hers, and I measured hers with mine, and soon we were both in tears.

'His is .06 of a millimetre longer,' sobbed Imelda.

'Hers is .0003 of a millimetre thicker,' I wailed. 'And her wrapping paper is wider too.'

When we started school, they put Imelda in one class and me in another. It didn't work.

'His teacher is bigger than mine,' wailed Imelda. 'I measured them.'

'Only round the tummy,' I sobbed. 'Hers is taller and has got much bigger feet.'

Every day it was the same.

'His fish fingers are bigger than mine,' sobbed Imelda one evening.

'Hers are,' I wailed.

'They can't be,' shouted Mum. 'They're made in a factory. With millions of dollars worth of equipment scientifically designed to make sure every fish finger is exactly the same size. That's why we have fish fingers four times a week.'

Imelda and me thought about this.

'It's the way you cook them,' wailed Imelda. 'You make mine shrink.'

'Mine shrink more,' I sobbed.

Mum grabbed our plates and dumped the fish fingers onto the chopping board.

'Right,' she said. 'Here's what we're going to do. You're each going to cut your fish fingers exactly in half. I suggest you use your tape measures. Then you're each going to choose which halves you want, one piece at a time, taking it in turns, so you both end up with exactly the same number of halves, which each of you will have chosen yourself.'

Mum gave a weary sigh.

'Let's see you find a reason for squabbling then,' she said. 'I should have thought of this years ago.'

Mum handed us a knife each.

Me and Imelda grabbed our tape measures and measured the knives.

'His is bigger than mine,' sobbed Imelda.

'Hers is,' I wailed.

The years passed. Nothing changed. Except Mum and Dad got wearier. Sometimes I felt guilty, but I couldn't stop. I couldn't give in. I couldn't let Imelda get more than me. You can't do that, not when you're a twin.

Whenever I thought about the future, I realised life would always be the same in our family. Until Mum and Dad got old and so weary they died. Then the undertaker would send us their ashes, and Imelda would claim I got a bigger share and I'd say she did.

That was our future.

Until last week, when we went on holiday.

I think it was the motel muesli that was the last straw. ('He's got bigger bran flakes than me.' 'She's got bigger particles of hydrogenated kelp.')

Or maybe the last straw was at the service-station cafe. ('She's got a bigger straw than me.'

'His 275-ml carton of chocolate milk is bigger than my 275-ml carton of chocolate milk.')

Or maybe it was the drive up the coast. ('He spilt more chocolate milk on the car seat than I did.' 'She did a bigger sick in the glove box than I did.')

Whichever it was, at lunchtime everything changed.

We were having a picnic in a carpark near the highway. Sandwiches ('hers is crustier') and bananas ('his is more bent').

'For the love of Pete,' said Dad wearily. 'When are you two going to grow up and stop whingeing and complaining?'

I looked around at the other families having picnics. Happy laughing families with kids who weren't squabbling and parents who weren't weary and miserable.

I looked at their cars. None of them had luggage on the roof like ours. Probably because they didn't have an extra bag full of tape measures and rulers and microscopes and weighing scales and surveyor's tripods and portable laser measuring devices.

Suddenly I felt weary and miserable too.

I wanted our family to be one of the happy ones.

We'd eaten most of our picnic. There were just two bananas left. You didn't need a measuring device to see that one was big and one was small.

Mum and Dad were pretending those bananas didn't exist. I could see they were hoping me and Imelda would do the same.

I picked up the big one and held it out to Imelda. 'Here,' I said. 'You have it.'

Imelda stared at me, stunned.

So did Mum and Dad.

'You want me to have the big banana?' said Imelda, amazed.

I nodded. I could see Imelda's mind working fast. Her eyes narrowed. I could see she was looking for the catch.

Then she grinned.

'No thanks,' she said. 'I don't need it.'

I was confused. Was she saying she wanted me to have it?

Before I could decide, Imelda jumped up, grabbed hold of my hand and dragged me round the other side of a big parked truck.

'I don't need your banana,' she said sweetly. 'I've got a bigger banana than you'll ever have.'

I stared.

In front of us was a gigantic banana. It must have been at least 30 metres long. And three times as tall as a grown-up. It looked like it was made of plastic. On the side of it was a sign.

The Big Banana, Coffs Harbour, NSW.

'I win,' said Imelda.

For a moment I hoped this was just a silly game. That we were having fun like the other families. But Imelda was looking at me in a very mocking way and I could see from her eyes that she was deadly serious.

I realised what had happened.

Imelda had listened to Dad and decided he was right. We were too old for whingeing and complaining. Now we were ten, she'd decided, we were old enough for gloating and winning.

Everything had changed, and nothing had.

She'd won with the banana. I knew there couldn't be a bigger banana anywhere in Australia. But that was only Round One.

Later that afternoon, further up the highway, we passed The Big Prawn and I spotted it first, which made it mine.

'I've got a bigger prawn than you,' I gloated.

Imelda seethed.

In the front of the car, Mum and Dad, who'd been feeling a bit light-headed from three whole hours without any whingeing and complaining, sagged into their seats.

The rest of the week was a nightmare.

As we toured around on our driving holiday, me and Imelda couldn't relax for a second. We hardly dared blink in case we missed something.

I got The Big Peanut, The Big Crab and I was in the middle of gloating to Imelda that I had a bigger bottom than her when Mum wearily pointed out that what I'd just seen wasn't The Big Buttock, it was a haystack covered with pink plastic.

Imelda got The Big Pineapple, The Big Cow and what she claimed was The Big Swimming Pool, which it wasn't because it was a lake.

'Cheat,' I sneered at her.

'Jealous,' she sneered back.

'Please,' sighed Mum wearily.

We'd never been more unhappy.

I started imagining big things and desperately hoping they'd be round the next corner so I could see them first and win.

The Big Flyscreen.

The Big Teabag.

The Big Blood Clot if we passed an abattoir.

Nothing.

Dad started going out of his way to avoid big things. He saw in a tourist brochure that the next town had The Big Tow Truck, so he took a dirt track through a swamp to keep us away from it.

We got bogged in the mud.

While Mum and Dad tried to get us out, me and Imelda gathered dry grass and branches to put under the back wheels. Except Imelda wasn't doing much gathering. She was too busy gloating.

'I've got bigger bosoms than you,' she said in a very cocky voice.

I looked up.

Imelda was sneering at me and pointing towards the horizon. In the distance, next to what must have been the highway, was a huge advertising billboard with an ad for a caravan park. Most of it was a woman with half her bosoms showing.

I stared at it for a long time.

Imelda kept on gloating for a long time.

I didn't care. I was thinking about a long time ago, when all this had started. When Imelda reckoned I had the biggest bosom and I reckoned she did.

We couldn't both have been right. Then another thought hit me. What if we'd both been wrong? What if Mum's bosoms were exactly the same size? All this whingeing and complaining and gloating and winning wouldn't be necessary anymore.

Suddenly I wanted to know the truth.

That night, in the motel, I took a peek.

Mum was having a shower. Dad and Imelda were watching a movie on TV. During an exciting bit when they were totally engrossed, I crept over to the bathroom, opened the door and peeped in.

Just as I did, the shower screen slid open and Mum stepped out.

She saw me looking.

'Oh, for Pete's sake,' she said, grabbing a towel and wrapping it around herself. 'Can't a person get a moment's peace in this family?'

My guts went tight and cold. Not because Mum was annoyed. Because of what I'd seen.

Mum's left bosom was slightly bigger than her right one. And it hung slightly lower. Which made it seem even larger.

'What's wrong, love?' said Mum.

She must have noticed my miserable face.

'Imelda was right,' I said sadly.

'Right about what?' said Mum.

'That my bosom was bigger than hers,' I said.

'Of course I was right,' said Imelda, coming over. She gave me a jealous look. 'Your bosom was always bigger.'

Mum frowned and looked puzzled.

Then she grinned.

'What a pair of nongs,' she said.

For a moment I thought she was talking about her bosoms. But then I saw she wasn't, she was talking about me and Imelda.

'You didn't have a bosom each,' said Mum. 'You couldn't. The right-hand one didn't feed properly. The milk kept getting blocked. So I fed you both with the left one, taking turns.'

I stared at her.

'But I can remember us both sucking at once,' I said. 'I can remember it.'

'So can I,' said Imelda.

Mum shook her head.

'Nope,' she said.

'Wasn't possible,' said Dad, joining us.

'When we get home,' said Mum, 'I'll show you the doctor's report from the baby health centre. I was a lefty. That's why it sags a bit now.'

I looked at Imelda. I could see she was as shocked as I was.

'The right one was a waiting and burping area,' said Mum. 'While one of you was feeding on the left side, I'd cuddle the other one of you on the right side.'

Me and Imelda stood there for a long time, just staring at Mum's towel-covered chest.

Mum let us. I think she could see that me and Imelda had some important things to think about.

'Don't you mind?' I said to Mum after a while. 'That we made one of them a bit saggy?'

'Course not,' said Mum. 'It's what it's for. Anyway, when I've got a pair of anything, I always like them both exactly the same amount.'

Dad nodded.

Mum gave me and Imelda a long look.

I realised she wasn't just talking about her bosoms.

I glanced over and saw that Imelda had realised this too. She opened her mouth to say something. I wondered if she was going to boast about having a worse memory than me.

For a moment I wanted to be the one to boast about having the worst memory.

But I didn't.

I decided to give Imelda the chance.

Imelda stayed silent.

After a while I realised she was giving me the chance.

We stood there, glancing at each other nervously. Then we swapped a little grin. Mum gave us both a hug. And at last there was no need for me or Imelda to say anything.

Harriet's Story

Harriet wakes up.

She can't see anything except the dull glow of her bedside clock.

3.14 a.m.

That explains why the rest of her bedroom is dark. Darker than the inside of a black sock that's been swallowed by a large bat who lives in a cave with very thick curtains.

Strange, thinks Harriet. I don't usually wake up in the middle of the night. And if I do, I don't usually lie here making up weird sentences about how dark it is.

She wonders what's going on.

Then she realises.

She's thirsty. Very thirsty. Thirstier than a blast-furnace operator lost in the middle of the Sahara desert who forgot to have a drink before he went on holiday.

Of course, thinks Harriet. That's why I've woken up. And that's why I'm making up these weird sentences. My brain's dehydrated.

Easily fixed.

Harriet switches on her lamp and reaches for the glass of water Mum always leaves on the bedside table.

The glass is empty. Emptier than a cave whose usual inhabitant, a large hungry sock-eating bat, has rushed off to the Sahara after hearing that an overheated blast-furnace operator has just taken off his shoes.

Harriet blinks.

This thirst, she thinks, is really making me think weird things.

Oh well, still easily fixed.

Plenty to drink in the kitchen. Water in the tap. Juice in the fridge. Long-life milk in the cupboard if I feel like a long life.

Harriet gets out of bed, opens her bedroom door and creeps out. She closes the door quietly behind her.

The hallway isn't as dark as her room. There's a faint haze of moonlight coming through a window.

This is more sort of gloomy than dark, thinks Harriet. As gloomy as a bat in the desert staring at two socks it can't eat because it's allergic to polyester.

Stop it, Harriet says to herself.

The kitchen.

She doesn't turn the hallway light on. Mustn't wake Mum and Dad. They both work hard and need their sleep.

As Harriet creeps past their room, she hears gentle snoring. And wheezing. And slobbering.

Muttley must be sleeping on their bed.

Just the thought of her beloved dog makes Harriet's insides go warm. Almost as warm as the polyester-sock soup a hungry bat might make to try and get some of the sock flavour without having to swallow any of the actual . . .

Harriet concentrates on getting down the stairs to the kitchen.

Luckily there are some glints of moonlight on the stairs. She goes down carefully, step by step, counting each stair silently to keep her mind from wandering.

. . . three, four, five . . .

She stops.

Gleaming on the next stair is a small plastic racing car.

Typical, she thinks. Younger brothers always leave their toys where other people could step on them and do triple backward somersaults down the stairs and land on their pelvises and sprain their anterior fibulate cartilages and miss out on selection for the school swimming team.

Harriet reminds herself that Billy is only four and probably didn't mean it.

Then the moonlight disappears.

The plastic racing car glows eerily. Particularly around the headlights.

Strange.

Harriet didn't think racing cars had headlights.

She stands in the darkness, feeling a bit spooked. She's read about this. Hallucinations. Seeing things. It can happen to people who are extremely thirsty. She read a story only recently about somebody dying of thirst in a desert who thought a large bat was eating his socks.

Mum. Dad. Help.

Harriet wants to call out. She wants Mum and Dad to wake up and switch on the light and stumble concerned out of their room and trip over Muttley and do triple backward somersaults down the stairs and land on their pelvises and sprain their anterior fibulate cartilages and miss out on . . .

No, she doesn't.

It's OK, Harriet tells herself. I'm not in the desert. I'm standing on the stairs at home. People don't usually die of thirst standing on the stairs, even when they feel like they might.

Slowly, carefully, she moves down the dark steps towards the kitchen.

. . . eleven, twelve, thirteen . . .

She knows there are fifteen steps because that's how Mum and Dad taught her to count, years ago. But she prepares herself for a few more now, maybe a few hundred more, because that's what happens when you're hallucinating from thirst.

. . . fourteen, fifteen . . .

She tests ahead with her foot.

No more.

Just flat floor.

Good, the hallucinations have stopped.

Harriet walks towards the kitchen, very slowly and carefully because this downstairs hall is darker than a . . .

Stop that.

She can't see the kitchen door, but she knows roughly how far it is from the bottom of the stairs. She holds her hands up in front of her in case the hallucinations start again and she bumps into a stuffed gorilla or a big pile of bat poo or the Eiffel Tower.

Bump.

Her fingers are touching something. It doesn't feel lumpy or pooey or French.

It feels like a door handle.

Yes.

The kitchen door.

At last she can get a drink.

Harriet turns the handle, steps into the kitchen and quietly closes the door. Now she can switch the light on without disturbing Mum and Dad.

She does.

At first the brightness hurts her eyes. She can't see anything. All she can think of is thirst. She wants to rush to the fridge and grab the bottle of juice and glug it down, blind and squinting. But she doesn't.

There are other bottles and jars in the fridge she wouldn't want to grab by mistake. Soy sauce. Dad's home-made ginger beer.

Instead Harriet turns away from the glare and waits for her eyes to adjust. Which they do. Soon she can see the back of the kitchen door clearly.

She can also see a big shadow looming over her.

Somebody else is in the kitchen.

Somebody big.

From the shape of the shadow, it doesn't look like Mum or Dad or Billy. It looks like a man with the sort of very broad shoulders a burglar would probably have. And over one of his shadow shoulders is what looks like a huge sack. Bulging with something very big inside it.

Probably the fridge, thinks Harriet.

She wants to run.

She wants to claw open the kitchen door and leap up the stairs and fling herself into bed with Mum and Dad.

But her hands are sweaty with fear and she knows that if she tries to grab the door handle her fingers will probably slip and she'll be fumbling and the burglar will have heaps of time to grab her and put her in his sack.

She has to think of something else.

Behind her, the burglar isn't saying anything.

He's probably in shock too, thinks Harriet. Burglars are probably cowards underneath, which is why they slink around stealing fridges in the dark.

Harriet has an idea. She decides to turn and face the burglar and pretend she's braver than she is. She'll offer him a deal. If she can have the juice, he can take the fridge.

She turns, guts twisted tighter than a polyester sock. And blinks.

There isn't a burglar.

Just Mum's ski suit, hanging from the light fitting. The hood has flopped over to one side and is making a big sack-shaped shadow.

Harriet remembers Mum saying the ski suit has to go to the drycleaners. She must have hung it here so she wouldn't forget.

Dizzy with relief, and thirst, Harriet pulls the fridge door open, almost tasting the cool sweet juice.

She grabs the juice bottle.

It's empty.

So's the milk.

Dad's ginger beer fermentation jar is lying broken in the bottom of the fridge. Most of the ginger beer has leaked out and been soaked up by the leftover curry and rice in the salad crisper.

Harriet stares, horrified.

There's only one person who'd drink everything in the fridge that carelessly.

Harriet knows she should be waking Mum and Dad and telling them the bad news so they can inform the insurance company and get some more ginger beer yeast for Dad and call the police to see if there's a Younger Brother Punishment Squad.

But first she absolutely must have a drink.

Harriet grabs a glass from the cupboard and goes to the sink and turns the tap on.

Nothing comes out.

She turns the tap on more. Still nothing. She tries the hot tap. Nothing.

The taps are completely dry. Drier than a pair of socks that have been lying in the desert sun so long you wouldn't even know a bat had tried to make soup out of them.

Oh no, thinks Harriet. I'm making up weird sentences again.

Another thought hits her.

Is it just a coincidence the fridge is empty and the water pipes are dry on the same night? Or is something else going on?

Like . . .

Like . . .

Harriet can't imagine what it could be. She thinks about the moonlight disappearing, and the plastic racing car going spooky, and the burglar-shaped shadow. And now suddenly here's a drought or a burst water main or a clogged valve at the reservoir. Everything that's happened since she got out of bed has made it harder for her to get a drink.

Getting a drink should be so simple.

Not a big problem.

Unless . . .

Suddenly Harriet has to sit down on a kitchen chair.

Could it be . . .?

Last week in class Ms Lovett was talking about stories and how they work. How in every story, the main character must have a problem. And how the character never solves the problem straight away, because that would make the story too short and too boring.

'In a story,' Ms Lovett said, 'things always come along to make the problem harder to solve. Things always get worse before they get better.'

Harriet thinks again about the empty glass and the racing car and the dark hall and scary shadow and the empty juice bottle and the dry taps.

Could it be, she thinks, that I'm in a story?

No, that's crazy.

Harriet goes to the cupboard, finds the long-life milk, and opens the carton. She tips the milk into the glass. Except she doesn't because nothing comes out. She shakes the carton. The contents feel solid. And now there's a cheesy smell.

She looks more closely at the carton to make sure Mum didn't buy long-life cheese by mistake. No, it says long-life milk. Right next to where it says *Use By September 2009.*

Harriet puts the carton down.

She's tempted to ring Ms Lovett for advice. But it's 3.25 a.m, and she knows teachers don't get paid overtime.

No, thinks Harriet, I'll deal with this myself.

She remembers something else Ms Lovett said.

As characters battle to solve their problems, they often discover they're braver than they ever thought they were.

Harriet isn't feeling particularly brave at the moment, but definitely more determined.

And thirstier.

My problem, she says to herself, is getting a drink. If I'm in a story, things will keep coming along to make it harder for me to solve my problem.

Let's put it to the test.

Harriet thinks about what she can do next.

Of course. If a person finds themself in a drinkless kitchen, there's an obvious solution. Go out into the garden and drink from the fish pond.

Harriet opens the kitchen window and peers out. The moon is glowing again and the pond is rippling, but the trees around it are full of bats. They're fruit bats and Harriet knows they're harmless, but she also knows it's best not to drink anything that's directly under a bat's bottom.

She closes the window.

OK, she thinks. I need another way to fix the problem. How about waking up Mum and Dad and asking them to drive me to the all-night supermarket? It's only a ten-minute journey.

Harriet takes a couple of steps towards the stairs, then stops.

She's thinking of all the things that could happen on the way to the supermarket to stop her solving her problem.

Dad crashing the car into the library.

The whole family being abducted by aliens and taken to a planet where the inhabitants live on a diet of really salty chips and curried sand.

Mum being pulled over for not wearing a seatbelt and then being charged with the desert murder of a sockless blast-furnace operator.

Mind you, there would probably be a water cooler at the police station . . .

No.

Harriet sits down again and thinks hard. She needs a way of solving her problem that won't put Mum and Dad in danger and cause them to lose sleep and/or their car and/or their freedom and/or their library tickets.

Of course, she says to herself. Why didn't I think of it before? I'll break into our neighbours' house and borrow a drink from them.

Harriet creeps out the back door, staying well away from the fruit bats, climbs over the fence and runs, crouching, across the neighbours' lawn.

At their house, trying to feel braver than she ever has before, she looks for a possible place to break in.

And finds one. An open toilet window. It's a bit high up, but if she stands on this garden table, and pulls herself up using this metal box screwed to the wall with the little red flickering light on it . . .

Oops, thinks Harriet as she jumps back down from the table. That burglar alarm wasn't there last time I looked.

Yet another thing making her problem harder to solve.

As Harriet hurries away from the neighbours' house, she remembers something else Ms Lovett said about stories. How trying to solve a problem can sometimes cause an even bigger problem.

She also remembers something Dad said about the neighbours. How they collect Olympic swimming medals, buying them from all over the world, and how they're always worrying that their priceless collection will be burgled.

That would have been a bigger problem alright, thinks Harriet. If the neighbours had caught me in their house and thought I was trying to steal their medals, and had rung the police. The Older Sister Crime Squad would have been round in a flash.

As Harriet crosses the lawn, she notices that a trench has recently been dug and filled in again. A trench from the street to the neighbours' house.

A cable's probably been laid, she thinks. A high-security burglar alarm cable that has to go under the ground.

Wait a minute.

When a deep high-security trench is dug, perhaps it can sometimes damage other things under the ground. Like water pipes.

Harriet hurries out to the street, to where the trench meets the footpath. She peers at the ground. And sees exactly what she was hoping to see.

A big patch of damp mud.

She's so thirsty now she's tempted just to fill her mouth with mud and see if she can suck any water out of it.

But she doesn't. She hurries to the shed, finds Dad's pickaxe, comes back and digs down into the mud.

Yes.

There it is.

Just as she'd suspected.

She's uncovered the place where the water pipe to her house joins the main pipe for the street. In the house pipe, near the join, is a crack with water trickling out of it.

Harriet drops to her knees and laps at the water. It's muddy and gritty, but she doesn't care.

All she cares about is there's not enough of it.

The tantalising taste of water is driving her crazy with thirst.

She grabs the pickaxe and swings it gently and makes the crack in the pipe just a little bit bigger. Mud and plastic putty ooze out of the crack.

Look at that, thinks Harriet. When they dug the trench, they not only cracked our pipe, they tried to hide what they'd done with plastic putty.

She swings the pickaxe again and makes the crack a little bit bigger again.

Well, quite a bit bigger actually, but Harriet doesn't care because now the water is bubbling out in a glorious fountain and she plunges her face into it and drinks and drinks and drinks.

And drinks.

Ahhhh, that's better.

Problem solved.

Suddenly Harriet is dizzy with tiredness. She has just enough strength to block the hole in the pipe with the putty and her socks, put the pickaxe back in the shed, and drag herself up to bed.

She flops down and closes her eyes, and as the warm tide of sleep carries her away, she has one last thought.

That's nice, she murmurs to herself. My story has a happy ending.

So deep is Harriet's sleep she doesn't hear the faint pop of a plug of putty and sock being expelled from a hole in a water pipe, and the soft gush of water fountaining high into the night sky and then cascading down a driveway and under the neighbours' front door.

Hours later she's still slumbering so soundly that even the harsh sound of a State Emergency Service diesel pump starting up on the other side of the fence doesn't wake her. Nor does the even harsher sound of the neighbours wailing about possible rust damage to their medals.

Somebody the noise does wake, though, in the next street, is Ms Lovett.

Hmmm, thinks Ms Lovett, stretching sleepily under the covers with the contentment of a person who loves her job. I think I'll talk to the class some more about stories today. Introduce them to irony.

Perhaps use the example of a character solving a problem and causing another problem that's the exact opposite.

She pauses, reflecting.

Are they ready for irony, this lot?

She stretches again, smiling.

Yes, I think so.

SNOT CHOCOLATE

King Ned

Ned opened his eyes and frowned.

Something was wrong.

It was daylight and he was still in bed.

How was that possible? Uncle Vern didn't allow sleeping in. The hovel was too small. Uncle Vern and Ned always got up at dawn in case the pigs needed a lie down.

Something else doesn't feel right, thought Ned.

I'm warm.

Deliciously warm.

Ned saw why. A blanket was draped over him. Uncle Vern's blanket. Ned recognised the sheepskin with the sheep's head still attached.

Which was very strange, because Uncle Vern didn't believe in young people being warm.

'Not good for ye,' Uncle Vern often told Ned. 'That be what caused the terrible infant mortality in the twelfth century, children bein' too warm.

Either that or too hungry, I can't remember zackly.'

Ned didn't care if being snug was dangerous.

He was enjoying it.

Anyway, he thought, this isn't the twelfth century, it's the thirteenth, so I'll probably survive.

Ned had never felt warm in bed before. It was lovely. He snuggled deeper under the blanket. The bed felt extra soft, as if somebody had stuffed extra straw and rags and fluffy dead mice into the mattress while he slept.

'Good mornin', sire.'

Ned jumped guiltily.

He'd assumed Uncle Vern had gone out to get some stoats for breakfast. But this was definitely Uncle Vern's voice.

Ned peered around. The hovel wasn't much bigger than a plague cart so it was strange that he could hear Uncle Vern but not see him.

Puzzled, Ned sat up.

And stared in surprise.

Uncle Vern was splayed out on the ground next to the bed, bottom in the air, chin in the dirt, staring up at him fearfully.

'I await your command, sire,' said Uncle Vern.

If Uncle Vern had been a different sort of person, given to light-hearted japes rather than scraping mould off damp trees for a living, Ned might have thought this was a merry jest.

But Uncle Vern didn't do merry jests.

What was going on?

'Uncle Vern,' said Ned, concerned. 'You shouldn't lie on the damp ground like that. You'll get skin rot.'

'No I won't,' said Uncle Vern, still looking at Ned fearfully.

'Millipedes might crawl up your nose,' said Ned, desperately trying to think of something to snap Uncle Vern out of it.

Uncle Vern shook his head. Ned wasn't sure if he was disagreeing or trying to dislodge millipedes that had already crawled in.

'Why are you doing this?' said Ned.

Uncle Vern was a stern and rather bossy uncle who spent a lot of time calling Ned a fool. Sprawling on the ground and twitching in terror just wasn't like him.

'I'm doin' this so as you won't be killin' me,' stammered Uncle Vern. 'Your Highness.'

Ned stared at him, very concerned.

Your Highness?

Poor Uncle Vern must have accidentally swallowed some tree mould while he was feeding it to the pigs and it must have given him a tragic affliction of the brain.

Slowly, so as not to scare Uncle Vern, Ned climbed out of bed.

Uncle Vern slithered further away.

'Uncle Vern,' said Ned gently. 'You only call people Your Highness when they're the king. I'm not the king.'

'Yes you are,' said Uncle Vern.

Ned wondered what to do.

They couldn't afford a doctor, and he wasn't sure if acorn tea could cure a brain affliction this bad. Perhaps if he used some of the really strong acorns, the ones that had been eaten by pigs and come out the other end . . .

He bent down to help Uncle Vern up.

Uncle Vern whimpered and tried to slither even further away. Which wasn't easy in a tiny hovel cluttered up with two beds and two stools.

Ned decided to humour Uncle Vern. He couldn't think what else to do.

'Sit yourself on a stool,' he said nervously. 'That's a command.'

Ned suspected that commands weren't usually issued in a wobbly voice, but Uncle Vern didn't seem to notice. He scrambled to his feet. Then hesitated. Ned guessed he must be terrified about sitting down when royalty was still standing.

Ned gave a regal nod.

Uncle Vern sat on a stool, still looking terrified.

'Don't be afraid,' said Ned. 'I'm not going to hurt you. Kings don't kill people.'

'Yes they do,' said Uncle Vern. 'The last king, God rest his soul, used to kill people all the time. That's why he was called King Rufus The People Killer.'

Ned hadn't known that. Plus it sounded like the king was dead, which he hadn't known either. Even after living with Uncle Vern for two years, Ned was still getting used to how much time news took to reach people living in remote bogs with pigs who had bowel problems.

Except, Ned reminded himself, Uncle Vern isn't thinking straight, so probably none of this is true. The king probably isn't dead at all. He's probably in his castle right now, handing out wise advice and food parcels to his subjects.

'The king didn't have any sons,' said Uncle Vern. 'So they've been looking for the next in line to the throne. They came round here in the middle of the night while you were asleep and said it was you.'

Ned sighed sadly.

Uncle Vern was in the grip of a terrible malady.

A sudden one. Like when Mum and Dad got the plague. One minute they were perfectly healthy, the next you were at their funeral.

Ned didn't want to think about that.

He also didn't want to think about what lay ahead for Uncle Vern if he couldn't be cured. Times were tough these days for brain-addled lunatics. They usually got drowned in duckponds, or locked in a cage and exhibited at fairs, or sometimes both.

Ned patted Uncle Vern on the arm and while Uncle Vern hid under a stool, he hurried out of the hovel desperately hoping there were some strong acorns in the pig pen.

Extremely strong.

He stopped at the doorstep, which wasn't so much a doorstep as a congealed heap of all the cold pig fat Uncle Vern had scraped out of the frying pan over the years.

Ned felt dizzy. He knew that dizziness could happen to people who didn't get enough fresh vegetables. Specially when they were short of sleep because of cold beds and noisy pigs who slurped tree mould all night. But Ned was pretty sure his dizziness was from something else.

The something that was in front of him.

Ned gaped.

Standing in the mud outside the hovel were six horses. Black ones. With silver plumes on their heads.

Behind them was a coach so golden and purple and gleaming that even a boy who'd never been to school knew instantly it was royal. Even before the two courtiers standing stiffly to attention bowed to him, opened the coach door, bowed to him again and murmured, 'Your Majesty'.

Ned had never been mistaken for a king before and it was making him feel a bit brain-addled himself. Which was why the coach journey was almost over before he realised his mistake.

Poop, thought Ned. Uncle Vern's right, I am a fool.

The only reason Ned had let the coach whisk him away, the only reason he hadn't explained to the courtiers that he was just the humble nephew of a mould farmer, was so he could get to the king and beg His Majesty to send a doctor with lots of strong acorns and leeches to cure Uncle Vern's brain.

Except, Ned now realised, Uncle Vern's brain didn't need curing. Because, unlike Ned, Uncle Vern wasn't brain-addled at all. This royal coach with its velvet cushions and silk curtains and delicate snacks on silver platters proved that.

The only brain-addled person, thought Ned, is whoever thinks I'm the king.

'Excuse me,' said Ned to the courtiers.

He wanted to explain his mistake and ask them to turn the coach round and take him home before he got into trouble for impersonating a monarch.

But the courtiers fell to their knees and held out the platters again.

Ned took one more quail drumstick and a couple more hummingbird nuggets, just to be polite. Plus, after two years of pig-nostril gruel, they were very delicious.

He ate them quickly so he could say what he had to say.

But by the time he'd finished chewing, the coach was clattering over a very large drawbridge and the courtiers were opening the curtains so Ned could see the majestic gleaming radiance of the royal castle.

Inside the castle walls, thousands of people stared at Ned. Well, hundreds, but when you lived in a hamlet with seven other peasants and eleven pigs, and the only time you had visitors was when the pigs had worms, even hundreds seemed scary.

Specially when they were all so well dressed. And kneeling down. And touching the muddy ground with their foreheads as you stepped out of the coach.

Well, not stepped.

Were carried.

'Your Majesty.'

The words rumbled around the huge castle courtyard in a mighty reverential whisper. Followed by a roar.

'The King Is Dead,' roared the crowd. 'Long Live The King.'

Oh, thought Ned. Uncle Vern was right about that too. I'd better get this whole misunderstanding cleared up.

Ned peered around the courtyard, trying to see who was in charge.

Whoever it was, he hoped they'd be wise and kind. The sort of viscount or bishop or admiral who understood that mistakes were sometimes made. And that a boy who made one or two of them shouldn't necessarily have his entrails boiled in oil.

'Sire.'

The two courtiers reverently placed Ned onto a red and gold carpet. But it wasn't the courtiers who had spoken.

Ned looked up.

Standing over him, bowing slightly, was the tallest man Ned had ever seen. He was very thin, but he must have been at least five foot six or even seven.

Amazing, thought Ned. People who don't live in bogs grow really tall. He could scrape the mould off a low branch without using a ladder.

'Welcome, Your Majesty,' said the man, and there was something about his haughty voice and dark pointy beard and the silver thread woven through his sumptuous clothes and the fur around the edge of his cloak and the jewels on the hilt of his sword and the way people lay down in the mud so he could walk on them without getting his boots dirty that made Ned think he might be the person in charge.

'On behalf of your worshipful subjects,' said the man, 'my humble greetings. I am your Lord Chamberlain, at Your Majesty's service.'

'Hello,' said Ned.

His voice came out squeaky, partly because of all the people listening, and partly because the Lord Chamberlain's eyes were making him feel nervous.

They were dark and darting and didn't look worshipful, humble or friendly.

'Actually,' stammered Ned, 'there's been a bit of a mistake.'

He was finding it hard to get words out, so he gestured towards the two courtiers from the coach. This would give the Lord Chamberlain an idea about the general nature of the mistake.

The Lord Chamberlain's eyes narrowed, which made them even scarier.

'A mistake?' he said.

Ned nodded.

'Please accept my apologies,' said the Lord Chamberlain. 'It won't happen again.'

Before Ned could say anything else, the Lord Chamberlain's sword flashed and the heads of the two courtiers plopped onto the ground, followed by the thud of their bodies.

Ned felt sick.

He decided to leave the topic of mistakes for a while, until he wasn't feeling so faint.

'What else does Your Majesty desire?' said the Lord Chamberlain.

'Can I sit down for a moment, please?' said Ned.

The royal throne was huge and uncomfortable. Ned's feet didn't even touch the ground, and jewels were poking him in several personal places.

He sipped the water he'd asked for.

The gold goblet was almost too heavy to lift, but at least the water didn't taste as though pigs had been washing in it.

Ned sighed.

He wanted to go home.

True, at home the water wasn't this clean and you had to drink it from the same mug as Uncle Vern. Verily, at home you didn't get to wear soft velvet robes like this, or real fur underwear. But at home you could be yourself and you were safe from murderous blades. Except when Uncle Vern was trimming pork giblets with a cleaver, but that wasn't often.

'Feeling better, Your Highness?'

Ned jumped.

The Lord Chamberlain had seated himself very close to Ned on a silver throne almost as big as the royal one.

Ned wasn't sure what to say.

A large number of other people were very close too. Courtiers mostly, anxiously hovering around with things a king might need, such as more gold goblets, whole roast oxen, maps of countries to invade, and great mounds of the exotic brightly coloured things Ned had heard about, called fruit.

The Lord Chamberlain stood up and clapped his hands.

The vast throne room emptied in a few seconds.

'Your Majesty,' said the Lord Chamberlain. 'My duty is to be your royal advisor, and my advice is that we should have a little chat.'

'Alright,' said Ned nervously.

'You are probably wondering, Your Most Royal Highness,' said the Lord Chamberlain, 'why you are the king.'

'Sort of,' said Ned.

'It's simple,' said the Lord Chamberlain. 'Your great-great-great-great grandmother was a distant member of the royal family.'

Ned blinked with surprise.

'Well,' continued the Lord Chamberlain, 'she wasn't exactly a family member, but she used to remove worms from the royal hunting dogs and those dogs were so grateful they treated her just like family. Peed on her hovel, dug up her garden, they truly loved her. Which we calculate makes you one million four hundred and sixty-three thousand two hundred and ninety-seventh in line to the throne.'

Ned struggled to take this in. Before he could ask the obvious question, the Lord Chamberlain answered it.

'The other one million four hundred and sixty-three thousand two hundred and ninety-six weren't available,' he said. 'Plagues, wars, overseas holidays, you can't imagine how relieved we were to find you.'

Ned could imagine, but it wasn't as simple as that.

'What if I don't want to be king?' he said quietly. 'Do I have a choice?'

'Oh, yes,' said the Lord Chamberlain. 'You most certainly do have a choice. You can choose to be the king, the most powerful person in the land whose every need, desire and whim is instantly satisfied and whose every law, command and proclamation is instantly obeyed. Or you can choose not to be the king, which means you're trespassing in the royal palace, an offence punishable by instant –'

The Lord Chamberlain drew his sword.

'I'll be the king,' said Ned.

'Wise choice, Your Highness,' said the Lord Chamberlain, putting his sword away.

Ned sagged miserably.

His head hurt. At first he thought it was the diamonds in his crown digging into his skull. But he realised it couldn't be that. The crown was too big so the royal housemaids had lined it with a couple of socks.

The Lord Chamberlain handed Ned a scroll of parchment covered in scrawly marks.

Ned wished he'd learned to read, but Uncle Vern had always said it was a waste of time given that pigs couldn't write.

'Our Constitution requires only two things of you, Your Highness,' said the Lord Chamberlain. 'One is that you behave like a king at all times, a special person of wealth, power and very white wrist ruffles so your loyal subjects can feel a glow of pride just thinking about you. The other is that you never leave the royal castle. We don't want you going outside like the last king and picking up some snotty peasant sniffle that turns fatal so we have to go through this whole tedious business all over again.'

Ned sagged even more.

Now he knew how the pigs at home felt, pampered with all the tree mould they could eat and all the lie-downs they fancied.

But utterly trapped.

The Lord Chamberlain was watching Ned closely again.

'As your royal advisor, Your Majesty,' he said, 'I advise you to make a start.'

Ned realised what the Lord Chamberlain meant.

Start behaving like a king.

Ned couldn't think of a single law, command or proclamation. He tried to summon up a need, desire or whim. Apart from going home, nothing.

The Lord Chamberlain's hand was resting on the hilt of his sword.

Ned suddenly remembered the anxious hovering courtiers and all the things they'd been offering him.

'Bring me a bandana,' he said in the most regal voice he could manage.

The Lord Chamberlain gave him a look.

'Your Highness wants a colourful scarf-like piece of fabric tied rakishly around his head? May I suggest that what Your Majesty wants is a banana.'

Ned sighed. It seemed he couldn't even get that right.

He wasn't a king, he was a fool.

Ned snuggled into the huge, soft, warm royal bed.

What a brilliant first command he'd finally come up with.

'I command,' he'd commanded, 'that I spend most of my time in bed.'

Nobody argued.

Maybe, Ned thought to himself, I'm going to be

quite a reasonably good king after all.

It was a magnificent bed, and easily big enough to hold all the things he might want to ask for.

So far there were just bananas. The first one had been so delicious, he'd asked for more. As the courtiers brought them in, the Lord Chamberlain explained that the bravest ships' captains in the land spent years on dangerous oceans to bring the bananas back from distant shores. By ancient royal command they sailed home the cold way, via the North Pole, so the bananas didn't get too ripe.

Ned was impressed.

He made a note to make sure his commands were that good.

The Lord Chamberlain also explained that a king shouldn't have to peel his own bananas, so they'd got him a trained chimp. Well, not a chimp exactly, but they'd found a very nimble-fingered monk with a protruding lower jaw.

Ned sighed contentedly. This was a wonderful experience, people being kind and considerate to him. The other people in his life had always been too busy for that, or too dead, and he was enjoying the feeling.

'Another banana please,' said Ned to the monk.

The monk got peeling.

'Your Majesty,' said the Lord Chamberlain, who was standing in the corner of the royal bedroom keeping an eye on things. 'You don't have to say please. You're the king.'

'Sorry,' said Ned.

'Or sorry,' said the Lord Chamberlain.

Ned covered his embarrassment by eating the banana.

He still had a bit to learn about being a king.

'I want to make a Royal Proclamation,' said Ned to the Lord Chamberlain.

The Lord Chamberlain raised an eyebrow.

Ned guessed why.

He'd been king for three days now and they'd both lost count of the bananas he'd eaten, and other fruit of all kinds, and vegetables and nuts except for acorns, and interesting colourful pork dishes from faraway lands.

But this was his first proclamation.

'I want to proclaim,' said Ned, 'that everybody in my kingdom be happy.'

Ned had been thinking about this all morning. He'd been thinking about how much power he had, which when he really thought about it was a humungous amount. He'd been thinking about how much good he could do with that power.

And suddenly it hit him.

He wanted everybody in his whole kingdom to be extremely happy.

'If I may advise Your Majesty,' said the Lord Chamberlain. 'A proclamation is a statement of how things are. If Your Highness wishes to proclaim universal happiness, what is required first are some means to make people happy. I suggest commands and laws, with the death penalty for people who don't obey them.'

Ned sighed.

With the Lord Chamberlain it was always the death penalty.

Ned could still hear scrubbing from the other side of the bed where the nimble-fingered monk was trying to get bloodstains out of the carpet after the Lord Chamberlain had beheaded a courtier who'd brought Ned a bruised apricot.

'Alright,' said Ned. 'Pass a law to make everyone happy.'

It was the Lord Chamberlain's turn to sigh.

'If I may advise Your Majesty,' he said. 'People may need a little more help than that.'

Good grief, thought Ned. Can't anyone think for themselves? Do I have to do everything around here?

'Alright,' he said. 'Law number one. Everybody must have enough to eat, including three types of fruit per week, two types of vegetable and at least one interesting colourful pork dish from a faraway land. Law number two . . .'

The Lord Chamberlain clapped his hands.

Several nervous courtiers came in with parchment, ink and quill pens.

For the rest of the afternoon, Ned made laws, the courtiers wrote them down, and the Lord Chamberlain frowned.

It was very hard work.

Ned needed a lot of strawberries and truffled pork ribs to keep his strength up.

The gentle chink of fine porcelain coaxed Ned out of his cosy slumber.

He opened his eyes.

At first he couldn't see where the sound was coming from. The bed was piled so high with buns that Ned took a few moments to spot the figure on the other side of the room holding a tray.

Was it another annoying courtier with yet another chamber pot?

No, it was a girl, a few years older than him.

He noticed how different she looked from the other females he'd seen in his weeks at the castle. She was wearing a simple white smock and apron, and her fair hair was tied back in a ponytail. She didn't have any of the ringlets or powder or lice that the other women wore in their hair.

'I'm Genevieve, Your Majesty,' she said, her eyes cast modestly downwards. 'I'll be serving you from now on.'

About time, thought Ned grumpily.

He'd issued the command to the Lord Chamberlain ages ago, before having his nap.

'No more courtiers,' he'd said. 'I'm sick of them flocking in here, bowing and scraping and leaving furrows in the carpet with their foreheads when they back out of the room.'

The Lord Chamberlain had seemed to agree. Possibly, Ned thought, because he'd had to behead several courtiers only that week for bringing Ned buns with thumb prints on them.

'From now on,' Ned had commanded the Lord Chamberlain, 'I only want to be served by one person.'

And here she was.

'What have you got for me?' said Ned, greedily eyeing the plates on Genevieve's tray.

'Lime and rose marmalade buns,' said Genevieve. 'Candied butterfly buns. Hazelnut and gold-leaf custard buns. And a new savoury bun that contains the stewed gizzards of some rare but delicious furry woodland creatures.'

'Yum,' said Ned. 'Give them here.'

With a regal wave of his hand he swept off the bed several dozen of the other types of buns he was already bored with. He grabbed the plate from Genevieve and started gobbling the new ones.

For a fleeting moment Ned remembered the taste of his very first bun. A simple warm yeasty ball of light-as-air dough with a bit of vanilla icing on top.

It had only been a few days ago that he'd proclaimed he was sick of fruit and meat, and a nervous courtier had appeared with his first bun on a tray, but it seemed like a lifetime.

Ned pushed another bun into his mouth and turned to Genevieve.

'You look like a reasonably intelligent person,' he said, spraying her with bits of hazelnut and gold leaf. 'What's the word from my kingdom? Are people happy yet?'

Genevieve glanced at the Lord Chamberlain, whose face stayed blank.

'Well, Your Majesty,' said Genevieve, 'it's early days yet. The Bedtime Story Law seems to be working quite well. And the Saying Please And Thank You Law seems to be very popular, except with Vikings and Goths. But the law requiring everyone to tell fifteen jokes a day is causing some difficulties. The murder rate is up alarmingly and people are saying they'd rather get the plague than hear another knock-knock joke.'

Ned scowled.

'Ungrateful scum,' he muttered. 'They're given the chance to be happy and they don't even take it. I'm working my fingers to the bun, I mean bone, for that selfish rabble. Maybe we should find a few of the really unhappy ones and make an example of them.'

Ned dragged a custardy finger across his own neck.

Genevieve glanced at the Lord Chamberlain again.

'It's an option,' said the Lord Chamberlain.

Ned opened his mouth to explain that he hadn't meant chop their heads off, he'd just meant make them uncomfortably sticky with custard. But he closed it again.

Sometimes a king had to be ruthless.

'Here,' said Genevieve. 'Let me clear away some of these stale buns.'

She made a small bag of her apron and started dropping buns into it one by one.

'Get rid of them all,' growled Ned, sweeping the remaining few hundred onto the floor. 'And tell those lazy curs in the kitchen that if they don't prepare fifty new types of bun by the morning, all delicious, I'll pass a Cooks Dangling Off The Battlements While Crows Peck Off Their Tummy Fat Law.'

Genevieve paused and furrowed her brow.

Then she leaned closer to Ned than any non-royal subject was meant to lean, including the Lord Chamberlain.

'Your Majesty,' she said quietly. 'You don't think being king is going to your head a bit, do you?'

She went back to picking up buns.

Ned stared at her.

He couldn't believe what she'd just said.

It was treason.

Didn't she realise that any second now the Lord Chamberlain would have his sword out and her head off?

Except that wasn't happening. The Lord Chamberlain was calmly watching as she calmly picked up buns.

Maybe the Lord Chamberlain didn't hear her, thought Ned. Or maybe I didn't hear her correctly.

Maybe she said something else. Or maybe she didn't say anything at all. Maybe I only thought she did.

But deep down Ned knew that she'd said it and he'd heard it.

And that there was one thing even a king couldn't banish.

The truth.

Ned closed his eyes and sank back onto his pillows. Several of which, he could feel, had buns stuffed inside them.

A tiny nagging thought started to form in the back of his mind, as far away as a jagged piece of crystalized ginger on top of a bun three pillows down, but just as impossible to ignore.

Maybe, he thought miserably, she's right.

Ned stared at the ceiling of the royal bedroom.

In the gloom of the early evening, he could just make out the unicorns and dragons on the royal crest, which was inlaid into the ceiling and was carved from rare timbers and mother-of-pearl and slices of the thigh bones of old enemies of the realm.

To Ned they looked like pigs dancing happily.

He couldn't stop thinking about what he'd left behind at home and how much he missed it.

Genevieve is right, he thought miserably.

Being king had gone to his head and he'd turned into a monster.

'Are you there, Lord Chamberlain?' said Ned.

There was no reply.

Ned couldn't see if the Lord Chamberlain was in his corner, or if he'd popped out to behead someone. The Lord Chamberlain was one of those people who could sleep standing up, Ned had seen it, but he always snored a bit and ground his teeth, and at the moment Ned couldn't hear either of those sounds.

Ned got out of bed.

His legs felt wobbly. Probably because he hadn't used them for several weeks, apart from kicking a few buns off the bed.

He headed for the door.

Wobbly or not, he had to do this. Apologise for his behaviour, starting with saying sorry to Genevieve, then the courtiers, then maybe even the Lord Chamberlain.

The corridor was very long.

Ned spotted a figure sitting on a bench against the wall in the distance. Some of the candles had blown out, and in the gloom Ned couldn't make out who it was.

As he got closer, he started to feel nervous.

What if it was one of the cooks, brooding about having to stay up all night inventing new buns. Pushed to the brink by exhaustion and custard fatigue. Desperate to use his knife on something more deserving than the internal organs of small furry forest creatures.

A power-crazed king, for example.

Ned shuddered.

The figure turned towards Ned and stood up.

Ned froze. He could see the silhouette of what the figure was holding. It looked like a huge knife. Ned turned to run. Then remembered he couldn't. He was wearing the royal nightgown, which was so big on him it flopped over his feet in folds.

'Ned?'

The figure had spoken. It spoke again, in a familiar voice.

'That nightgown's wa' too warm, lad. Ye'll be dyin' of infant mortality in that thing.'

'Uncle Vern,' shouted Ned, running towards him.

He tripped and fell into Uncle Vern's arms. They'd never actually hugged before, and it was a bit awkward at first, specially as Uncle Vern was also holding his pig-lard-shaping stick which he'd brought with him for self-defence. But they settled into it after a while and both enjoyed it.

'What are you doing here?' said Ned.

'I came to see you, bitty lad,' said Uncle Vern. 'Beseech ye to stop sendin' the trees.'

Ned stared at him, puzzled. Then remembered. Way back, in his first week as king, he'd issued a command that damp trees should be delivered to Uncle Vern in large numbers. The royal army had departed the same day to carry out the order.

'It were a nice thought, Your Highness,' said Uncle Vern nervously, and for a moment Ned thought he was going to prostrate himself on the floor. 'But them army lads planted 'em, and the forest got too big like. I was out there scrapin' last week and it took me two days to find my way home.'

'Sorry,' said Ned in a small voice. 'Being king went to my head.'

'Aye,' said Uncle Vern, putting a sympathetic hand on Ned's shoulder. 'That can happen.'

'How did you get in here?' said Ned.

'Bribed the guards wi' some pork chops,' said Uncle Vern. 'Then some Lord Chamberlain was about to remove my bonce, but the queen turned up and saved me.'

Ned stared at Uncle Vern.

'The queen?' he said.

'Aye,' said Uncle Vern. 'A slip of a girl, but nice.'

Ned felt faint.

'She's in there,' said Uncle Vern, pointing to a huge pair of doors. 'Welcoming guests at a royal ball or summat. But after that she said she'd take me to see you.'

Ned tried to speak, but all he could do was stand with his mouth open.

'Ye alright, lad?' said Uncle Vern. 'Ye be lookin' a bit like a brain-addled piglet.'

Things didn't improve for Ned when the doors of the royal ballroom swung open and light and noise and merriment spilled out, followed closely by a young woman in a dazzling ballgown and a mass of glittering diamonds and a crown.

Ned blinked.

It was Genevieve.

'It's alright, Your Highness,' said Uncle Vern to Genevieve. 'Ye don't have to trouble yerself. I've found him.'

Ned's mouth stayed open.

'Ned,' said Uncle Vern, 'this is Her Royal Highness Queen Genevieve as I was telling ye about.'

Ned tried to say something, but all that came out was a squeak.

'Poor Ned,' said Queen Genevieve, 'I owe you an apology. I'm afraid I've used you selfishly for my own purposes.'

Ned didn't understand what she meant, but he suddenly found he could speak, so he did.

'That's alright, I don't mind,' squeaked Ned. 'Your Highness.'

He wasn't sure if it was really alright, but what else could you say to a queen?

'I should explain,' said Queen Genevieve. 'As you know, my father the king died suddenly and I was crowned much earlier than I'd been expecting. So I decided to do what my grandfather did when he was crowned very young. Allow a young commoner to be king for a while and witness what happens to us all if we have too much power and aren't careful with it and start behaving like a power-mad froth-brain.'

Ned digested this, and the more he did, the more foolish he felt.

'I'm sorry to have deceived you, Ned,' said Queen Genevieve. 'But you have done me a great service. Throughout my reign, if ever I feel power going to my head, I'll think of you.'

'That be nice, ent it, Ned?' said Uncle Vern.

Ned didn't think it was nice at all. He wanted to crawl under a large stone for ever.

'I can see you have mixed feelings about this, Ned,' said Queen Genevieve. 'I'm sorry.'

'I don't have mixed feelings, Your Highness,' said Ned. 'I have very clear feelings. I'm a fool.'

'No, Ned,' said Queen Genevieve, 'you're not a fool. You're a Fool, and that's a very different thing.'

Ned didn't have a clue what she was talking about.

'A Fool,' said Queen Genevieve, 'is a very important person in a royal household. He's the person who, if the monarch is in danger of turning into a power-crazed dunce, says or does something to bring that monarch to their senses. Just like you've done for me these past few weeks.'

'I'll be a pig's nostril,' said Uncle Vern.

Even though Ned was still stunned, he could see the sense in what the queen was saying.

'Ned,' said Queen Genevieve, 'I'm going to reign for a long time if I can stop peasants sneezing on me. The longer I have absolute power, the greater the risk I'll turn into an addled-headed twit. So I very much need a Fool, and I'd like it to be you. It's a very well-paid job. I do hope you'll accept.'

* * *

Ned did accept.

People had been calling him a fool for so long that it was an easy decision to make. Except, as he quickly discovered, the Queen was right. This was very different.

It was hard work, but very satisfying.

The Queen got a bit tetchy with him at times, but that's when he knew he was doing his job well. Other times he could see in her eyes how much she valued him.

There were times when it almost felt like he was running the country. That's when he needed somebody to take him down a peg or two, and luckily he had someone.

Uncle Vern, the new Lord Chamberlain.

'I'ope them pigs is alright,' Uncle Vern would sometimes say.

'Don't fret, Lord Chamberlain,' Queen Genevieve would say. 'The old Lord Chamberlain was born to farm pigs. When slaughter time comes, he'll have their heads off and they won't feel a thing.'

Sometimes Ned did feel a little sorry for the old Lord Chamberlain, having to scrape damp trees with such a fine sword. But at least he had plenty of trees to scrape.

'That's as maybe,' Uncle Vern would reply. 'But them pigs'll be missin' Ned summat rotten. He has a way with them pigs, does young Ned, specially when their nostrils gets blocked.'

And Ned would give a small smile, partly from

the fond memories, and partly because he knew how lucky he was to have Uncle Vern.

With Uncle Vern around, there was no chance of a young man getting full of himself and ending up with a head like a custard bun. A big one with silly gold leaf on top.

And that's just how Ned wanted it.

I might be a Fool, he thought happily, but I'm not a fool.

Troll

'Look at that,' says Gavin, putting his hot chocolate down and tapping the screen of his tablet indignantly.

None of us look.

We're not being rude. We like Gavin a lot. But getting indignant is Gavin's hobby. And when he says 'look at that', he doesn't really want anybody to actually look.

Gavin's a good step-dad and we're glad he's got a hobby he enjoys. He spends hours each evening flicking around the news sites on his tablet, looking for things to make him feel indignant and stunned and outraged by what people get up to.

He loves it. He likes nothing better than finding something that makes his voice go squeaky with indignation.

'Look at that,' he says again, his voice squeaky with indignation.

We still don't look.

Mum stays dozing on the settee in front of the TV because that's her hobby.

I stay on the floor sending texts because that's my hobby. Well, not so much a hobby. I've got several friends whose lives would be a total mess without advice from me, so it's more of a job except I don't get paid.

Trump our dog stays on the floor next to me licking his bottom, which is his hobby. Like Gavin, he doesn't expect other people to do his hobby either.

'Look at that,' says Gavin for the third time. He usually says it three times.

We still don't look because we know he'll tell us about it.

'This report here in *The Guardian*,' says Gavin. 'It's about a nun helping injured children. She's devoted her life to setting up a clinic in Miami to treat children with serious head injuries.'

'Mmmm,' says Mum in the tone she always uses, the one that means 'that's terrible'.

'Exactly,' says Gavin. 'They mostly get the head injuries from walking into things while they're looking at their phones.'

You've got to hand it to Gavin. Most of the things that get him worked up are pretty interesting.

Except it turns out that this time it isn't the phones that have got him indignant. Or the children.

'As you'd expect,' says Gavin, 'the comments are

mostly nice ones about the nun. *God bless you, sister.* Stuff like that. But look what some miserable, sour-minded troll has written. *You smell, fat bum.*'

Suddenly I'm not smiling.

I go over and look at Gavin's screen.

Oh, no.

I'm shocked, and I can see Gavin is too. Though his shock might mostly be because I've actually come over for a look.

I'm feeling shocked for another reason. And horrified. But not by the comment on the screen. By the username.

Beansprout.

He's at it again.

'Trolling a nun,' says Gavin. 'It's a sick world.'

I go back to my spot on the floor, trying not to show how I'm feeling. I casually send a message on my phone to the friend I was giving advice to before this happened.

Sorry, family emergency. If the vinegar doesn't work, try the hair dryer. Don't squeeze them. Catch you later.

Then I casually get to my feet and head towards the door.

'Back in a sec,' I say.

The others don't even look up from their hobbies.

I sprint down the hallway to Nate's room. I don't check if his door's unlocked. It won't be. I give it several thumps.

'Nate,' I hiss. 'You're gunna be in big trouble if you don't stop that right now. Let me in.'

A long silence.

Then Nate's voice. 'Go away.'

'Open this door,' I say, 'or I'll unscrew the lock.'

He knows I could. His history project in term three was on convicts and I helped him make convict chains out of Mum's metallic link belt and the lock from the shed door.

I listen, trying to tell if he's coming to open his door.

He's on his feet, I can hear him. It sounds as though he's moving things around. If he's trying to hide his computer, that's stupid. We all know he's got it. Gavin bought it for him to do his homework.

What a mistake that was.

The door opens. Nate glares at me.

'What?' he says.

He knows what. I steer him back into the room and close the door behind us.

'You said you'd stop,' I say.

'Stop what?' says Nate, his blond curls flopping into his eyes which he does when he wants to look innocent.

'This,' I say, stepping over to his computer which is still on his desk and still switched on.

I peer at the screen and see that Nate's been looking at a YouTube video of an Olympic weight lifter. There's a list of comments under it. The last comment is from Beansprout.

You're weak.

I click into the computer's history.

More comments under a cute cat photo.

Beansprout: *You're ugly.*

Click. The Prime Minister talking about bilateral free-trade negotiations.

Beansprout: *You're stupid.*

Click. A news report about sick kids in Finland.

Beansprout: *You're Finished.*

I turn and give Nate a look.

'It's my hobby,' he says quietly.

I sigh. Poor kid. In a way I don't blame him, but I can't tell him that. If Mum finds out what he's doing she'll go ballistic.

'It's alright for you,' says Nate. 'You and Mum and Gavin have all got your hobbies.'

'I don't call this a hobby,' I say. 'Adding to the anger and unhappiness and bad feeling in the world.'

'It's what Dad does,' mumbles Nate.

He looks so sad I want to hug him.

Instead I grab his shoulders.

'Dad's got his own shock-jock radio show,' I say. 'Adding to the anger and unhappiness and bad feeling in the world is his job. You're a nice kid who's not on the radio, so stop being a troll.'

'I'm not a troll,' says Nate.

'Yes you are,' I say.

'You don't know anything about trolls,' says Nate.

I'm about to say 'I know a troll when I see one', but I'm distracted by a noise from inside Nate's wardrobe.

Two noises. A thump and a snort.

'What was that?' I say.

'Nothing,' says Nate, too quickly.

There's another snorting sound from inside the wardrobe.

I step over and open the wardrobe door.

I don't know what I was expecting to see in there. A schoolmate, maybe. Or Nate's iPod running a podcast of Dad's radio show, which Nate secretly listens to sometimes.

But not this.

'Get lost, big nose,' growls a raspy voice. 'This is flosshead's room.'

For a second I think it's some sort of animatronic toy. An amazingly lifelike robot, waist-high with dirty green rubbery skin and about sixteen batteries.

But when it rolls its eyes at me and screws up its snout and then snorts again and strings of snot flop onto the floor, I know it's a living creature.

'Are you deaf,' it rasps, 'as well as thick as a toilet roll?'

I don't reply. Just sort of gape.

'You can stand there with your stupid mouth open all week,' says the creature. 'I'm not throwing you any fish.'

I turn to Nate. I still can't speak, but I can see he's imagining the questions I'd be asking if I could.

'I told you I'm not a troll,' says Nate quietly. 'This is a troll.'

'Mr Troll to you, toilet brush,' says the troll.

'Where did it come from?' I squeak, my voice suddenly back.

'It climbed in through the window about two weeks ago,' says Nate.

I stare at them both. Two weeks? No wonder Nate's been keeping his door locked so much lately.

'Dropped in to visit a workmate,' says the troll. 'But the flabby big-mouth's done a runner.'

Does he mean Dad?

Must do, the rest of us are still here.

Which is gobsmacking. We've met some pretty horrible friends of Dad's, but nothing like this.

I start to ask the troll how long he's known my father, then stop myself. I must still be in shock. Only people in shock would try to have a normal conversation with a creature that could be from outer space for all I know.

'W-where are you from?' I stammer to the troll.

'Adelaide,' says the troll. 'At least, that's where my last job was. Insult adviser to some meathead in the state government. Got bored. Same old crapola. There's thousands of us trolls in this country and most of us work in politics. I fancied going back to radio for a bit. Not that it's any of your business, mudflap features.'

'He's been helping me with my hobby,' says Nate.

'Helping you?' sneers the troll. 'Get real. You

haven't written a word, fluffhead. All you're good for is scraping the dog's bum.'

'He likes dog poo,' says Nate. 'On cracker biscuits.'

I stare at Nate again. That explains the smell in his room, and why there's never any cracker biscuits when I get home from school.

I turn back to the troll.

'Well that's all over now,' I say. 'You're leaving.'

The troll gives a snort and another blob of something stringy flops onto Nate's carpet.

'I'll leave when I want to, darling,' says the troll.

I see red. We'll have to clean that carpet now. And nobody with yellow teeth calls me darling unless I let them.

I pick up the troll.

He's heavy, but no heavier than a big plastic garbage bag full of garbage.

'OK, Mr Garbage Bag,' I say. 'Listen carefully. We've got friends up north. Last visit they showed me how they kill cane toads. Lots of salt, then into the freezer. If the toads struggle on the way to the kitchen, sometimes a cricket bat is used. Nate, grab your cricket bat.'

Nate doesn't move. He's staring open-mouthed at me and the troll.

'Now,' I say.

Nate grabs the cricket bat.

The troll is swearing at me and spraying me with stringy stuff, but I don't let that distract me.

'So,' I say to the troll, 'here's your choice. Go now, or we'll be paying a visit to the spare freezer in the garage.'

I carry the frothing troll over to the window.

'Open it, Nate,' I say.

Nate opens the window.

I throw the troll out.

He lands on his head on the lawn, scrambles to his feet and yells at me.

'Interfering cow,' he splutters.

'It's my hobby,' I say.

The troll takes a couple of steps towards me.

I take the cricket bat from Nate and grip it in both hands.

The troll stops and snorts again.

'I'm done with you dopey frothheads anyway,' he says. 'I've got more important things to do. Policy advisor to the education minister probably, so I can get your school shut down.'

Muttering, the troll stomps away into the night.

I close the window.

Nate is looking at me like he thinks I'm going to yell at him.

I don't.

'Let's sit down and have a chat,' I say.

'Don't want to,' says Nate.

'If you really want to get Dad's attention,' I say, 'I can tell you a better way of doing it.'

Nate sits down and we have a chat.

* * *

That was a month ago.

Things have been very different since.

For some of us, anyway. My friends are still mostly disasters and I still have to put in overtime to stop them ruining their lives and their skin.

Mum has started helping me, which is great. She knows some great healing ointments and natural moisturisers for people who've tried to get rid of pimples with a nail file.

I still have to spend a lot of time on the floor with my phone, which is what I'm doing now.

Gavin still spends a lot of time being indignant, which is what he's doing now.

'Look at this,' he says indignantly, putting his hot chocolate down and tapping the screen of his tablet.

Nate goes over and has a look.

For a moment Gavin looks pleased, which is one of the things that are different now.

Then he goes back to being indignant.

'More state schools being closed down,' he says. 'And at the same time they're giving more cash to private schools.'

Nate nods thoughtfully.

'Probably be closing ours next,' he says.

'Exactly,' says Gavin. 'Elitist mongrels.'

Nate thinks some more.

'Why don't we write a letter,' he says to Gavin. 'To the education minister. Explain to him in simple words why this'll harm the future of our country.

We'll put it on your Facebook again. That letter we wrote last week to the health minister got twenty-seven thousand likes.'

'OK,' says Gavin to Nate. 'Let's do it.'

I smile, in a relieved sort of way.

It was a risk, but I'm glad it's working out. Anyone can be a troll, look at Dad. But our world needs us to use our hearts and brains instead of our spleens and bile and other stringy bits.

I said this to Mum the other day.

She agreed.

'All our futures depend on it,' she said.

She paused and smiled.

'Plus,' she said, 'it's so nice to see Gavin finally sharing his hobby.'

The FDC

Archie wanted to go home, but he couldn't.

There was too much blood.

It was dripping through his fingers. If he didn't do something fast, his school uniform would look like a year-one art project.

An elderly man walking past gave Archie a sympathetic nod.

'I had nosebleeds when I was a lad,' said the man. 'Frozen peas, that's what you need.'

Archie didn't reply. He kept his hands over his nose and gave the man a grateful look.

I need more than frozen peas, thought Archie. A bag of frozen pineapples would be better. Then next time Rosco Kruger picks on me, I can flatten him with them.

Trying not to drip too much, Archie hurried into the kids' playground behind the public library. He went over to the rubbish bin next to the monkey bars. The only useful thing he could see in the bin was a half-eaten Big Mac. He kept one hand on his nose and with the other he squished bits of the bun into two balls and stuffed them into his nostrils.

The blood stopped. For now.

Archie glanced around. At least the playground was empty. At least he didn't have to put up with little kids pointing at him and saying 'Mum, why has that boy got a bun up his nose?'

Archie wondered if his nose was bent. It felt bent. Rosco Kruger always twisted it hard, but today he'd twisted it extra hard.

That's all Mum and Dad need now, thought Archie. The expense of nose surgery on top of everything else.

He peered at his reflection in the shiny metal rubbish bin. His nose looked swollen but not bent or broken.

Archie waggled it cautiously.

Pain flashed through his head. So did a jolt of anger.

That vicious bully.

If there was any justice in the world, Rosco Kruger would be hanging upside down from these monkey bars now with the chains from the swings wrapped tight around his body, sobbing about how sorry he was while Archie stuffed McDonald's buns up his bully-boy nose till his head exploded.

Calm down, Archie told himself. Violent acts of revenge only happen in movies.

Mum was always saying that. Just like Dad was always saying how sometimes life does a poo on your head and you just have to wear it.

Archie sighed.

The bun balls were starting to feel like quarter pounders. Carefully Archie unplugged his nose. He waited a while to make sure the bleeding had stopped, then scuffed a hole in the ground and buried the bun balls hygienically under the slide.

He decided not to go home yet.

Best give the swelling a chance to go down.

Archie headed towards the library, trying not to think about what a happy place this playground had been for him and Mum and Dad before all their problems started.

As he passed the adventure sand-pit, he noticed a red blob on one of the white-painted car tyres.

Oops, he thought. That was probably me.

Archie crouched down, spat on the dried blood and rubbed at it with the strap of his school bag. He didn't want hungry dogs licking the tyre and developing a taste for them and then chasing cars and getting run over.

The blood was really dried on.

He rubbed it as hard as he could.

'G'day,' said a gruff voice behind him.

Archie turned and peered up.

A large bloke in a work singlet and shorts was standing there, holding out his hand as if he wanted to shake.

Archie stood up nervously. Mum and Dad were always warning him to be careful of strangers.

'You're probably wondering who I am,' said the bloke.

No I'm not, thought Archie, but he didn't say that. He just gave a shrug, which he hoped made him look not that interested without being rude.

'I'm your FDC,' said the bloke.

Archie tried to work out what that meant. FDC?

'Fairy Demolition Contractor,' said the bloke.

Archie stared at him.

'I'm sort of like a fairy godmother,' said the bloke. 'Except I demolish things.'

Archie took a step back. Mum and Dad had warned him to be very careful of strangers like this. Ones with sad mental conditions who'd been released into the community without adequate medical support.

The bloke grinned.

'Dunno what I'm talking about, do you?' he said.

Archie shook his head. He wished his school bag was over his shoulder instead of on the ground behind the poor unfortunate deranged person. Then he could run.

'It's simple,' said the bloke. 'Everyone's got a fairy somebody.'

Archie didn't say anything.

Best not to encourage him.

'Which you probably didn't know,' continued the bloke, 'cause you've never met me before. We only turn up when you really really need us. Then you get your three wishes.'

Archie wondered if he should offer to go to the chemist and fetch some medication.

'With me you get three demolitions,' said the bloke. 'You choose three buildings, I knock 'em down.'

Or food, thought Archie. If there's any more McDonald's in the bin, I could distract him with that.

'We can start now, if you like,' said the bloke. 'I've got the rig with me.'

He pointed to something over Archie's shoulder.

Archie turned.

And almost fainted.

Behind him, parked in the library carpark, was a huge semi-trailer with a massive crane on the back. Hanging from the crane was a giant metal ball.

Archie sat down on the roundabout. It wasn't moving, but he felt like everything else was whirling around.

'I've got explosives in the truck,' said the bloke. 'And a sledgehammer for small jobs. You choose.'

Archie struggled to get his thoughts straight.

Would a sick person in the grip of a tragic fantasy actually have a truck like this? With a metal ball this size?

Archie didn't think so.

Perhaps it's me, he thought. Perhaps I'm hallucinating from loss of blood.

'I can see you're having a bit of trouble digesting it all,' said the bloke. 'What say we get started on the first one, so you can see how it works.'

Archie waggled his nose again.

Pain, just like before. Real pain, which meant this was almost certainly really happening.

Most of Archie still wanted to run, but part of him was beginning to feel a tiny bit curious.

Alright, very curious.

'What'll it be?' said the bloke. 'Flatten an old shed? Knock your school down? How about Parliament house? Wouldn't mind giving those mongrels a shake-up.'

Archie's mind was racing.

'By the way,' said the bloke, 'the name's Noel.'

He held out his hand again. Archie shook it cautiously. It was a big muscly hand with ginger hair on the back. Warm and solid.

It felt completely real.

Archie let go of Noel's hand and sat there for a few moments, waiting for a very strong feeling to leave him.

It didn't.

He looked up at Noel's big weatherbeaten face.

'Do you do violent acts of revenge?' he asked.

The Krugers' place was a big two-storey house in a posh street.

At one side of the house, next to the swimming pool, was Rosco's cubby.

Gang headquarters, that's what Rosco called it. But Archie knew a cubby when he saw one, even when it had gang members in it.

Archie could see the shadowy shapes through the cubby window as he peered out from his hiding place inside the front hedge. He could also see Noel's huge truck and gigantic wrecking ball filling up most of the Krugers' driveway.

Mr Kruger was coming out of the house, looking bewildered.

'What's going on?' he demanded.

Noel wound his window down.

'I'm here to demolish the cubby,' he said. 'Mind yourself.'

Mr Kruger stared up at him, dumbfounded.

Noel revved the huge engine and drove through a fence and across several flower beds and parked next to the swimming pool.

Mr Kruger yelled angrily.

'You can't do that!'

Somebody else screamed. It was Mrs Kruger, coming out of the house with a small dog and a terrified expression.

On the semi-trailer, winch motors howled and the giant metal ball started to move.

Archie tried to yell at Rosco to get out. But his voice was in shock. All he could do was croak, and that was muffled by the hedge and drowned out by the grinding of heavy machinery.

'Rosco,' yelled Mr Kruger.

Rosco's face appeared at the cubby window. He looked up at the metal ball and his mouth fell open.

The two gang members scrambled out of the cubby. Rosco followed, frantically trying to push them out of his way. One of the gang members fell into the pool.

Archie held his breath as the metal ball whooshed down. It hurtled over Rosco's head and smashed into the cubby.

Fragments of gaily-painted wood and brick-textured plastic were flung across the garden, slicing the heads off flowers and shredding the washing on the line.

For a moment everything went quiet, except for the sound of a heavy-gauge chain being rewound into its storage position.

Archie realised his hands were hurting from gripping the hedge.

Rosco looked as stunned as if the metal ball had hit him. So did his parents and the gang members.

While Mr and Mrs Kruger dragged the dripping boy out of the pool, Rosco stared at his own wet clothes.

From the miserable expression on Rosco's face, Archie could see that the big wet patch on Rosco's pants hadn't come from the pool.

Noel was whistling an Abba tune as he backed the truck out into the street. He stopped next to Archie and held something out of the driver's window for Archie to take.

'When you're ready for your other two,' said Noel, 'ring this number.'

It was a business card.

Noel Watson, it said. *Demolition Contractor (Fairy)*. And a very long phone number. Heaps of digits.

Archie didn't count them.

He was too busy diving back into the hedge as Mr and Mrs Kruger sprinted out of the garden after Noel's truck.

And too busy watching them come back in a daze because when they'd got round the corner, the truck had vanished.

'Mum,' said Archie in a small voice. 'Can I ask you something?'

Archie hated disturbing Mum while she was doing her paperwork. She needed all her energy and concentration for the letters she got back from the insurance company. For swearing at them and wheeling herself up and down the backyard till she'd calmed down.

But this was urgent.

'Course you can, love,' said Mum. She swung her wheelchair round to face him. 'What is it?'

Archie took a deep breath.

'Do you believe . . .?'

He couldn't say it.

Mum looked at him, concerned.

Archie blurted it out.

'Do you believe in fairies?'

Even as he heard himself say the words he knew it was a dopey question to ask a woman whose whole life had been ruined by a harsh world.

Except Mum didn't look like it was a dopey question. She was staring at him with a strange expression, concerned but sort of fascinated, and Archie was pretty sure it wasn't because his nose was still swollen.

'Has yours come?' she said quietly.

Archie stared at her.

She sounded like she'd almost been expecting this to happen.

Archie felt a bit faint. All he could do was nod.

'No details,' said Mum quickly. 'Don't tell me any details. This has to be your secret. You mustn't ever say who your fairy person is or what he or she does.'

Archie sat down on the settee. He could barely take this in. *Your fairy person?* Did that mean that everyone had a . . .?

Dad came in from the kitchen. He and Mum swapped a look.

Mum gave him a nod.

Dad blew out his cheeks. He sat down next to Archie and gave Archie's shoulder a squeeze.

'It's a shock, isn't it, mate?' he said. 'It is for all of us when we first find out. But it has to be a secret, son. Between you and your fairy whatever. If you break the secret, they go and they don't come back.'

Archie managed to find his voice.

'Does everybody have one?' he said.

Mum and Dad nodded.

'Everybody in the world?' said Archie.

'Sooner or later,' said Dad.

Archie felt like he was back on the roundabout.

'Are you OK, love?' said Mum.

'I think so,' said Archie, hoping he wouldn't faint or throw up from the shock. 'Why didn't you tell me? When you told me where babies come from, you could have tacked it on the end.'

Mum and Dad both sighed.

'All the parenting experts say it's best not to tell,' said Dad. 'Otherwise kids'll waste their childhoods wondering when their fairy person is going to turn up.'

Archie thought about this. He could sort of see the sense in it.

Sort of.

'Plus,' said Mum, 'some fairy experts reckon that knowing in advance, you run the risk of wasting your three wishes. Letting little problems get on top of you. So your fairy person appears too early and you use up your wishes before you really need them.'

Archie saw Mum and Dad give each other a sad glance.

He stared at them.

'Is that what happened to you?' he said.

They both nodded.

'I got a Fairy Chef,' said Mum quietly. 'Dad was up for a promotion at work and his boss was coming here for dinner and I was desperately worried that I wouldn't impress him with the meal. Then Marco appeared. Three delicious courses.'

She shook her head sadly.

Archie looked at Dad.

'Fairy Golf Instructor,' said Dad miserably. 'When I got the promotion, they told me I had to join the golf club, same as the other managers. What a waste. I only won the first three holes.'

Archie gave Mum and Dad a hug each. He knew exactly why they were so miserable. How awful it must be, to have used up all your wishes before the really bad things happened.

Mum and Dad were both looking at him.

Archie wanted to tell them that he wasn't going to waste his wishes. He was going to make the most of his. He was going to use his to bring a smile back to both their faces.

He was about to tell them how, then he remembered the rules.

So he kept quiet.

This was between him and his Fairy Demolition Contractor.

Archie stared up at the building. He'd forgotten it was this tall.

Eighty-six storeys.

Could Noel manage eighty-six storeys?

'G'day, Arch,' said Noel's voice behind him.

Archie jumped and turned round. Noel was standing at the kerb in front of his truck.

Amazing. He'd only rung Noel two minutes ago. And two minutes ago there hadn't been a single parking spot available.

'This one here, is it?' said Noel, squinting up at the insurance company building.

Archie nodded, trying to look more determined than he suddenly felt.

'Right oh,' said Noel. 'Better stand back a bit. Next street might be best.'

Archie didn't move as Noel heaved himself up into the cabin of the semi-trailer. The winch motors started whining and the chain started clanking.

'Wait,' yelled Archie.

The winch and the chain went silent. Noel leaned out of the driver's window.

'What is it, boss?' he said to Archie.

Archie tried to look like a boss. Like he wasn't having doubts.

Which he wasn't. Not really. It was just the people coming in and out of the building. People with their breakfast and their phones and their friends.

Ordinary people.

'No rush,' said Noel. 'Couple of minutes if you like. You probably want to take some photos, right? Before and after.'

Archie didn't want to take photos.

He had all the images he needed in his memory. Images of Mum's and Dad's sad and anguished faces.

Archie stared up at the top floors of the tower. On those floors, in those offices, the people weren't ordinary. They were the monsters who'd ruined Mum's and Dad's lives.

The insurance company managers.

'Just say the word,' called Noel from the cabin, 'and we'll get this one knocked over by morning tea.'

Archie clenched his teeth and kept staring up at the top of the building. He imagined the faces of the insurance company monsters when they realised their luxury offices didn't have floors any more. He imagined their screams as they plummeted down, surrounded by disintegrating concrete and other howling managers. He imagined the hundreds of other employees on the floors below, all plummeting too. All crashing down onto the people visiting the building, like this lady just going in with a toddler in a stroller.

He turned away.

'Right to go?' called Noel.

Archie looked up at his Fairy Demolition Contractor.

'Noel,' he said. 'Can I have a word please?'

The inside of the Noel's cabin didn't seem very luxurious for a fairy workplace. The vinyl on the seats was cracked and the whole cabin smelled of chips.

Archie only noticed this once he'd stopped talking and was waiting anxiously for Noel to reply.

Noel was frowning, perplexed.

'Never been asked that before,' he said. 'Just the top three floors? That's all?'

Archie nodded.

Noel rubbed his stubbly chin, still frowning.

'Nah,' he said. 'Sorry. Can't do it.'

Archie didn't understand. Before, when he was telling Noel the terrible story of what the insurance company did to Mum, how they'd refused to pay for the special operation that could have got her walking again, Noel had been outraged.

'The slimy mongrels,' Noel had said. 'If some maniac chucks a rock off a freeway footbridge and smashes your car windscreen and you stop and get out and another rock hits you, that's a car accident as far as I'm concerned, end of story. Only a slimy mongrel would quibble about that.'

And when Archie had told Noel how Dad, who worked for the insurance company, had tried to stand up for Mum and had been fired on the spot, Noel was ropeable.

'Don't quote me on this,' he'd said, 'because I'm just a Fairy Demolition Contractor not a Fairy Hit Man, but those scumbags deserve to be whacked.'

Archie had been pleased to hear it.

So why had Noel gone all doubtful just because Archie didn't think the bottom eighty-three storeys deserved to be whacked?

'It's structural,' said Noel. 'To whack the top bit, you have to whack the bottom bit. The crane won't reach past the eleventh floor.'

Archie couldn't argue with that.

He looked out the window and saw the lady with the toddler leaving the building. He wondered if they were the family of one of the monster managers. Even if they were, did they deserve to be whacked?

'Do the lot, then, eh?' said Noel.

Archie struggled to give Noel the go-ahead.

He couldn't.

'What about all the innocent people?' he said.

Noel shrugged.

'I'm just a demolition contractor,' he said. 'Not a philosopher.'

'I'm not a philosopher either,' said Archie. 'But it doesn't seem right, whacking innocent people.'

Noel gave a long sigh.

'Sorry, Noel,' said Archie. 'Sorry I dragged you out for nothing.'

'You didn't,' said Noel. 'See, there's a rule. Once you make the call, I have to knock something down.'

Archie stared at Noel.

Noel shrugged apologetically.

Somebody tapped on the cabin door.

'Jeez,' said Noel, suddenly rigid with alarm. 'If that's a Fairy Inspector, I'm cactus. Duck down, I'm not supposed to have clients in the cabin. Haven't got the insurance cover.'

The knock came again, louder.

Looking ashen, Noel slowly opened the cabin door.

Standing there, blinking up at them nervously, was Rosco Kruger.

'Hi Archie,' said Rosco. 'Sorry to disturb you.'

Archie stared.

'How did you know I was here?' he said to Rosco.

'I saw you hiding in the hedge yesterday,' said Rosco, 'after my cubby got demolished. And I came to see you this morning at your place. As I was arriving you were leaving, so I followed you here hoping you were coming to see . . . him.'

'The name's Noel,' said Noel gruffly.

He'd obviously decided Rosco wasn't a Fairy Inspector.

'What do you want?' said Archie.

Rosco didn't reply at first, just took several deep breaths.

While he was doing that, Archie had a sudden thought. If he told Rosco all about Noel now, his name, what he did, what he'd done to Rosco's cubby, then Noel would have to immediately disappear forever and nothing else would need to be demolished.

Except, Archie remembered with dismay, Rosco already knew all that.

Archie tried desperately to think of something he could tell Rosco about Noel that Rosco didn't know.

Before he could, Noel gave an exasperated snort.

'We're busy people here,' he said to Rosco. 'What do you want?'

Rosco took one more big breath and spoke up.

'I want you to demolish our house,' he said.

The big metal ball smashed through the upstairs of the Kruger house, hurling handmade convict bricks, chunks of high-quality plaster, slivers of Italian bathroom tile and bits of genuine roofing slate across the garden like shrapnel, where they made a complete mess of the Balinese gazebo.

'Yippee,' squealed Rosco, jiggling up and down and clapping his hands. 'I've wanted this for ages. My Fairy Sports Coach was hopeless. Get good at squash, he said. Win tournaments. Make your parents notice you. Make them as proud of you as they are of their house.'

Rosco suddenly scowled.

'As if,' he said.

Archie looked anxiously at the disintegrating house.

'You're totally sure your parents aren't in there?' he said to Rosco.

'I told you,' said Rosco. 'My mother's at the designer lighting shop and my father's at the art dealer's. As usual.'

Archie saw that neighbours were starting to assemble along the front fence. He could hear the distant sound of a police siren, coming closer.

Rosco gave the neighbours a glance.

'Don't worry,' he said to Archie. 'My parents spend their whole time re-decorating the house. People'll think they've just decided to go one step further.'

The big metal ball smashed into one of the downstairs rooms. Fragments of antique furniture, sections of lime-bleached floorboards, parts of designer lamps and bits of genuine original oil paintings flew across the lawns.

Archie could hear the police siren getting closer.

'Arch,' called Noel from the cab of the truck. 'You'd better pop off home. I'll finish up here. Been nice working with you.'

He gave Archie a wave.

Archie waved back, said thank you to Noel one last time, and turned to head home.

Rosco blocked his way. And grabbed him. Not by the nose this time. By the hand.

'Thanks for saving my family,' Roscoe said to Archie, shaking his hand emotionally. 'When I get a new gang headquarters, you're invited.'

Mum and Dad were both watching the TV news when Archie came in.

On the screen was the Kruger house. Which was strewn all over the Kruger garden. Neighbours and police and State Emergency Service teams were milling around.

Mum and Dad looked at Archie.

'That's the Kruger place,' said Dad.

'Rosco Kruger,' said Mum. 'Isn't he the boy who's been bullying you?'

Archie didn't know what to say.

'You don't have to say anything,' said Dad gently. 'That's the deal, remember.'

Archie did want to say something.

'Mine was a Fairy Demolition Contractor,' he said.

Mum and Dad both nodded slowly, as if they weren't surprised to hear this given what they'd just seen on the news.

Archie saw they were trying not to show their feelings, which didn't look like very happy ones.

'I suppose Rosco Kruger deserved it,' said Dad. 'But still, to knock his whole house down . . .'

'No Dad,' said Archie quietly. 'The bullying wasn't why Rosco's house got knocked down. His cubby, yes, but not the house.'

Mum and Dad weren't hiding their feelings now. They were both looking very puzzled.

'Rosco wanted the house knocked down,' explained Archie. 'His parents were so obsessed with it, they didn't have any time for him. I reckon that's why he bullied me. He was jealous of what great loving parents I've got.'

Mum and Dad swapped a glance.

'So even though Rosco had hurt you, you gave him one of your three wishes?' said Mum.

'I gave him two,' said Archie. 'His dad's a workaholic. Prefers a car dealership to his own son.'

Archie pointed to the TV screen, where the news reporter was standing in front of the wreckage of a car sales yard.

Mum and Dad swapped another look.

Archie was pretty sure he knew what they were thinking. This was the moment he'd been dreading. Having to confess and tell them the truth. That he hadn't been able to do the most important demolition of all.

'I'm sorry,' he said to them. 'Noel and me went to the insurance building and . . . I tried, I really did, for both of you, but . . .'

Archie could hear how small and sad his voice had got.

'But it was full of people,' he whispered. 'I'm sorry.'

He felt even worse now that Mum was reaching for a tissue and was dabbing her eyes.

'It's OK, son,' said Dad.

Archie suddenly felt a stab of indignation at how unfair it all was.

'What I don't understand,' he said, 'is why I got a dumb Fairy Demolition Contractor when if I'd known about this whole fairy thing, what I'd really have wanted, a million times more, is a Fairy Leg Surgeon for Mum.'

'Oh, love,' said Mum.

She blew her nose and looked at Archie.

'We're glad you got a Fairy Demolition Contractor,' she said.

Archie wasn't sure he'd heard her right. She said it again. Archie still didn't understand.

'Because,' said Mum, 'it's reminded me that there's something more important in life even than being able to walk.'

'Or having a job,' said Dad.

Archie still didn't understand.

'It's knowing that your son has a wonderful heart,' said Mum.

She beckoned Archie towards her, and just before her arms wrapped around him, he saw on her face something he hadn't seen there for a very long time.

A smile.

The hug lasted for ages, with Dad joining in. Mum cried some more. Soon all three of them were wet, and Archie noticed that Mum's mascara was making his school shirt look like a year-one art project.

Archie didn't mind.

He wouldn't have stopped her tears of happiness for anything, not even if he had a McDonald's bun.

Wipe Out

We're so anti-bacterial at our place.

Mum and Dad hate bacteria big time. Their main hobby is killing them.

I'm glad bacteria are just very tiny microbes the human eye can't see, because if they were any bigger we wouldn't be able to move at our place for the dead bodies.

'Callum,' Mum and Dad are always saying to me, 'wash your hands before dinner, then spray the bathroom. And after that, spray your bedroom, and your shoes, and the next-door's cat's bottom.'

We are the most anti bacterial family I've ever met.

Here's what happens if you come to visit us.

You ring the doorbell by pressing a button that gets sprayed at least once a day with anti-bacterial bell-spraying fluid.

Mum answers the door using a handle that gets

wiped more than a bum. You follow her down the hall on a carpet Dad cleans with an anti-bacterial shampoo that me and my brother Troy aren't even allowed to touch in case it kills us and turns our fingernails green.

Dad's in the kitchen, wiping. Mum does some wiping too, then offers you a cup of tea. Don't have it, the cups taste of chemicals.

Why is Mum looking at you like that? She wants you to take your clothes off so she can run them through the machine using a laundry detergent that's soft, fragrant and very very anti-bacterial.

Get the picture?

Except it's not the whole picture. Because sometimes Mum doesn't want you to take your clothes off. Sometimes instead she clutches her tummy.

'Ow,' she says. Then she says it again, louder. 'Ow. Ow. Ow.'

Mum gets a lot of bad tummy pain.

Dad says it's not fair. We live in a house that's a death-zone for bacteria. In other parts of the world bacteria tell each other scary stories about our house. Yet Mum still gets terrible pain from tummy bugs.

I hate to see Mum in such pain. So do Dad and Troy. But we don't know what to do, so we just do more wiping.

Dad says it's a mystery, scientifically speaking.

I'm not a scientist, not yet. But I've been thinking

that maybe it isn't such a mystery.

Look at my friend Newt.

His house isn't anti-bacterial. I had tea at his place last week, and there was a lump of dried snot stuck to the dining table. OK, it might have been creamed spinach, but it definitely wasn't anti-bacterial.

His fridge has furry jam in it. So does his bathroom, on the taps.

His bedroom is like a sandstorm when you jump on the bed. It's mostly dandruff, but some of it's mouse poo from his pets, you can tell from the taste.

Newt's house must be the most bacterial place on the planet. But his mum never gets tummy pains, and nobody there gets headaches like Dad gets, and Newt doesn't have anxious dreams at night like me and Troy.

Ms Easton at school has just said something amazing.

She reckons some people are too anti-bacterial.

'Having a few of those bad bacteria around is good for us,' says Ms Easton, which sounds crazy but it's got to be right cause she's a teacher. 'They give our immune system something to practice on.'

'What's an immune system?' says Newt. 'Have I got one?'

Ms Easton gives him a look. She nods.

I think she's been to his house.

'We all have one,' she says. 'It's an important part of our body cells. The part that keeps us alive. Protects us against infection and disease.'

This is very interesting, scientifically speaking.

Specially to me.

'You said having a few of those bad bacteria is good,' I say to Ms Easton. 'How many's a few?'

'With those bad bacteria you don't want too many,' she says, glancing at Newt's hands. 'A billion. Two billion tops.'

That sounds like quite a lot to me.

Which is why I'm putting all the different bacteria things I can find into this health shake for Mum, so her immune system can get some practice at keeping her healthy.

I'm putting in old orange juice that's gone fizzy. Blue bits off some cheese I found in my camping bag. Milk that's had a furball from a cat soaking in it. Some stuff from under my fingernails. Some other stuff Newt kindly gave me.

There, all nicely blended.

I'll give it to Mum now before it curdles.

That didn't go very well. Dad says that what Mum just did, scientifically speaking, is called projectile vomiting.

'You said it was a heath shake,' wails Mum.

'It was,' I say. 'And it would have totally perked your immune system up big time, if you hadn't projectile-vomited it on Dad.'

'What's in it?' says Dad, peering suspiciously at his very messy shirt.

'Just some orange juice and cheese and other stuff,' I say. 'Stuff that's good for immune systems.'

'That's mouse poo,' says Troy, sniffing Dad's shirt. 'You can tell by the smell.'

I hate it when younger brothers try to be scientists.

'And what's this?' says Dad angrily. 'It looks like snot.'

'It could just be spinach,' I say. 'Or some other creamed leafy green vegetable with bacteria on it.'

But nobody hears me because Mum is clutching her stomach and moaning loudly. Her face is squished with pain.

Poor Mum, it's never been this bad.

I've got an awful feeling that part of it might be my fault.

We all hold her hand and stroke her arm and look anxious, and some of us say sympathetic things and some of us (me) say apologetic things, but it doesn't make her feel better.

Dad calls an ambulance.

The ambulance men gave me rude looks, and so did some of the other people here at the hospital. Cleaners mostly, because when they heard what I did, they sympathised with Mum and Dad. What Mum and Dad do for a hobby, they do for a living.

Dad has hardly spoken to me since we left the house.

I don't blame him. I'd be furious too if I had a son who'd poisoned his own mother.

I'm very worried about Mum. The emergency doctors and nurses took her away as soon as we arrived, straight after I confessed. We haven't seen her since, and that was hours ago.

One of the emergency doctors is coming back now.

Dad jumps up.

'How is she?' he says to the doctor.

Dad is pale with worry.

I know why. When Mum was a girl, she nearly died. Her immune system went seriously cactus and she had to spend weeks in hospital in an anti-bacterial ward.

People couldn't even bring her grapes.

Not even washed ones.

She got better in the end and was allowed to go home, but I think that's when she started wiping door knobs.

'She's asleep,' says the doctor to Dad. 'A couple of the tests we gave her required a minor anaesthetic.'

I can see Dad wants more information, but I get in first.

'Is she going to be OK?' I say. 'From the bacteria poisoning?'

The doctor looks at me.

I make a silent promise that if Mum gets through this, I'll be the most anti-bacterial person in our street. The germs won't stand a chance. Door knobs, carpets, next door's cat, I'll wipe and spray them all ten times a day. I'll stay home from school to do it. Ms Easton won't be able to stop me, not after her advice nearly killed my mum.

The doctor puts her hand on my shoulder.

I go very tense.

Can doctors arrest people for being badly informed and slightly too bacterial?

'You weren't totally off the beam, Callum,' the doctor says. 'If you'd given your mum the right kind of bacteria, it would have helped her, because some bacteria are good.'

I look at her, confused. I turn to Dad.

He's staring at the doctor, gobsmacked.

'Good bacteria?' he says.

We're both struggling with the idea.

'It's a bit complicated, scientifically speaking,' says the doctor. 'But basically there are good bacteria and there are bad bacteria. Your teacher was right, we need a few bad bacteria around so our immune systems don't get lazy. But to be really healthy we need billions of the good bacteria living inside us.'

That is amazing.

Wait till I tell Ms Easton.

Dad is open-mouthed, which I don't think is just so that good bacteria can find their way in.

'One of the tests we did on your wife,' says the doctor to Dad, 'involved putting a tiny camera inside her. It lets us see what's going on. What we saw was lots of swelling and inflammation. So we did some other tests which told us she's hardly got any good bacteria inside her at all.'

Dad doesn't say anything.

I can see what he's thinking.

Somebody has to say it.

'Is it cause our house is too anti-bacterial?' I ask the doctor.

The doctor frowns.

'Probably not,' she says. 'Your poor mum's got something that's called inflammatory digestive-tract disease. You can be born with it or you can just develop it, but it's always made worse by stress.'

'There's a lot of that in our house,' says Troy. 'Anti-bacterial stress.'

I love it when younger brothers back you up.

'Try not to worry,' says the doctor. 'We'll work out the right medicine for your mum and she shouldn't have the pains any more. And you can help by making her some yoghurt health shakes. Be sure to get the yoghurt with the good bacteria in it.'

I give Dad a nervous look.

I know he was planning to tell me that if I ever made Mum another health shake, he'd have me arrested.

Dad is frowning, which he does sometimes when he's thinking.

'Look at it this way,' the doctor says to him. 'What Callum did with the mouldy cheese and the mouse poo was a scientific experiment. Even when scientific experiments go wrong, they can still help us discover important things for the future.'

'I agree,' I say. 'And we've discovered something very important for Mum's future, bacterially speaking.'

Dad is staring at me, and he's still frowning.

But he's starting to look just a little bit proud.

We are so bacterial at our place.

We love bacteria big time. Our main hobby is making millions of yummy drinks with them. I'm glad bacteria are just tiny microbes, because if they were any bigger we wouldn't be able to fit them into our blender.

Or into our mum.

I told Ms Easton everything the doctor said, and she was very interested.

I told Newt too.

He was even more interested. He's planning to be a billionaire when he grows up, so he's always looking for business opportunities to get him started. He reckons this is a top opportunity.

He's invited kids from anti-bacterial homes round to his place to give their immune systems a workout.

He even put a sign in his front yard.

Germ Gym.

His mum made him take it down, but the anti-bacterial kids are still paying him two dollars a visit.

When I tell Mum, she laughs a lot and her tummy doesn't hurt even a tiny bit. She gives me a squeeze, and then she says something I'll never forget.

'I'm glad you don't want to be a billionaire,' she says. 'I'm glad you want to be a scientist. Because one day I reckon you'll do some experiments that won't just make one person's insides a better place, they'll make the whole world a better place.'

Dad and Troy are listening.

And nodding.

For a few moments I have inflammation of my whole body, but in a good way.

'Thanks,' I say.

Then we all sit down and watch TV, and we don't wipe the remote, not once.

Cumquat May

Walking to school, May wondered if she would be hit by a truck.

It didn't seem likely.

May was pretty sure trucks hardly ever came down Dumaresq Street, because of the speed bumps and the lollipop lady and the lack of truck-stop fuel and refreshment facilities.

So as usual she felt happy and safe. The sun was shining gently between the houses. The bamboo steamer she was hugging to her chest felt pleasantly warm inside its tea towel.

May wished Nan was here.

'See, Nan,' she'd say. 'Ancient Chinese wisdom isn't always right. We don't always have to be on guard against bad things. The lotus flower of happiness doesn't always have the slug of misery chomping away at it. And most days the truck of doom is miles away, stuck in a traffic jam.'

Actually she wouldn't say that. Nan got furious when she thought people were disrespecting ancient Chinese wisdom. And when Nan was furious, sometimes she used her knowledge of ancient Chinese swearwords.

May grinned.

Poor Nan.

She wished she could cheer Nan up with some traditional Australian wisdom. Dad was great at that. For a Chinese bloke his knowledge of traditional Australian wisdom was awesome.

'It's Friday,' Dad would probably say to Nan. 'Best day of the week, Friday. Thursday's over and the weekend's whistling at ya.'

If Nan scowled and started making a list of what could go wrong on a Friday, May would get in first.

'It's Friday and I've got two best friends and nine prawn-and-ginger dumplings,' she'd say. 'How good is that?'

With a carefree skip, May went in through the school gate. And discovered it wasn't as good as she'd thought.

Nowhere near as good.

At first, as May went across the playground, nothing seemed miserable or doomed at all.

Just a bit different.

She saw that somebody else was with April and June. A girl. The three of them were sitting in the

Calendar Club meeting place under the climbing frame. The place where April and May and June always had breakfast together.

May squinted, trying to see who it was.

The girl was a bit taller than April and June, and looked a bit older.

'Hi, May,' said April.

'Lo, May,' said June. 'This is Julie.'

'Julie's joining our club,' said April.

May felt shocked. And annoyed. Nobody had asked her.

'We had a vote,' said June. 'Me and April voted yes, so there wasn't any point waiting for you to vote, cause you'd be a majority.'

'Minority,' said Julie, looking May up and down.

'Julie's Dad's got an amazing car,' said April. 'It's a Jugular.'

'Jaguar,' said Julie.

May didn't need to be told about the car. She recognised Julie now, the new girl who was repeating year six and who people said had been expelled from her last school.

Each morning her father dropped her off in the No Drop-Off Zone and then did a wheelie in the staff carpark.

'Hello,' said May quietly.

Julie didn't reply. Just stroked her very elegant hair which May calculated must have taken about a million hours to do. Unless going round corners very fast in a Jag made your hair get elegant by itself.

‘So,’ said Julie after a while, staring at May’s tea-towel bundle. ‘This must be the dumpling.’

There was something about the way Julie said it that didn’t sound very friendly to May.

She saw June and April glance at each other nervously.

‘Not dumpling,’ said May to Julie. ‘Dumplings. I’ve only got nine, which doesn’t really divide into four. But you’re the guest, so me and April and June will have two each and you can have three.’

May unwrapped the tea towel.

Julie looked the steamer up and down.

May was shocked to see she was doing it with what looked like a sneer. Nobody sneered at Nan’s dumplings. They were famous throughout the district. Well, maybe not the whole district, but they were famous throughout the Calendar Club.

‘We’re having organic sourdough toast,’ said Julie.

She stood up and pulled a toaster out of the most expensive-looking schoolbag May had ever seen. It was also the most expensive-looking toaster May had ever seen. Gleaming. Elegant. Not a crumb on it.

‘Where can I plug this in?’ said Julie to April and June.

April and June scrambled to their feet.

‘Over there,’ said April, pointing to the porch outside the library.

‘It’s where the teachers plug the loudspeaker

system in for jazz dodgeball,' said June. 'I'll show you.'

May wrapped the steamer back up to keep the dumplings warm.

Dumplings and toast. Quite nice actually. She'd often had it.

She watched June and April setting off towards the library porch with Julie and reminded herself of another piece of Dad's traditional Australian wisdom.

You're a mug if you don't give people a second chance.

Julie was probably just nervous about being in a new school and anxious about making friends.

After a few steps, Julie stopped and turned back to May, holding out some very expensive-looking bread.

That's nice of her, thought May. She's going to ask how I like my toast.

'I've only got nine slices,' said Julie. 'Not enough for you. But you've got dumplings. Enjoy your dumplings, dumpling.'

She headed off to plug in her toaster.

May stared.

What did she just say?

April and June were looking shocked too.

The year before, when May had started at the school, the head teacher had taken her aside.

'We're a friendly and very inclusive school community, May,' she'd said. 'So I don't expect you to have any trouble. But if anybody does call you a name, you must tell me, OK?'

May had been puzzled.

'What sort of name?' she said.

The head teacher looked uncomfortable.

'Oh, I don't know,' she said. 'Dumpling, for example. Something like that.'

May was still puzzled.

'My mum and dad call me dumpling all the time,' she said.

The head teacher looked more uncomfortable.

'Yes,' she said, 'but if someone calls you that here, it'll be different. They'll be trying to hurt your feelings. On account of where your family comes from and you being a bit plump. If anyone calls you dumpling here, I need to know, OK?'

Nobody had. Not the whole year.

Until now.

May glared at Julie, who was crouching by the jazz dodgeball socket.

That was your second chance, thought May. I'm starting to think you're not just an anxious new girl, I'm starting to think you're also an extremely rude person.

She waited for April and June to give rude Julie the flick and come back over to the climbing frame and have their Calendar Club breakfast as usual.

So far they weren't moving.

Julie turned from the jazz dodgeball socket and called to them.

'Toast'll be ready soon,' she said. 'You'll love this marmalade. It's from Paris.'

May snorted.

This new kid didn't have a clue. If she thought a bit of organic toast and Paris marmalade was going to break up the Calendar Club, she was dreaming.

Except April and June still weren't coming back.

They were looking at May guiltily.

April was giving her a shrug.

May felt a chill wind touch her deep inside. The sort of wind you feel when a truck's brakes have failed in the distance and the truck is hurtling towards you.

It wasn't actually a truck, but when April and June walked away from her and over to Julie, it felt like one.

May sat under the climbing frame, miserably chewing a dumpling.

She felt numb.

How could they do it? Invite an outsider to join the Calendar Club? A rude pushy outsider who didn't even like dumplings. And who didn't even have the right name.

May had always known that April and June were hopeless at spelling, but April, May, June, Julie? That was ridiculous.

The things people do, thought May, for the chance of a ride in a Jag and the hope of non-frizzy hair.

Pathetic.

'Nice dumplings,' said a voice.

May looked up.

A boy was grinning down at her from the top of the climbing frame. May recognised him from one of the other year-six classes. She didn't know his name and she didn't particularly want to, not at the moment.

'We have dumplings too where I come from,' said the boy. 'They're called Mantu. Those look good.'

May remembered that the boy was from Afghanistan.

'What's in those?' he said.

May could see he was hoping she'd offer him one.

She was tempted to say prawn toenails and pigs' bumholes to get him to leave, but she didn't. They might be delicacies in Afghanistan.

'Do you mind?' she said. 'I've got important things to think about.'

'Sorry,' said the boy.

He was still looking at the dumplings and his dark eyes were so wistful that May suddenly grabbed a dumpling and held it up to him.

'Thanks,' he said, taking it. 'My name's Karim.'

May realised to her horror that he was climbing down towards her, probably to sit next to her.

That's all she needed. Word getting around that poor pathetic Dumpling May was so desperate for a friend, she was hanging out with a boy.

'I'm very busy,' she said.

The boy's face clouded.

'OK,' he said quietly. 'Thanks for the dumpling.'

As he headed off across the playground through the yelling kids, May felt a twinge of guilt. She pushed it away.

She'd been telling the truth. She was very busy. Waiting for her best friends to come to their senses. To remember who their real friend was. To spot the difference between a real friend and a pig's bum-hole.

'Nan,' yelled May, rushing into the kitchen. 'I need dumplings.'

Nan came in from the backyard with the scrap bucket, frowning and deep in thought.

'The chooks have stopped laying,' she said. 'I think it's global warming.'

May sighed.

'They haven't stopped laying, Nan,' she said. 'I collected the eggs before school.'

Nan took this in and looked at May sternly.

'We've talked about this, Mabel,' she said. 'I don't want you getting up so early. You must sleep in as late as you can on school mornings. Knowledge seeks a rested mind.'

May resisted the temptation to argue. Or to remind Nan how much she hated being called Mabel. This was more urgent.

'I need your help, Nan,' she said. 'I need you to help me make some very good dumplings.'

'What about the ones we made yesterday?' said Nan. Her eyes widened with alarm. 'Did they get stolen? I told you to watch out for thieves on the way to school.'

'Trucks, Nan,' said May wearily. 'You told me to watch out for trucks.'

'Those as well,' said Nan. 'Why do you need more dumplings now?

May told Nan about Julie and the toast and the Jaguar and the Paris marmalade.

She told her about all the times during the day she'd thought April and June would come to their senses.

And how they hadn't.

Nan put her arms round May and hugged her for a long time.

'I understand now,' she said softly. 'You want special dumplings.'

May felt relief seep through her like the broth in freshly steamed Xiao Long Bao, which when Nan made them were dumpling magic.

'You want dumplings so special,' said Nan, 'so delicious, so tantalising, so irresistible, that all who smell them will fall under their power and no toasted breakfast treat in the world will stand a chance of stealing your friends away.'

May felt tears of gratitude filling her eyes.

Sometimes ancient Chinese wisdom was a wonderful thing.

'You want superdumplings,' murmured Nan.

'Megadumplings. Dumplings that will blow July out of the water.'

'Her name's Julie,' said May. 'But apart from that you're spot on.'

Nan gave a long sigh.

May felt a stab of anxiety. She'd heard that sigh many times before. The relief started to trickle out of her like the broth in a Xiao Long Bao that some idiot has tried to pick up with a fork.

'Oh Mabel, Mabel, Mabel, Mabel,' said Nan. 'Dumplings aren't weapons of war. And even if they were, no friendship has ever been won with a weapon of war. Trying to win friendship with a weapon of war is like trying to pick up water with chopsticks.'

May gave a despairing groan.

For Nan, everything in the world that she didn't agree with was like trying to pick up water with chopsticks.

'Please,' said May. 'I'm desperate.'

Nan grabbed a pair of chopsticks and reached over to the sink and tried to pick up water with them.

May gave another groan.

Nan gave her another hug.

'If a friendship is a friendship,' said Nan, 'it will be a friendship. Now help me get dinner. We're having fish fingers.'

May slumped back in her chair.

It was hopeless.

She'd never hated ancient Chinese wisdom as much as she did now.

Faintly, through her despair, May heard the distant sound of Dad's voice in her memory. The advice he'd given her the day she'd left to come to the city to live.

'Pay attention to the wisdom of others,' he'd said, 'but listen even more carefully to your own heart.'

She'd almost forgotten that.

Now she was glad she hadn't. Because he was totally right.

'Thanks, Dad,' she whispered.

May sat on her bed, deep in thought.

A new club. That's what she needed. A new Calendar Club with really good friends in it. Friends who wouldn't dump her the first time French marmalade came along.

Trouble was, there were only three girls in the whole school with Calendar Club names.

April, May and June.

May stared at the wall, desperate.

So desperate that for a few crazy moments she seriously considered letting boys join the Calendar Club. And making them only use the first few letters of their names.

Augie.

Septimus.

Declan.

Maybe one of them would even have a pet called Octopus.

For a brief moment it all seemed possible. Until she remembered she didn't know any boys called Augie, Septimus or Declan. And even if she found some, they were boys, so what would she talk to them about? Plus she was pretty sure boys liked marmalade even more than girls did.

No, it would have to be dumplings. And if Nan wouldn't help her, she'd make them herself.

They would be the most amazing dumplings anyone had ever seen. Dumplings that April and June wouldn't be able to resist. Dumplings that would have them begging to be let back into the Calendar Club.

Strawberry dumplings.

Chocolate dumplings.

Marmalade dumplings.

May grabbed her school bag to find a pen to make a list. There was usually one somewhere in the bottom of the bag. It just took a bit of rummaging.

She rummaged. And felt something.

It wasn't a pen, it was a small piece of paper, folded tight.

She unfolded it. A note.

Dear May,

Sorry we broke up the club, but we got sick of dumplings. Totally sick. We're over them. We never want to eat another dumpling in our whole life.

Sorry.

April and June.

May stared at the note for a long time.

She thought about Mum and Dad and how happy they'd be if she went back to live with them on the farm. And did school on the computer like before and told them she didn't mind living hundreds of kilometres from civilization and never seeing another kid in actual person.

Happy, but they would know it wasn't really true.

'May,' Dad would say gently. 'Friendship's not a hobby, it's a job. And you don't get to knock off early on Fridays.'

'Life isn't meant to be easy,' Mum would say, because she was an expert at traditional Australian wisdom too. 'Fun, but not easy.'

May felt tears stinging her eyes.

Mum and Dad wanted the best for her, she knew that. They loved her so much they were prepared to only see her during school holidays, so she could have the best. A real school. And real friends.

They'd be really sad if they knew how lonely she felt right now. And really disappointed.

May heard a sloshing sound coming from the backyard.

She knew what it was, but to take her mind off Mum and Dad, she peered out the window.

Nan was doing what she did every night. Tipping the washing-up water onto the roots of her cumquat tree. Well, Nan called it washing-up water, but it wasn't the ordinary sort. For a start it had veggie water in it, plus the water Nan soaked her fermented bean curd in. And floating in it were leftover bits of the dried Chinese herbs and twigs Nan boiled up to make ancient potions that cured flu and kept cutlery shiny.

'Very good for the cumquats, this water,' Nan often said. 'Look at them. Supercumquats. Megacumquats.'

May looked at the cumquats now, small orange fruit glowing against dark green leaves in the light from the kitchen.

They didn't look particularly super. Or mega. They never did. Just like small oranges really.

But May knew they were different. And quite unusual. She hadn't heard of a single other garden in the whole district that had a cumquat tree.

Perhaps, thought May, it's not the size that makes them super and mega. Perhaps it's their flavour.

Except the flavour of cumquats was bitter.

Which was why people made marmalade from them.

'Mabel, what are you doing? This is not sleeping. Knowledge will not seek a mind that is banging around in the kitchen at three o'clock in the morning.'

Nan stood in the doorway, glaring.

May sighed.

She'd tried to be as quiet as she could, but obviously she hadn't been quiet enough.

Nan was staring at the pile of cumquats on the kitchen table. All washed and some of them cut into pieces.

'What are you doing?' said Nan again.

May suddenly wished she'd talked to Nan about this before she'd started. Got her permission to pick the cumquats.

'I'm making marmalade,' said May quietly.

She knew exactly what Nan would say next. A cumquat picked sneakily in the dead of night is an unhappy cumquat. Marmalade isn't a weapon of war. Things like that.

'Marmalade,' said Nan, 'isn't a victim of war.'

May looked at Nan.

That wasn't what she'd expected, and she wasn't exactly sure what it meant.

'Those cumquats you've cut up,' said Nan. 'They look like they've been stabbed and shot. To make marmalade you need to slice the fruit very thin. And where are the pips?'

'I threw them out,' said May.

'You need the pips,' said Nan. 'The pips make the marmalade set. Don't throw any more out. And cut the fruit thin. Here, let me show you.'

Nan rolled up the sleeves of her nightie and started slicing a cumquat.

May watched, feeling a bit dazed and not just because it was three in the morning.

'Nan,' she said after a while. 'You know why I'm making this marmalade, don't you?'

Nan nodded. She handed May the knife. 'Now you do it.'

May started carefully slicing.

'So you don't think,' she said to Nan, 'that making this marmalade to win my friends back is like trying to pick up water with chopsticks?'

Nan shook her head.

May sliced silently, a bit confused. After a while she looked at Nan again.

'Why did you change your mind?' she said.

Nan gave her a little smile.

'Modern Chinese wisdom,' she said.

Walking to school on Monday, May felt like she'd been hit by a truck.

Well, her arms did.

She'd never chopped anything for so long.

But it was worth it. As she walked, she could hear the jars of cumquat marmalade clinking gently in her schoolbag.

May smiled, even though her insides were prickling with anxiety.

If this didn't work, she'd still be grateful that Nan had discovered modern Chinese wisdom.

But she hoped it would work. Which was why she'd set out earlier than usual. To make sure her toaster, the one Nan had pulled out from under the house and dusted off for her, was set up and plugged in before Julie arrived.

It felt good, arriving at school this early.

With a hopeful skip, May went in through the school gate.

And discovered she wasn't early enough.

Julie was over by the jazz dodgeball socket, behind a very large folding table.

Hundreds of paper plates were laid out on the table. And tubs of butter. And bags of bread. And jars of marmalade.

Good grief, thought May. She's making toast for the whole school. She must want friends even more badly than me.

April and June were with Julie, crouching over several toasters.

May felt like giving up. Turning round and going home. Telling Nan she felt ill, which was true.

But the thought of doing that made her feel even worse.

What a sad waste of so much hard work and cumquat marmalade and modern Chinese wisdom.

Instead, May stood behind a tree and waited.

After a while, Julie went into the girls' toilet.

She's probably feeling nervous, thought May. With so much at stake. Or else she's got a few cappuccino machines plugged in there.

May, feeling quite nervous herself, went over to April and June. They looked startled when they saw her.

'You shouldn't be here,' said April. 'This is embarrassing.'

'I just wanted to give you these,' said May.

She took the jars of cumquat marmalade out of her bag and put them on the table.

April and June stared at them.

'Julie's already got marmalade,' said June. 'From that France place. This is really embarrassing.'

'Taste it,' said May.

April and June looked doubtful.

May took the lid off a jar and held it out to April.

April glanced around nervously to check that Julie was still in the toilets. Then she stuck a tiny part of the tip of one finger into the cumquat marmalade and tasted it.

Her eyes widened.

She tasted some more.

June tasted some too. Her eyes widened as well.

'These jars are for you,' said May to April and June. 'But if you want to use them this morning, that's fine with me.'

She walked away, back to the tree.

After a while, Julie returned to the table.

May watched as April and June showed her the jars of cumquat marmalade. They didn't point to the tree, so it didn't look like they were telling Julie who the marmalade came from.

Julie was frowning, annoyed, probably because she could see this new marmalade didn't come from Paris. But there wasn't time to do anything about it.

Kids were arriving at school. Coming over to the table, curious. Helping themselves to toast.

More and more of them, arriving in groups.

April, June and Julie were suddenly frantic with the toasters, keeping up the supply.

Kids were buttering their own toast. And, May saw, smearing on their own marmalade. Some chose Paris, some cumquat.

May forced herself to keep breathing as she watched. Her insides were aching.

There was a swarm around the table now and the toast-makers were barely keeping up. The playground was buzzing.

Still more kids were arriving.

And teachers.

For a moment it looked like the teachers were going to stop the whole thing, until one of them nibbled a slice of toast that a student handed her and then stared at it, amazed.

May guessed it had cumquat marmalade on it.

Gradually, she saw, the crowd was realising that the two marmalades were very different. People were grabbing jars of cumquat marmalade and sticking their fingers in and having another taste.

Telling their friends to taste it too.

May couldn't hear what was being said in the hubbub, but she could see lots of kids talking to Julie with excited hand movements that looked grateful and very enthusiastic.

Julie, glowing, was responding with the sort of hand movements people use when they're boasting that their marmalade comes from Paris.

May knew this was the moment.

The moment to go over and tell everyone the truth. Tell them who they should be thanking for the marmalade. And then it would be her that everyone would be excitedly crowding around, desperate to be her friend, begging her to bring cumquat marmalade every morning.

And she could. There were thirty-seven more jars of it at home.

She'd be Cumquat May, the leader of the Cumquat Club, the most popular girl in the whole school.

It was a wonderful thought, and May was tempted.

Very tempted.

She took a step forward.

Then stopped.

She thought about Nan. About friendship and weapons of war. She thought about Dad too. About listening carefully to your own heart.

May felt lucky to have so much wisdom in her life. And so much love.

Perhaps though, she thought, it's time I started working out some wisdom of my own.

The thought glowed inside her, warm as the filling in a just-made dumpling.

May stood there a while longer.

Then she gave one last look at the clamouring mob of excited marmalade fans, turned, and walked slowly away across the playground.

When she was halfway across, she saw that over on the other side a solitary figure was sitting against the fence, eating from a plastic lunchbox.

As she got closer, he looked up and gave her a friendly grin.

It was Karim.

May smiled back, went over and sat down next to him.

He offered her his lunchbox.

She took it.

'Nice dumplings,' she said.

The Tortoise And The Hair

Vic didn't slow down when he reached the pet shop.

'Mind your backs,' he called out as he sprinted straight inside. 'Urgent delivery coming through.'

Vic knew kids weren't meant to run in shops, and he knew at this speed there was a danger of tripping over a kennel and ending up nose-first in a sack of pigs' ears. But he had to take the risk. He was seriously late.

Nothing must slow him down.

Please don't stutter, thought Vic as he thudded into the counter. Please don't stutter, please don't stutter, please don't stutter.

Behind the counter, Mr Pappadopoulis looked up, frowned at Vic and began to stutter.

'H – h – h – h – h – h – h – h – h –'

No, thought Vic. Please. I haven't got time for this.

‘H – h – h – h – h – h – h – h – h –’

Vic knew what Mr Pappadopoulis was trying to say.

‘Hello,’ said Vic, getting in first to save Mr Pappadopoulis the trouble and more importantly to save time.

‘W – w – w – w – w – w – w – w – w –’

Please, begged Vic silently. Let me do the talking.

Mr Pappadopoulis didn’t.

‘W – w – w – w – w – w – w – w – w –’

Once again, Vic guessed what Mr Pappadopoulis was trying to say.

‘What,’ said Vic, ‘can you do for me? Thanks for asking.’

He reached into his sports bag and took out Monty.

‘Gran’s tortoise needs a clip,’ he said.

Mr Pappadopoulis peered at Monty and frowned again.

‘T – t – t – t – t – t – t –,’ he said. ‘T – t – t – t – t –’

‘Toenails, that’s right,’ said Vic. ‘Gran’s hoping you can do it. Her hands shake too much and the last time I tried, I accidently dropped Monty into a laundry bucket full of starch.’

Monty blinked.

So did Mr Pappadopoulis.

‘I know,’ said Vic. ‘Poor Monty. The last thing a tortoise needs is to end up stiffer and even slower. But I was in a rush and I slipped.’

‘S – s – s – s – s – s – s –,’ said Mr Pappadopoulis.

Vic was puzzled for a moment, then got it.

'Sling him over to you? Thanks, Mr P,' said Vic, handing Monty to Mr Pappadopoulis. 'Sorry I can't stay to chat, I'm in the school athletics team and I'm late for the District Championships. My phone number's on Monty's tummy. Bye.'

As Vic sprinted out of the shop, he glimpsed puppies, fish, guinea pigs and terrapins all looking at him disapprovingly.

That was a bit unkind, the pets' faces said. *Don't you know anything about stuttering? Don't you know that rushing a stutterer is the worst thing you can do?*

Vic pushed the guilt away and sprinted down the street. Those puppies and fish and guinea pigs and terrapins obviously didn't know anything about being in a district championship relay team.

Vic glanced at his watch.

Twenty-eight minutes till the team bus left.

Enough time.

Probably.

The tortoise was done, only the hair to go.

Please don't gossip, thought Vic as he rushed into Uncle Riad's hair salon. Please don't gossip, please don't gossip, please don't gossip.

Uncle Riad was with a customer, blow-drying a cascade of Beyoncé curls. He looked up, saw Vic and gave him a grin.

'How's the champ?' he said. 'I was just telling

Leonie here what a killer you are on the track. How you're gunna blow the opposition away today. Wipe the track with 'em. Bring home a fistful of trophies. Even better, those engraved silver carving platters.'

'I'm only in the relay team,' muttered Vic.

'Vic runs the final legs of all the relays,' said Uncle Riad to Leonie. 'The four times one hundred metres, the four times two hundred metres and, wait for it, the four times four hundred metres. Creams 'em every time.'

Leonie looked impressed.

'Thanks, Uncle Riad,' said Vic. 'But I'm in a bit of a hurry.' He took Gran's wig from his sports bag and held it out. 'Gran says it needs a trim.'

Uncle Riad didn't even look at the wig, just kept on gossiping to Leonie.

'You'd never have guessed,' said Uncle Riad, 'if you'd seen his wobbly thighs when he was little. He didn't walk till he was two and a half.'

Vic wondered if Uncle Riad had heard any part of 'needs a trim' and 'bit of a hurry'. Maybe Uncle Riad had a build-up of hair clippings in his ears.

'Vic's parents would be so proud if they could see him now,' Uncle Riad was saying to Leonie. 'Be a winner, that's what they always told him. That's why they called him Victor.'

Take the wig, begged Vic silently. Please take it.

'Throw yourself at life,' said Uncle Riad, looking fondly at Vic. 'That's what his dad always said. Go full pelt. Do whatever it takes to get in front of the other mongrels.'

Take it, pleaded Vic. Take it, take it, take it.

'If only his parents were still here to see what a champ their son has turned into,' said Uncle Riad. He sighed. 'If only they hadn't driven quite so fast. Through that red light.'

Vic glanced at his watch.

Thirteen minutes till the bus left.

He stuffed the wig into Uncle Riad's hands. Uncle Riad stared at it, frowning.

'What happened?' he said.

'Got a bit melted in the toaster,' said Vic. 'I was in a hurry, making Gran's toast and trimming her split ends at the same time. Bye.'

He turned and sprinted out of the salon.

The sounds of the hair dryer and Uncle Riad's voice drifted after him.

'Blow 'em away, champ.'

Please don't be gone, thought Vic as he ran towards the school gate. Please don't be gone, please don't be gone, please don't be gone.

If the bus was gone, so was his place in the team. Mr Callaghan the sports teacher was fanatical about being on time. He didn't like lateness at the finishing line, or anywhere.

Vic's chest was hurting with effort and stress.

Thirteen minutes from Uncle Riad's salon should have been plenty, he thought bitterly. It would have, if the streets hadn't been jammed with dawdlers and slowcoaches.

Old people who needed to peer into every shop window, probably looking for a product that would get starch out of their pants.

Gangs of teenagers meandering along, gawking at their phones, probably checking the Guinness Book Of Records website to see if they'd broken the record for the slowest dawdle through a shopping centre.

Families pausing all over the footpath to taste each other's ice-creams.

Vic had very nearly crashed into a mum and dad and kids with chocolate and pistachio moustaches, and he'd felt a bit jealous. Then, as he'd pushed past them, a bit sticky.

Please don't be gone, begged Vic again.

He sprinted through the school gate and round the corner of the library to the staff carpark.

There it was. The team bus.

He'd made it.

'Victor,' said a voice. 'What are you doing here?'

Vic stopped and turned round.

Mr Downie the principal was coming out of the library.

'Didn't you get our message?' said Mr Downie.

Vic looked at him, confused.

'We sent you a text last night,' said Mr Downie. 'You're not running today. Sorry.'

Vic stared.

Not running?

'I discussed it with Mr Callaghan,' said Mr Downie. 'We agreed you haven't been putting in your best times lately and you could do with a rest. Didn't you look at your phone?'

Vic was so dazed he could hardly think.

He had to admit he probably hadn't looked at his phone last night, what with his evening training program and cooking Gran's tea and Uncle Riad coming round and challenging him to an arm wrestle.

'Have the weekend off, Victor,' said Mr Downie. 'Do something relaxing. Take it easy.'

The principal went back into the library.

Vic slumped against the wall. It was true, his times had dropped lately. But he'd hoped it was just temporary while he was saving up for new running shoes. Which had taken longer than he'd planned because he hadn't wanted to put extra financial pressure on Gran. It was hard enough for her, with all the debts Mum and Dad had left.

The strange thing, though, was that even when Uncle Riad had found out he needed new running shoes and bought him a pair, plus a luminous green singlet that said *Champ*, his times hadn't picked up.

That was very strange.

And worrying.

Vic stared numbly across the carpark.

Mr Callaghan was getting onto the bus. He gave

Vic an embarrassed wave. The bus door closed behind him. Vic could see the faces of the athletics team silhouetted in the windows.

The bus started to drive away.

Vic heard a voice inside his head.

'Be a winner,' said the voice. 'Because if you're not a winner, you're a loser.'

He wasn't sure if it was his dad's voice, or Uncle Riad's, or Donald Trump's.

Vic didn't care.

He gripped his sports bag and ran after the bus.

By the time Vic caught up with the bus, it was going quite fast.

It had started slowly, turning a few corners, but now it was on a long straight downhill street and was already in third gear.

Vic was running the race of his life.

He'd stopped feeling the pain in his legs several hundred metres back. All he could feel now was a searing fire in his chest and the blood pounding in his head and his eardrums about to explode.

And lower down, in his guts, sadness.

Which he wasn't surprised by.

He'd been dumped. Dumped by the team he'd done so much for. Including giving up ice-cream because of the risk of flab.

Vic was tempted to stop running and give the sticky patch of chocolate and pistachio on his shoulder a good lick and just enjoy it.

But he didn't.

He forced a last spurt of effort into his legs, ignored the agony in his lungs, caught up with the bus and pounded on the back window.

In the driver's-side rear-vision mirror he saw the driver's face go wide-eyed with shock, and Vic remembered just in time to drop back as the driver hit the brakes.

As Vic staggered up the steps onto the bus, he saw it wasn't just the driver who was in shock.

Mr Callaghan and all the kids were staring at him too. Mouths almost as wide as his, and he was the one gasping for air.

As soon as Vic saw Mr Callaghan's face, he knew he was going to get his place in the team back. And he did. Mr Callaghan started giving it to him even before the bus door was closed.

'That was amazing, young man. An amazing piece of running. In the light of such an improved performance . . .'

Vic tried to let Mr Callaghan know that he needed to sit down.

He couldn't speak for the moment, so he let Mr Callaghan know by getting very dizzy and dropping his bag and almost fainting.

Mr Callaghan jumped up and lowered Vic into his seat.

'Head between your legs,' said Mr Callaghan. 'Get some blood back to your brain.'

Vic leant forward and lowered his head.

He found himself looking at his bag on the floor between his feet. It was half open and he could see his phone.

There was a message on the screen from Mr Pappadopoulis.

The bus was moving again now and Vic was still a bit dizzy, so the words in the message were blurry and hard to make out.

Monty must be finished, thought Vic. Trimmed and ready to be picked up. Gee, that was quick.

He blinked a few times and suddenly he could read the message clearly.

Have you thought of slowing down?

Winning isn't the only thing in life.

Take time to decide what's important to you.

Silly boy.

Vic stared at the message. There was something about the first letter of each sentence . . .

Then he remembered what Mr Pappadopoulis had stammered in the pet shop.

H – h – h – h – h –

W – w – w – w – w –

T – t – t – t – t –

S – s – s – s – s –

Vic had thought in the shop he'd known what Mr Pappadopoulis was trying to say, but he hadn't.

He did now.

It was here, in the message.

Vic read the message again. And again.

He kept on reading it until Mr Callaghan started booming in his ear.

'How are you feeling, lad? Back to your senses?'

'Yes, Mr Callaghan,' said Vic quietly. 'I am.'

'Good to hear,' said Mr Callaghan. 'Because in the light of your performance today, you're back in the team.'

Vic looked around the bus. All the kids were nodding. Except one.

Garth Watson.

Garth must be his replacement.

'What about Garth?' said Vic to Mr Callaghan.

'Garth won't mind stepping down,' said Mr Callaghan. 'In the circumstances.'

Vic could see that Garth did mind.

A lot.

Vic zipped up his sports bag.

'Thanks for the offer,' he said to Mr Callaghan. 'But I've decided not to be in the team any more.'

Mr Callaghan stared at him.

'Can I get off the bus please?' said Vic.

'No,' said Mr Callaghan. 'You can't.'

Vic could see from Mr Callaghan's face that Mr Callaghan was going to try to make him stay in the team. Vic didn't want to have to sit through that. He had more important things to do.

He stood up and smashed the emergency glass panel with his phone and pulled the emergency lever.

An alarm went off and the driver swore loudly

and pulled over to the side of the road. The bus door opened with a hiss. Even as the driver was turning round to see what the trouble was, Vic was stepping past him and out the door.

'Sorry about the glass panel,' said Vic.

'Make sure you haven't left anything on the bus,' muttered the driver.

Vic didn't reply.

He had left some things on the bus. Not his sports bag or phone. A couple of things he didn't need any more.

Years later he would tell his own kids how much better his life had been after he'd left those things on the bus. After he'd left behind the dopey idea that if you run fast enough, you can get away from sadness. And after he'd ditched the desperate hope that if you run even faster, you can catch up with what you've lost and get it back.

Get them back.

Vic walked slowly away from the bus.

He ignored Mr Callaghan's angry shouts, which stopped eventually when the bus engine started up again.

There was no hurry.

Vic had the whole day ahead of him. With not a lot planned.

He fancied some quiet time with Gran. Washing her wig, with a bit of conditioner to add bounce and vitality.

Then a stroll with Monty, who'd probably be

keen to check out the back garden now his toenails were in working order.

And this evening, a couple of hours on his own with Gran's family photo album.

Just taking it slowly.

But first, a cup of tea with Mr Pappadopoulis. And a relaxed chat.

It didn't have to be a long one.

Vic didn't need to say much. He didn't need to say please don't stutter or please don't gossip or please don't be gone.

Just two words.

Thank you.

Chips That Pass In The Night

When I ask for fifty dollars worth of chips, the man behind the counter in the fish and chip shop gives me a funny look.

'No salt, thanks,' I say.

Ernie isn't meant to eat salt. He's not meant to eat chips either, but they won't kill him. They won't be able to. Something else is doing that.

'Fifty dollars?' says the man. 'Are you sure?'

He's looking at me very suspiciously. I don't know why. There's no law against kids buying chips.

I'm tempted to tell him about Ernie. How much Ernie loves chips. How Ernie has said more than once that in his opinion, chips are magic.

I decide not to say anything in case he thinks Ernie is a silly old man.

Instead I show him my fifty-dollar note. It's the first fifty-dollar note I've ever had. I wait to see if it works like I always imagined it would.

It does.

The fish and chip man grunts and shovels chips into a big wire basket.

I hope this won't take long. If anyone sees me here, such as Mum or Dad or Uncle Mal or Auntie Liz, I'm history. And poor Ernie will die disappointed.

'Bags or box?' says the fish and chip man.

'Can you wrap them in newspaper?' I ask.

I think Ernie will enjoy them more that way. They might remind him of his childhood. When he was happy. Before everything happened.

'We don't do newspaper,' says the man.

I don't believe him. He looks almost as old as Ernie. He's got nose hairs, plus elastic straps over his shirt holding up his very baggy trousers. I don't think he's modern enough to get his news online.

A woman who's battering fish behind the counter glares at him.

'Stop being a grump,' she says. 'There's some in the kitchen.'

She must be the man's wife because he doesn't start an argument, just rolls his eyes and goes out the back.

'Thanks,' I say to the woman.

The woman gives me a look.

'Your mum needs to do some cooking classes, young man,' she says.

Which is a cheek because she doesn't even know Mum.

I'm tempted to tell her that Mum doesn't need to cook because she's got all Ernie's money and she and Dad can afford home delivery every night.

But I don't. It's bad enough that Ernie is poor and sick, without all his personal financial details being made public in a fish and chip shop.

A girl is standing near the shop.

'Do you want a chip?' she says.

She's holding out a small bag of them.

It's nice of her, offering one to a complete stranger. But a bit surprising. Can't she see I've just come out of the same shop that she must have been in? And that I'm holding a huge parcel that smells very strongly of exactly what she's offering.

'No thanks,' I say.

The girl's shoulders sag.

She looks so disappointed I'm tempted to take one. But my parcel is heavy and droopy and I need both hands to hold it.

Plus I've got to get these chips to Ernie before it's too late.

'Why doesn't anyone want one?' mutters the girl.

She doesn't look disappointed any more, just angry. Which makes me feel nervous. She's about my age, but bigger and I'm pretty sure she'd be stronger.

My life savings are invested in these chips. If she starts any rough stuff, this newspaper could easily split open.

'Sorry,' I say. 'I would have one of your chips normally. Probably a few. But I've already got some and I'm in a hurry. Thanks anyway. Bye.'

I walk away.

After a couple of moments I realise the girl is walking next to me, staring at my parcel.

'You must have a seriously big family,' she says. 'And pets that like chips.'

She doesn't sound angry now, just sort of wistful.

'These aren't for my family,' I say. 'They're for someone else.'

The girl frowns as if she doesn't believe me.

She might have a point. Ernie is Mum's ex-husband, so in a way we're related. Even though he and Mum got divorced before Mum and Dad had me.

'You're right,' I say. 'Ernie is sort of my family. Well, he feels like he is.'

Why am I telling her all this?

'Why are you giving him so many chips?' says the girl.

She's very nosy for a complete stranger. But there's something about the way she's looking at me. Like she really wants to know.

I blurt it out.

'People have been very mean to Ernie,' I say. 'And now he's very sick. Before he dies I want him to see that at least one person really likes him.'

Now that I've said it out loud, it sounds sort of dumb.

If Mum and Dad heard me say it, that's the word they'd use. Dumb. And stupid. And feeble brained.

The girl gives a soft whistle. She doesn't sound like she thinks it's dumb.

'You must really like him,' she says. 'To give him that many chips.'

I look at her. For a person who's a complete stranger she's extremely understanding.

I want to ask her why she was giving away chips. And why she was so disappointed and angry that people wouldn't take them. But I don't know how to put the question into words. I'm not very good at asking girls personal things.

All I can think of is what Mum and Dad would say if they were here.

'That's not how the world works, Jackson,' they'd say. 'Only imbeciles and con artists give things away. Ditch that little twerp now.'

I hope the girl can't tell from my face what I'm thinking.

Probably not. She isn't looking hurt or cross. She's staring at the ground, her hands in her coat pockets, frowning thoughtfully.

Then suddenly, as if by magic, the words come out of my mouth.

'Why were you doing that?' I say. 'Being so generous with your chips?'

The girl looks at me for a few moments. As if she's not sure whether to answer me.

'I'm trying to learn a hard thing,' she says softly.

'What?' I say.

'To forgive potatoes,' she says.

I try not to stare at her. From the tone of her voice I can tell it isn't a joke. It sounds like it's something very important to her. I try not to let her see that I haven't got a clue what she's talking about.

This always happens when I talk to girls, me ending up feeling awkward and embarrassed.

The girl is looking like she doesn't know what to say now either. She's staring at the ground again.

Suddenly I'm feeling even more awkward and embarrassed at the idea that she might be feeling awkward and embarrassed. I wish we could just say goodbye and leave it at that.

It'll have to be me who says it, to get both of us out of this.

I rehearse it in my mind.

'Very nice meeting you. I have to go now. Bye.'

I try to say it.

I can't.

The girl turns to me.

'Can I come with you?' she says. 'To see Ernie?'

As we head towards the hospital, I hope I'm not doing the wrong thing.

What if Ernie doesn't want a stranger seeing what's happened to him and where his life has ended up?

And what if I get even more embarrassed and

stressed from being with this girl and I have to be hospitalised?

In a different ward to Ernie?

'What sort of very mean?' says the girl.

I look at her, not sure what she's asking.

'You said people have been very mean to Ernie,' she says.

I open my mouth, then close it again.

It's a hard thing to explain, that a person can take another person's pet-grooming salon away from them out of anger and greed and unkindness and out of having a brother who's a very experienced lawyer and a new husband who's a member of the local council so they know how to do it.

Actually it's not that hard to explain.

It's just hard to say out loud that your mum is greedy and unkind.

'What sort of mean?' says the girl again.

'Just mean,' I say.

The hospital entrance is crowded, but the security guard still sees us.

'What have you got there?' he says.

'A present for a patient in Ward Six,' I say.

The security guard steps towards us, takes the parcel, and sniffs it.

'No hot food in the wards,' he says.

'It's just chips,' says the girl. 'For a family member. Take a look if you don't believe us. Taste them for identification purposes if you need to.'

I look at the girl.

The security guard looks at us both.

'Come this way,' he says sternly.

We follow him to a small room full of floor-cleaning machines. Two other security guards are sitting at a table drinking mugs of tea.

'You're not gunna believe this,' says the first security guard to the others. 'This pair want to bribe us to let them take hot chips into a ward.'

The other two security guards look at me and the girl as if we're criminals.

The first security guard plonks the parcel onto the table and rips it open. All three of them stare at the mountain of chips inside.

'Jeez,' says one. 'It'd need to be some bribe to get this lot in.'

'Help yourself,' says the girl.

I give her another look. She just can't resist giving chips away. What is this weird thing with her and potatoes?

The security guards look at each other. They reach forward and take one chip each. Then the first security guard bundles the parcel back up and puts it in my arms.

'Ward Six is on the tenth floor,' he says. 'Don't get grease on the furniture.'

In the lift, two doctors get in.

They don't need their stethoscopes to tell what's in my parcel because it's hanging open and I'm only just managing to stop chips falling onto the floor.

The doctors look at me and the girl.

'Where are you going with those?' says one.

'Ward Six,' I say.

'It's a present for a family member,' says the girl.

The doctors think about this.

'I used to live on chips when I was at med school,' says one.

'Same here,' says the other.

I know what the girl will say next. So I say it first.

'Help yourselves.'

The girl gives me a grin. I don't grin back. Uncle Mal has got a friend who's a doctor, and when he comes to dinner he always has multiple helpings of everything.

The doctors take two chips each and eat them.

They don't take more, which is a relief.

'Nice,' says one. 'Not from the canteen here, eh?'

I shake my head.

'From a real chip shop,' says the girl. 'Where they use real potatoes.'

The other doctor nods thoughtfully.

'All that erythromycin and metronidazole we pump into patients,' he says. 'Sometimes I think they'd be better off with chips.'

Ward Six must be having a quiet night because the nurses are standing around chatting.

'Hello, Jackson,' says one of the younger nurses. 'You here to see Ernie?'

I nod.

The nurse gives me and the girl a sympathetic look.

An older nurse is staring at the chips.

'You do know,' she says, 'you're not meant to bring hot food into the ward.'

'It's a present for Ernie,' says the girl.

She must be leaving the rest for me to say.

I look around at all the nurses.

'And for everyone who's caring for him,' I say.

I glance at the girl. I expect her to give me a look that says good one, we're a team. But she's wincing and frowning at me as if I've just done something wrong.

The nurses are all grinning with delight.

'That is so kind,' says one.

'I wish all our patients' families were so thoughtful,' says another.

'You two are our favourite visitors,' says the older nurse, beaming at me and the girl and taking the parcel of chips from me and putting it on the nurses' table.

The nurses all help themselves. Not just one or two chips each.

Handfuls.

They all gobble happily and some are already onto their second fistful.

I'm about to throw myself across the dwindling pile of chips to protect Ernie's present with my body.

Before I can, the girl tugs at my arm.

'Come on,' she says. 'We won't get them back now. Let's go and see Ernie.'

'No,' I want to yell. 'They're Ernie's chips. He's lost enough in his life already.'

Before I can get the words out, someone else arrives.

It's the head nurse, who can be very strict.

She stares at the chips and the munching nurses and she doesn't look happy.

Then she blinks.

Now she's staring at the girl.

'I know you,' she says. 'You're Gabby Fletcher. You poor love. A friend of mine works in the hospital that sent the ambulances for your family.'

The girl looks at the floor.

I can see she'd rather not be recognised.

A buzz is going around the nurses. A muffled buzz because they're still eating. But I can make out a few words through the mouthfuls of chips.

'She's been put in a home.'

'Tragic.'

'Both parents and her brother and sister.'

'On the Hume Highway.'

'Out-of-control potato truck.'

The girl turns to me and grabs my arm hard.

'Let's go,' she hisses.

She drags me away down the ward. I don't ask anything because some questions are too painful to think about, let alone answer.

Instead I point to Ernie's room.

We go in.

The other two patients in Ernie's room are asleep. I assume he is too at first because his eyes are closed and the machines plugged into him are beeping very slowly and quietly.

Then he opens his eyes.

He sees me and smiles. Sort of. I can see it's an effort for him to move even a few face muscles.

I go over and put my hand gently on his arm.

It's all I've got now the chips are gone.

The girl comes over too.

'Hello, Ernie,' she says softly. 'I'm Gabby. Would you like a chip?'

From her coat pocket she takes her small bag of chips and holds it out to him.

Ernie looks at the chips blankly for quite a while. Then he smiles. A proper smile this time. He takes one.

'Thank you, Gabby,' he says quietly. 'Are you a friend of Jackson's?'

Gabby looks at me.

I nod.

Gabby's eyes glow softly like the machines around the bed. She turns back to Ernie.

'Yes,' she says to him. 'I am.'

Ernie eats the chip.

It must be cold but he doesn't seem to mind.

I get a chair from the corner and put it next to Ernie's bed so Gabby can sit down. Then I go and lean against the wall, partly because there's only one chair, but mostly because it feels like the right thing to do.

I can't hear everything Ernie and Gabby are saying, but I don't mind. The more they talk, the more their faces relax and the more they smile.

I'm glad just to watch.

You don't often get to see two people without much happiness in their lives having some of it right in front of you.

I realise I'm smiling too.

It's not just the pleasure of watching Ernie and Gabby. I'm thinking about everything that's happened tonight, and I reckon Gabby was pretty smart using chips to forgive potatoes.

Because Ernie was right all along.

Chips are magic.

Secret Diary Of A Dog

Maddy doesn't usually get angry, but she did today.

'Ralph,' she yelled at me.

'*Woof*,' I said, to remind Maddy that if she wags her tail, well bottom, it might help her feel a bit better.

She was shouting so loudly she didn't even hear me. Young humans make a lot of noise when they get worked up.

'Spit that out, Ralph,' Maddy yelled, 'and don't ever let me catch you using the dental floss again.'

She must have spotted some white thread hanging from my jaws. I opened my mouth and the dental floss flopped out. So did a soggy pair of Dylan's underpants.

Dylan wailed.

He's eight, so he's very fond of his Spider-Man underpants.

'That does it, Ralph,' said Maddy. 'You're grounded. No sniffing other dogs' bottoms for a week.'

Maddy obviously couldn't see that I was simply trying to help out around the house. That I was on my way to remind Dad he urgently needed to do some shopping because the dental floss had almost run out and Dylan's undies had developed serious elastic-droop.

'Bad boy,' Maddy yelled at me.

I was shocked. Maddy had never called me that before, not ever.

That's when I started to realise just how much she's feeling the stress of Mum being away.

What happened next showed it even more.

Both cats tried to slink out of the room.

'Stay right where you are, both of you,' shouted Maddy. 'Did we or did we not have an agreement?'

The cats frowned as if they were trying to remember.

'We agreed,' said Maddy, 'that if I found any more dead birds in my sock drawer you would be punished. So, no TV for a month, not even if *Animal Hospital* has a stir-fry chicken segment.'

The cats were looking confused. Not surprising, poor things. I've tried to tell them, but they still think a dead bird is the best present you can give a person.

Both the goldfish were smirking.

'As for you two,' said Maddy, 'I've had enough of your smug insolence.'

To our horror and amazement, Maddy put the goldfish over her knee and gave them a spanking.

We glanced at each other, me and Dylan and the cats, and waited for Maddy to realise that spanking isn't good, plus it wasn't really working because she had to leave the goldfish in the water and she couldn't smack the bowl too hard in case it broke.

I barked a few times, advising her of this.

'Be quiet,' yelled Maddy.

Dad came in, just as I hoped he would, and saw what Maddy was doing.

'What on earth is going on?' he said.

Dad loves all living creatures. He's a very kind man. He refuses to eat tuna if dolphins have been caught in the same net. I'm pretty sure he'd refuse to eat dolphins if tuna had in any way suffered.

'Well?' said Dad.

Maddy didn't say anything. Just stared at the goldfish guiltily.

'Alright, everyone,' said Dad. 'Calm down. I know this isn't easy, Mum being away. But we're all doing our best.'

Maddy gave him a long look.

Then she said something that helped explain why she was behaving so unlike the Maddy we know.

'Dad' she said. 'We know you're trying your best, and we love you, and we know Mum asked you not to let the house get messy, but is it really necessary for you to be the most painfully organised dad in the whole world?'

Dad frowned at her.

'What do you mean?' he said.

'The lists,' said Maddy. 'They're stressing us out. Why can't you do anything without making a list? What other parent needs a list before they do the gardening?

(1) gardening gloves

(2) gardening hat

(3) lawn mower

(4) lawn.'

Dad was still frowning.

'I'm sorry,' he said. 'I just want you to feel the house is in safe hands.'

'We want to feel that too,' said Maddy. 'Right, Dylan? Right, Ralph?'

'Yes,' said Dylan.

'*Woof,*' I replied.

'But Dad,' said Maddy. 'Can't you see? The more mega-organised you get, the more nervous we get that deep down this is all too much for you. Look at the way you put food into the fridge in alphabetical order. If Mum doesn't come home soon, I'm going to have a nervous breakdown.'

Dad didn't say anything else for quite a few moments.

Just kept on frowning, concerned and sad.

Then he perked up.

'I think we all need a day off,' he said. 'Let's go to the zoo.'

Dylan and Maddy looked stunned.

Today was a school day, and a work day for Dad.

'Come on,' said Dad. 'Car leaves in ten minutes. Ralph can come too if he stays in the backpack.'

Maddy opened her mouth as if she had more to say.

Then she changed her mind, and she and Dylan ran off to get ready.

Dad picked me up and tickled my tummy. But he wasn't grinning like he usually does when he tickles me.

'Wish me luck, Ralph,' he muttered.

He put me back down and went off to get ready himself.

I watched him go. I had a heavy lump in my tummy. It wasn't a fur ball, or one of those white balls you eat when you go to a golf course.

It was a ball of anxiety.

I took my own advice and wagged my tail to calm myself down.

Chill, I said. There's nothing to worry about. We're just going to the zoo for a fun day out.

Woof.

I love the zoo.

When you live in a house with humans, you don't get to meet many other creatures from the wild. Meeting noble creatures from the wild makes my heart soar with pride. It makes me feel a bit noble and wild myself, even if I am wearing a crocheted tartan doggy smock.

Trouble is, dogs aren't allowed to run around at the zoo. They're not even meant to be there. Which is why I had to stay in Dylan's backpack.

Oh well, at least it gave me time to do my diary.

People think dogs don't keep diaries, but we do. In our heads. It's quite hard work. That's why we spend a lot of time panting. Having your tongue out cools your brain down.

I wish humans knew how to do that. Maddy could have done it today during the dental-floss incident. And at the zoo when Dad sat her and Dylan down for a little chat.

'You're probably wondering,' he said to them, 'why I've brought you here.'

'Dad,' said Maddy. 'This is the zoo. There's only one reason people come to the zoo.'

'To look at animals,' said Dylan. 'And have ice-cream.'

I peeked out from the backpack, hoping Dad would say, spot on, that's it, absolutely right.

But he didn't.

He seemed to be having trouble getting the next lot of words out.

'Except,' said Maddy to Dad, 'last time we were here, we did spend quite a lot of time trying to get your camera back from that orangutan.'

The kids both chuckled at the memory.

Dad wasn't chuckling. I could see he had something serious to say and wasn't sure how to say it.

I growled a couple of times, softly, to encourage him to spit it out, whatever it was. The birds and animals chattering and screeching and grunting around us all agreed.

'Tell them,' snorted the zebras.

'You can't pull wool over kids' eyes,' screeched the toucans.

'Only a fool would try,' grunted the hippos. Though that might have been, 'Only a fool would try to get an orangutan to take a photo of him and his family.'

Both Maddy and Dylan were looking at Dad, concerned.

'Are you alright?' said Maddy.

'Would you like a lick of my ice-cream?' said Dylan. 'When you've bought it?'

'Mum rang late last night,' said Dad. 'I'm afraid she's going to be away longer than we thought.'

Maddy and Dylan stared at him.

'Longer?' said Dylan.

'How much longer?' said Maddy.

They both looked so shocked, I wanted to hug them. But dogs can't hug. We can only lick. And it's a bit hard when you're in a backpack.

I did my best with Dylan's ear.

'Grandad's not getting better as quickly as we'd hoped,' said Dad quietly. 'Mum will tell you about it tonight when we skype, but she could be away a few more months.'

Maddy and Dylan were looking at Dad in horror.

My stomach was knotted. Over my left shoulder I could hear a pale-throated sloth regurgitating its lunch. I knew how it felt.

'A few months?' said Maddy.

Dad nodded.

Everything went very quiet. Even the sloth.

'I want to go to Scotland,' said Maddy. 'I want to be with Mum and Grandad.'

'Me too,' said Dylan.

I didn't woof 'me too' because I knew what Dad's reply would be. Plus when dogs fly they have to spend weeks in a cage with only suitcases to talk to.

Dad sighed.

'I'm sorry, loves,' he said. 'We can't afford it.'

Maddy glared at him.

I knew what she was thinking.

Sell the car. Sell the house. Sell Dylan's Lego.

But she didn't say any of that because she knew it was impossible. There was school to go to and work to do and me to feed.

Dad struggled to put on a cheerful face.

'It's not the end of the world,' he said. 'We'll still skype with Mum every day. And maybe it'll only be one or two months.'

Poor Dad.

I knew that despite his brave face his heart must be heavier than a buffalo's bum flap.

Maddy and Dylan looked like theirs definitely were.

'Sometimes,' said Dad, still struggling to sound

positive, 'every family has to be apart for a while. Like those kids at your school who live with their father.'

'Their mum's dead,' said Maddy.

'Oh,' said Dad.

'And it's easier for them,' said Dylan. 'Their dad's got an apartment with a swimming pool and a housekeeper and a speedboat.'

'Oh,' said Dad.

I've never heard him sound so miserable.

Poor humans. They're always worried that other humans are better than them. Dogs don't have that problem. It's because we're allowed to sniff each other's bottoms.

'I know how hard this is for you,' said Dad to Maddy and Dylan. 'I wanted to soften the blow a bit. That's why I brought you here today. To your favourite place.'

'Too see the animals,' said Maddy. 'And take our minds off the fact that we're living with a parent who uses a tape measure to make toast fingers.'

Dad looked hurt. But he knew it was true.

'I'll get some ice-creams,' he mumbled and hurried away towards the kiosk.

Maddy took me out of the backpack and buried her face in my fur.

'Oh, Ralph,' she sobbed. 'I don't want months without Mum. I miss her. It wouldn't be so bad if Dad would just relax and be a normal dad, instead of trying to be so ridiculously organised and tidy.'

'I don't want him to buy me new undies,' wailed Dylan. 'He'll buy organised ones.'

'We can't even tell Mum,' said Maddy. 'She'll worry.'

I was tempted to offer to bite Dad's bottom, not hard, just enough to snap him out of it. But I knew Maddy and Dylan wouldn't be comfortable with that, and Dad definitely wouldn't.

'Dad used to be so relaxed and confident,' said Maddy. 'Before Mum went. I want that Dad back.'

'Me too,' said Dylan. 'I'm scared to eat the toast fingers.'

I had an idea. Perhaps I could just gently pull a few of Dad's leg hairs out with my teeth.

Then I had a better idea.

Of course.

I wriggled out of Maddy's arms, jumped to the ground and without looking back, I ran.

It was risky. I'd heard rumours that if zoo keepers catch dogs running around the zoo, they feed them to the pythons. But it was worth the risk.

I reached the lion enclosure and stuck my head between the bars.

'Excuse me,' I woofed to a magnificent male lion from the wild who was stretched out in the sun. 'Could you do me a favour? In a few moments a couple of human kids will arrive. Could you demonstrate how in the natural world daddies are very good at looking after children? Just be big and strong and kind and gentle, but very fierce when it comes to protecting cubs.'

The lion gave me an unfriendly stare. He didn't look like a creature who did many favours. Not kind and gentle ones.

I peered around, trying to see his family.

'Where are the cubs?' I asked the lion.

At the back of the enclosure was a cave. Perhaps they were inside, watching TV or chewing on a wildebeest.

A female lion came out of the cave.

'The kids are in a separate enclosure,' she growled. 'So Daddy Big-Chops here won't eat them.'

I stared at her, horrified. What sort of psychopath was she married to?

The female lion rolled her eyes.

'Don't ask,' she growled. 'They all do it. Quirk of nature, they reckon. They don't mention it when they first ask you out, of course.'

I heard yells and saw Maddy and Dylan sprinting towards me.

'Sorry to bother you,' I said to the lions, and dashed over to the elephant compound.

'Quick,' I barked at a herd of elephants. 'All you dads. Look loving and capable. I want these kids to see you and think, behold the mighty elephant, reliable and patient and never forgets a birthday.'

Several female elephants gave me a look.

'They may never forget a birthday,' said one, 'but they usually forget their kids. Last year one of the big boofheads rolled over and squashed a few to death.'

I gave the mummy elephant a cross look.

Honesty is good, but there's a time and a place.

'If you want to see the champion dad of the natural world,' said another female elephant, 'try the insect pavilion. There's a beetle in there that eats its own poo so his kids won't catch germs from it.'

That sounded promising, but I wanted Maddy and Dylan to see that big creatures, human-size ones, could be good daddies too.

Maddy and Dylan were very close.

I veered over to the hippo pit.

'Guys,' I said. 'Please. Work with me. Be good dads.'

Maddy and Dylan arrived, panting and angry.

'Ralph,' yelled Maddy. 'What are you thinking? You know you don't run off like that. Bad boy.'

I winced, then pointed my nose towards the hippos.

We all looked at a large male hippo lying in a pool of mud. Unfortunately he didn't look like a great parent. He wasn't cuddling his kids, or giving them tips on personal hygiene, or listening to their problems, or training them in their chosen sport, or helping them with their homework. Forget being relaxed and spontaneous with toast fingers, he didn't look like he knew what a toast finger was.

'His kids are over there,' said Dylan. 'He growls at them if they try to get close.'

This wasn't what I'd hoped for.

The only individuals the daddy hippo would allow near him were some white birds with long beaks who were clambering all over him, eating things off his tummy.

'He's organised them,' said Maddy, disgusted. 'To groom him. Pick fleas off him while he has a snooze. Trim his dry skin. Make him all neat. That'll be us soon, forced to collect our dad's dandruff and count it.'

Dylan gave a groan of despair.

I felt like groaning myself.

I could see Dad heading towards us, ice-creams safely cradled in his hands. Nobody organises ice-creams better than Dad.

Sometimes, when you're desperate, you don't think, you just act.

Well, we dogs do.

I squeezed between the bars of the enclosure and flung myself down into the hippo pit.

The mud was deeper than it looked. And stickier. And smellier. And the hippos' teeth were yellower than they looked, and more crooked, and much sharper.

Even the young hippos' teeth were.

The young hippos were grunting and squealing with indignation. So were the birds. They glared at me and I knew how the daddy hippo's fleas must feel.

Except the fleas weren't having to struggle to keep their heads above the mud like me.

'Cool,' said the daddy hippo. 'We normally don't get fed till four o'clock. Hey, you're a seriously plump swamp rat. Nice tartan packaging too.'

Other daddy hippos lumbered towards me, and a few mummies. All licking their lips.

I started to think I should have given this plan a bit more thought.

Then I heard my name being yelled, louder then it had all day. Not angrily, like before. Heroically.

And not by Maddy.

By Dad.

Suddenly he was in the mud next to me, just as I'd hoped, thrashing around, driving the hippos back with big sweeps of his arm and sprays of mud and dollops of ice-cream.

'Woah,' said the first hippo. 'Take it easy, dude. We're a protected species. Is that vanilla?'

The next few moments were a blur. Dad dragged me out of the mud, and while he heaved us both over the railings, I spent a bit of time upside down in his armpit, which was much nicer than the hippo pit.

Then Maddy and Dylan were hugging me and neither of them seemed to mind how muddy they got or how many other zoo visitors took photos of their muddiness.

'Ralph,' said Maddy, 'why did you do that?'

I didn't try to tell them. Sometimes it's better to keep quiet, specially when your mouth's full of hippos' lounge room.

Then Maddy and Dylan hugged Dad for ages, which made them even muddier.

'You saved Ralph's life, Dad,' said Dylan.

'And you risked yours,' said Maddy.

After the hugging, Dad went back to checking me over for injuries. There weren't any, luckily. But Dad didn't stop till he'd made absolutely sure.

He didn't seem to care that mud and slime and hippo poo were oozing out of my doggie smock, even though he'd crocheted it himself.

While he checked me over, I saw the way Maddy and Dylan were looking at him. At his sticky hair and his ripped shirt and his one shoe missing and at the mud and slime and hippo poo oozing out of his pockets.

I could see in their eyes they'd realised something.

Something that, if only I could speak, I could have told them a long time ago.

That their dad is a brave and noble creature from the wild, and no matter how long Mum is away, they'll be OK.

'Dad,' said Maddy. 'After you've persuaded the zoo officials not to call the police, can we go home and have toast fingers?'

'And after that,' said Dylan, 'can you buy me some new underpants?'

Snot Chocolate

It's been a long trial. Nearly two weeks so far. Mum must be exhausted. I think that's why she's doing the amazing thing she's doing now.

'Ms Beckwell,' growls the judge. 'Are you eating?'

Everyone in the courtroom stares at Mum. A couple of people snigger. The prosecutor rolls his eyes. The jury looks jealous.

Mum swallows whatever she's got in her mouth.

I'm shocked. When Mum started letting me come here after school to watch her work, the first thing she said was never eat in a courtroom.

The judge is glaring at Mum.

Mum hesitates. I'm pretty sure she'll own up. The truth is important to her. She spends a lot of time advising her clients to tell it.

'Sorry, your Honour,' says Mum.

The judge growls.

The jury looks wistful.

The prosecutor, whose tummy looks like he does a lot of eating himself, goes back to questioning one of the defendants about the alleged crime.

I'm sitting up the back in my favourite seat, the one that lets me see everything Mum does. I can see what she's doing now. Fiddling with something under her table.

It's a chocolate wrapper.

Now I'm really shocked.

Mum's eating chocolate in court. Which is a bad thing to do in any courtroom, but a really bad thing to do in a courtroom where the two defendants' alleged crime is stealing three hundred and twenty-eight thousand dollars worth of Easter animals.

Chocolate ones.

'I put it to you,' the prosecutor says to one of the defendants, 'that the nine hundred and three boxes of chocolate bilbies found in your storage unit came from the same hijacked truck as the five thousand two hundred and seventeen boxes of chocolate bunnies also found in your storage unit, or should I say, in your storehouse of crime.'

'It's not a storehouse of crime,' says the defendant. 'No way.'

I look across at Mum to see if she's going to object to what the prosecutor said. She's a brilliant defence lawyer and she doesn't let prosecutors get away with anything. But this time she stays silent. Mostly because her mouth is full.

I can't believe it.

If I was a defendant, I'd be ropeable that my barrister couldn't speak up because she had a gobful of Dairy Milk.

The defendants don't seem to have noticed.

Neither, luckily, has the judge.

The jury has. All twelve of them are staring at Mum. A few are licking their lips. It's ages since lunch and I don't think the criminal justice system includes afternoon tea.

Then the chocolate penny drops.

I realise what Mum is doing.

She's reminding the members of the jury how irresistible chocolate is. So that if they find Theodore Conway Tucker and Christopher Waylon Tucker guilty of stealing a truckload of it, they'll be a bit understanding and recommend a light sentence. Weekend detention picking up chocolate wrappers in a supermarket carpark, something like that.

Phew, I was worried there for a moment.

I thought Mum was being a greedy pig, but she's just being a good lawyer.

'Mum,' I groan. 'What are you doing?'

I stagger into her bedroom. It's the middle of the night. I was fast asleep until the noise from her bedroom woke me up.

'Sorry, love,' says Mum. 'Have I got it up too loud?'

She's in bed with her iPad. Sometimes she can't sleep so she watches movies. But it's not the iPad

I'm staring at. It's the chocolate wrappers all over her bed.

'What are you doing?' I say.

'I was a bit peckish,' says Mum.

'Peckish?' I say, still staring at the remains of half a chocolate shop on her duvet. 'That's not peckish, that's being a greedy pig.'

Mum loses it.

'Jemma,' she says angrily. 'How dare you speak to me like that. Go back to bed.'

But I don't. I stand there, glaring at her. Just like I've seen her do to a cop in court who won't give her a straight answer.

Finally Mum sighs.

'I felt like a bit of chocolate,' she says. 'Is that a crime?'

'A bit of chocolate?' I feel like saying. 'A bit?'

But I don't because this isn't a courtroom and it's not a good idea to cross-examine your own parent when she's already furious.

'You don't even like chocolate,' I say quietly.

'I just got out of the habit of eating it,' says Mum. 'I used to love it when I was a kid. And last week, when I had to sit through all those hours of expert witnesses testifying how the bunnies and bilbies in the defendants' warehouse had exactly the same smooth and creamy cocoa butter content as the stolen chocolate, I started tasting it again. My imagination started salivating. My taste buds went crazy. So I got myself a bar.'

I don't know what to say.

That actually sounds quite reasonable.

'But when you eat it in court,' I say, 'that's for the jury, right? So they're reminded how easily people are tempted by chocolate, specially eleven and a half tonnes of it.'

Mum looks at me, frowning.

'That is the reason you've been eating it in court,' I say. 'To get your clients a lighter sentence?'

Mum grins.

'That is so clever,' she says. 'I didn't think of that. You're going to make a great lawyer one day.'

It isn't the reason.

There's another reason Mum's eating chocolate in court, and it's making me sick in the stomach just thinking about it.

We're in court now and the jury's been sent out because they're not allowed to hear a legal argument that has to happen between Mum and the prosecutor.

Mum has explained to me that these legal arguments are a very important part of a trial. And she's very good at them. But today her words aren't flowing like they usually do. Mostly because she popped three squares of Lindt Extra Creamy into her mouth just before she started speaking.

'Are you alright, Ms Beckwell?' says the judge. 'Do you need a glass of water?'

'I'm fine, thank you, your Honour,' says Mum, swallowing.

She's not fine.

I've just realised the horrible truth. My own mother is addicted to chocolate. Which is putting her career seriously at risk. Not to mention her health. We did it at school. Sugar is poison. Too much gives you diabetes, tooth decay and chocolate stains on your sheets.

Well I'm not sitting here and letting it happen.

Mum might not be able to save Theodore Conway Tucker and Christopher Waylon Tucker, but I'm going to save her.

Mum's gone to bed.

I thought she never would.

When Mum decides we need a family talk, it can go on for hours.

At least this evening she confessed. Admitted she's been overdoing the chocolate lately. Though it wasn't so much a confession as an excuse. She reckons she needs cheering up because things have been a bit bleak since Dad left.

I could have told her that.

'Mum,' I said. 'If work's not bringing enough joy into your life, find yourself a hobby or a project. Weeding national parks or volunteer dog walking or something.'

I didn't tell her what my new project is.

Getting her off chocolate.

Good, it's melted.

I give the rich smooth liquid a stir, careful not

to rattle the saucepan on the cooktop. Mum's bedroom is right up the other end of the house from the kitchen, but sounds travel more at night and a chocolate addict can probably hear chocolate from streets away.

Now for the magic ingredient.

I sprinkle a big spoonful of dried chili powder into the melted chocolate and give it another stir.

We learned about this at school too. If you have a very painful experience, it can turn you off nice things you were doing at the time. Like if you're wearing green shoes and a dog pees on your feet, it can put you off wearing green shoes ever again. Specially if the yellow pee turns the green shoes blue, which is my least-favourite colour.

It's called psychology.

I pour the molten chocolate and chili into the ice-cube mould and put it into the fridge.

It'll be set by morning. I'll get up very early and put the squares back into the gourmet-chocolate-shop bag. When I give it to Mum as a sorry-for-calling-you-a-greedy-pig present, it'll look like ordinary chocolate.

The man in the gourmet chocolate shop said this type of chocolate is perfect for melting and re-setting.

'Are you going to make shapes?' he asked. 'Easter bunnies?'

I shook my head.

The only shape I'm interested in making is

Mum's mouth screwed up into a I'm-never-eating-chocolate-again shape.

I still can't believe it.

'Thank you, sweetheart,' said Mum on our way home from court yesterday. 'Your present was delicious. How did you know I love chili chocolate?'

I stared at her, but she didn't notice.

Just gave me a kiss.

Her breath smelled of chocolate. And chili.

I waited till we'd had dinner and watched TV and she was in bed, and then I crept into the kitchen again. I peered into the fridge.

To save Mum I needed something that would make chocolate taste truly revolting.

I saw the perfect thing.

Fish.

A piece of leftover raw snapper from the fish cakes Mum and I made for dinner.

I chopped it into tiny pieces, melted some chocolate and stirred the fish in. I added a slurp of Asian fish sauce just to make sure.

What a waste of time.

When I got to court this afternoon, Mum wasn't looking even a tiny bit like she wanted to vomit.

She was busy questioning the driver of the chocolate truck. Gently, because he looked upset. He'd lost his job and said that since the trauma of being robbed he'd also completely lost his appetite for chocolate.

Mum didn't comment on that, but I could see she felt very sorry for him.

'Did you see the faces of the individuals who robbed you?' she asked him.

'No,' he said. 'They had Donald Duck masks on.'

'Would you recognise them from their clothes or the shape of their bodies?' asked Mum.

In the dock, Theodore Conway Tucker and Christopher Waylon Tucker both tried to make themselves look very small.

'No,' said the driver. 'They were wearing bumble bee onesies.'

Mum said 'no more questions' and sat down and while the judge was telling the truck driver he could go, she popped a piece of fish chocolate into her mouth.

And sucked it happily.

I had to control myself. You're not allowed to scream with frustration in the public seats of a courtroom.

I wondered if Theodore Conway Tucker and Christopher Waylon Tucker would be interested in robbing Mum of all her chocolate.

Probably not.

On the way home I didn't want to talk.

Mum did.

'That chocolate you gave me this morning,' she said. 'It was very different to the last lot. A very complex and delicious flavour. What was it?'

'Gourmet,' I muttered.

'You certainly know how to come up with yummy chocolate,' said Mum. 'But love, please, maybe not quite so much. I don't want to get fat.'

I was tempted to remind her about something else she doesn't want to get.

Fired.

If the judge had seen Mum stuffing her face with fish chocolate, her career would be in worse shape than Exhibit A27 on the evidence table, which is a yellow and black striped ski glove that got dropped at the scene of the crime and squashed by a bus.

I didn't say that to Mum.

Mothers who are lawyers just love arguments, and Mum's problem is too serious to waste time squabbling.

It's so serious, I'm doing something I never thought I'd do.

Creeping into Mum's room at two a.m.

Checking she's asleep, which she is, I can tell by the snoring.

Hoping she's had a sleeping pill, which she often does, specially since Dad hasn't been around.

Keeping my torch pointing to the carpet as I reach out and very carefully insert a cotton bud into Mum's nostril.

And gently turn it.

If this doesn't get Mum off chocolate, nothing will.

* * *

It's slow work, gathering somebody else's snot in secret. You don't get a lot for your efforts. Specially not the solid bits you need to make snot chocolate. Solid bits are extremely important if you want the person who eats the snot chocolate to really taste the snot.

After three nights I still don't have enough.

I've agonised about this, but I'll have to do it.

Add some of my own.

I can't risk waiting any longer. The harder Mum works to prove that Theodore Conway Tucker and Christopher Waylon Tucker didn't steal all that chocolate, the more chocolate she eats.

Today she ate heaps, just after Theodore and Christopher told the prosecutor they'd lost the address of the caravan park in East Gippsland where they say they bought the chocolate.

She ate some more when the prosecutor asked them about the colour of the caravan they say the seller had the chocolate stored in.

'I can't remember,' said Theodore. 'It was just an ordinary colour.'

'Brown?' said the prosecutor with a sneer.

Mum put four squares of chocolate into her mouth at that point, I saw her. I think the judge might have seen her as well.

I need snot chocolate and I need it fast.

So here we go, in goes some of mine, straight from the nostril into the saucepan.

I'm her daughter, after all.

It would only be a health risk if it was from a stranger. One living in a caravan park in East Gippsland, for example.

This is weird.

It's the first day of the school holidays and I've been here in court all day and Mum hasn't eaten a single piece of chocolate the whole time. I can see the bag from the chocolate shop sticking out of her briefcase under the table, and it hasn't even been opened.

Mum seems pretty stressed.

Maybe that's why she hasn't eaten any chocolate.

She has to do her closing speech to the jury soon, and things aren't looking good for Theodore Conway Tucker and Christopher Waylon Tucker.

Theodore and Christopher aren't looking good either.

Every day of this trial, they've looked more and more guilty. Sitting slumped in a guilty way. Staring at the floor in a guilty way. And if anyone mentions a bunny or a bilby or a baby chocolate animal of any type, the defendants look like they're going to burst into tears.

Mum's about to stand up, I can tell by the way her shoulders are going tense.

Hang on, they're relaxing again. She's reaching under the table. Opening the chocolate bag. Popping a piece of chocolate into her mouth.

A piece of snot chocolate.

She's sucking it. Chewing it.

Thinking about it with a frown.

I wish she wasn't eating it right now. The judge is instructing her to present her closing remarks to the jury. But I can see she's more concerned with what's in her mouth.

As you would be if you were having your first taste of snot chocolate.

Mum stands up. Starts speaking to the jury. Stops. Moves her tongue around her teeth. Frowns again, as if there's something she can't work out.

'Ms Beckwell,' growls the judge, louder than he's growled this whole trial. 'Are you eating again?'

Mum looks at him, startled. She doesn't reply.

'I'm a patient man,' says the judge, angrily and even more loudly. 'But your behaviour throughout this trial has been, I don't know how else to describe it, a trial. You're very lucky I don't dismiss you from these proceedings. One more transgression and I will refer you to the disciplinary board.'

Poor Mum has gone pale.

It's like she's suddenly realised what she's been doing these last few days. Risking her career. Risking her clients' defence.

Or maybe she's just suddenly realised what she's eating.

'Thank you, Jemma,' says Mum suddenly across the dinner table.

She's been very quiet since we got home, and I

haven't said anything because I wanted to give her enough time to digest the judge's warning today, and the snot.

I'm not sure what she's thanking me for. Peeling the veggies? Offering to stack the dishwasher?

'I know what you've been doing, love,' says Mum quietly.

My blood runs colder than chocolate ice-cream.

Mum doesn't look angry, but her eyes have got that look in them. The lawyer's look that says nobody will leave this room until the truth is admitted.

'If you wanted to put me off chocolate,' says Mum, 'you should have used coriander. It's about the only thing I hate the taste of.'

I could kick myself.

How could I have forgotten about a simple herb? And Mum reckons I'll make a great lawyer.

Forget that.

Forget everything, except what's going to happen now.

Mum knows what I did.

Will she get ill and depressed again, like she did with Dad when he did bad things?

'That was rough luck,' says Mum, 'forgetting how much I love chili. And fish, specially used in creative ways. But what was that last flavour? It was salty and bitter and sweet at the same time. Some kind of salted caramel?'

I don't say anything.

She looks at me, hard.

I've seen politicians in court flinch when she does that. Tough politicians. Politicians who don't even flinch when they tell lies about drowned refugee children.

I can't help it, I have to tell her the truth.

'Snot,' I say.

Mum keeps looking at me for a long time.

Then she smiles.

'I love you,' she says.

We're waiting for the jury to come back in and give their decision.

Mum's not eating chocolate today, or doodling on a legal notepad like the prosecutor.

She looks calm.

Sad but calm.

I know now why she's sad. She explained last night. Theodore Conway Tucker and Christopher Waylon Tucker stole the chocolate bunnies and bilbies for a reason. Their sister's baby was very sick and needed an operation that could only be done in America and would cost two hundred and eighty thousand dollars. Theodore and Christopher were going to sell the chocolate to raise the money. But before they could, the baby died.

I glance over at Theodore and Christopher.

No wonder they're sitting slumped and staring at the floor.

I look around, trying to see their sister.

Her name's Eileen and she's been in the public

seats every day of the trial. She always looks sad too. I thought it was just because she was worried about her brothers.

Eileen isn't here today.

She probably can't bear the thought of seeing Theodore and Christopher being found guilty and sent to jail.

The judge comes back into the courtroom.

This means the jury are on their way back to give their verdict.

The judge sits in his big seat.

Mum sits back down and stares at her table. I know what she's doing. Trying to stay composed. She explained last night that this is the saddest trial she's ever worked on. Every time she looks at Theodore and Christopher and Eileen, she wants to burst into tears. The only way she's stopped herself is by eating chocolate. It's something she used to do as a kid when she was very sad.

She's not eating chocolate now.

She's staying composed without it.

I think she's doing the mental exercise I told her about last night. The one where you forget where you are and travel in your mind to a happy place.

When I do it I go to Cairns where Mum and Dad and I had a holiday when I was little.

I don't think Mum's in Cairns. Her shoulders aren't in the right position for whitewater rafting. She's probably planning what she's going to say after Theodore and Christopher are found guilty.

She couldn't say in the trial why they did it, because she was trying to convince the jury that they didn't do it. Now she's hoping that when she explains, the judge will give them a light sentence.

Her elbows are on the table and her cheeks are cupped in her hands.

Except what's happening?

One of her hands is moving round to the front of her face. Her finger is going up her nose. And out again. And into her mouth.

Oh no.

She's still gazing at the table.

She's chewing, but I can see from her glazed expression she doesn't know what she's chewing.

The judge does. He's staring at her. But he doesn't say anything. I don't think he can believe what he just saw. A top lawyer picking her nose and eating it.

If she does it again though, he will believe it.

She does it again.

Oh no.

What have I done?

I gave my mother snot chocolate, and now she's developed a taste for snot.

I couldn't stay in the courtroom.

I needed quiet time to think, and there wasn't any quiet time after the jury came back in and said 'not guilty'.

People clapped and cheered. They must have

been friends of Theodore and Christopher. The court officials yelled at them to be silent.

It was chaos.

Theodore and Christopher looked as stunned as Mum.

But now I've had a chance to think, I reckon I know what happened.

The jury must have felt sorry for Mum because of the way the judge yelled at her after she ate the snot chocolate. They must have thought it was unjust. So when they found they had some doubts about the case, to do with the Donald Duck masks and the bumble bee onesies and the black and yellow striped ski glove, they must have decided to give Mum and her clients the benefit of those doubts to make up for the injustice.

Which is a great result for Theodore and Christopher.

But not so great for Mum. When word gets around that she eats her own snot, she'll probably never work again.

The thought of that makes me do what Theodore and Christopher did. Not steal eleven and a half tonnes of chocolate. Slump and stare at the floor.

I pull myself together and sit up straight. I got Mum into this, I've got to get her out of it.

I look around, desperate for ideas.

And see somebody else, over on the other side of the courthouse foyer, also slumped and staring at the floor.

And crying.

It's Eileen. Theodore and Christopher's sister.

I've never spoken to her. I don't know what to say to her now. But she looks so miserable, I can't just ignore her.

I go over.

She looks up at me.

'You're Despina Beckwell's daughter, right?' she says, wiping her eyes.

I nod.

'Tell your mum thank you from me,' says Eileen. 'She did a good job. Shame she couldn't tell the jury why the boys did it. Might have stopped them going to jail.'

She starts crying again.

'They're not going to jail,' I say.

Eileen looks at me.

I tell her about the not guilty verdict.

Eileen stares at me as if I'm a kid making things up. Then she remembers I'm not just any kid, I'm the daughter of a senior barrister.

Her face lights up.

Then falls again.

I can see what she's thinking. Her brothers were found not guilty, but she just told me they did it.

'It's OK,' I say quietly. 'I don't talk about my mum's work. Plus you can't be found guilty of something once you've been found not guilty.'

Eileen's face shows that she's having a lot of different feelings. Relief, but a lot of others as well.

I can't imagine what she must be going through. Well, sort of, but not really.

'It's a mess,' says Eileen. 'All that stolen chocolate. Our mum's gunna kill Theo and Chris. They'll wish they were in jail by the time she's finished with them.'

I try to think how I can help.

Theodore and Christopher don't deserve to be killed. Perhaps there's something I can do to help their mum calm down. Perhaps by putting all that chocolate to good use.

You can probably guess the first idea I had.

Take all the chocolate to our place so Mum can eat it every time she's tempted to pick her nose.

I thought seriously about doing that, but then I had a better idea.

One that might help Eileen, just a bit.

Here at the Children's Hospital they can't believe it. The nurses and kids are agog.

Eleven and a half tonnes of chocolate.

The nurses are letting us give an armful to each kid. And a bedful to the ones who can't sit up. They can't eat it all now of course, but the doctors have said they'll prescribe some each day to everyone who's allowed. And give lots to their families. Enough to cheer everyone up.

Theodore and Christopher are looking very cheered up.

And their mum seems to like the idea too. She

hasn't tried to kill Theodore or Christopher once.

Eileen hasn't said anything, but she's been giving lots of the children hugs and just now she gave me one.

So I think it might have helped a bit.

I keep glancing nervously at Mum. She's standing with a couple of the doctors, watching us, smiling.

She hasn't picked her nose yet.

I take a chocolate bunny over to her.

'In case you're feeling a bit emotional,' I say. 'And need something to eat.'

She takes it, but doesn't eat it.

'I want to feel emotional,' she says quietly. 'Seeing all this. Knowing it was your idea.'

I see her eyes are wet. But she looks so proud at the same time that I feel myself glowing. In an anxious sort of way.

Mum looks at me for a moment and sees what I'm thinking. She puts her finger up her nose. Just briefly. Then smiles.

'The nose-picking was for the jury,' she says. 'I wanted to show them I wasn't scared of the judge. So that when they thought about their verdict, they'd know they didn't have to be scared of him either.'

I'm so proud of my mum. She is a great lawyer.

Plus I feel very relieved.

'If you want something to worry about,' says Mum, 'my next case is defending somebody who's been accused of forging a rare and expensive painting. So chances are I'll develop a craving for oil paint and turps.'

She gives me a wink.

I grin back.

'When you've finished your work here,' says Mum, 'I'm going to take you to a very posh restaurant to show how proud I am of you. We'll order anything you want. Fillet steak, lobster, giant pizza, anything.'

'Thanks,' I say.

I have a thought.

'And when we get there,' I say, 'we can toast the great job you did in court.'

'You're a bit young for wine,' says Mum.

I give her another grin.

'I know,' I say. 'So let's both have hot chocolate.'

ALSO BY MORRIS GLEITZMAN

Ludo helps other people.
It's how he was brought up.

When Dad is elected to Federal Parliament, Ludo grabs the chance to make Australia an even better place.

But he soon discovers it's not the homeless of the national capital who most need his help – it's the rich and powerful.

The funny and moving story of a boy and his friends managing not to lose heart in a sometimes heartless world

ALSO BY MORRIS GLEITZMAN

WATER WINGS
Pearl needs a gran and she needs one now. Luckily she's got Winston to help her. You can do anything when your best friend is the world's brainiest guinea pig. Well, almost anything.

ADULTS ONLY
Jake is an only kid.
He's the only kid in his family.
He's the only kid on his island.
Or that's what he thinks.

GIFT OF THE GAB
It's a normal week for Rowena Batts. A car full of stewed apples. A police cell. A struggle to keep Dad off national TV. Then her world turns upside down.

TEACHER'S PET
Ginger is allergic to cats. And possibly to her family as well. She's also not keen on the cat food in her breakfast bowl or the school principal trying to kill her best friend. The question on everyone's lips is - will Ginger snap?

THE OTHER FACTS OF LIFE
Ben stared at the TV.
He'd never seen anything like it.
Fascinating. Incredible. Awful.
He had to do something.

SECOND CHILDHOOD
Mark and his friends discover they've lived before. Not only that – they were Famous and Important People. Which is lots of fun. At first.

WORM STORY
Wilton has a bad feeling in his tummy. The one he lives in. Can one worm discover new worlds and save his friends from destruction? Wilton is about to find out.

ARISTOTLE'S NOSTRIL
Aristotle just wants to be happy. And, if possible, have the biggest adventure of his life. With no sneezing. Is that too much for a germ to ask?

ALSO BY MORRIS GLEITZMAN

BUMFACE
His mum calls him Mr Dependable, but Angus can barely cope. Another baby would be a disaster. So Angus comes up with a bold and brave plan. That's when he meets Rindi. And Angus thought *he* had problems . . .

DOUBTING THOMAS
Thomas has an embarrassing secret. Is it a rare and special gift or the worst thing that could happen to a boy? A story about best friends, surprising adventures and itchy nipples.

TOAD RAGE
The epic story of one slightly squashed cane toad's hunt for the truth. And the fun and games that result.

TOAD AWAY
The heroic tale of one slightly squashed cane toad's travels across oceans and continents. And some really busy roads.

TOAD DELIGHT
The jaw-dropping details of one slightly squashed cane toad's adventures in TV. And the shock when he discovers what's cooking.

TOAD HEAVEN
The stirring saga of one slightly squashed cane toad's dreams of a safe place. And what happens when he wakes up.

TOAD SURPRISE
The eye-popping yarn of one slightly squashed cane toad's search for friendship. And the surprising place he finds it.

ALSO BY MORRIS GLEITZMAN

BOY OVERBOARD
Jamal and Bibi have a dream. To lead Australia to soccer glory in the next World Cup. But first they must face landmines, pirates, storms and assassins. Can Jamal and his family survive their incredible journey and get to Australia?

GIRL UNDERGROUND
Bridget wants a quiet life. Including, if possible, keeping her parents out of prison. Then a boy called Menzies makes her an offer she can't refuse and they set off on a job of their own. It's a desperate, daring plan – to rescue two kids, Jamal and Bibi, from a desert detention centre. Can Bridget and Menzies pull off their very first jail break, or will they end up behind bars too?

EXTRA TIME
A young Aussie soccer genius and his 10-year-old manager take on the world. And win. For a time.

GRACE
In the beginning there was me and Mum and Dad and the twins. And talk about happy families, we were bountiful. But it came to pass that I started doing sins. And lo, that's when all our problems began.

LOYAL CREATURES
They were loyal creatures, the men and horses of the Australian Light Horse, but war doesn't always pay heed to loyalty. The powerful story of a 16-year-old volunteer and his horse in World War One. And of a journey towards his own kind of bravery.

TOO SMALL TO FAIL
What do you do when your mum, your dad and sixteen camels are in trouble – and only you can save them? The sometimes sad but mostly funny story of a boy, a girl, a dog and four trillion dollars.

ALSO BY MORRIS GLEITZMAN

AN UNFORGETTABLE SERIES THAT HAS TOUCHED HEARTS ALL OVER THE WORLD

ONCE

Once I escaped from an orphanage to find Mum and Dad. Once I saved a girl called Zelda from a burning house. Once I made a Nazi with a toothache laugh. My name is Felix. This is my story.

AFTER

After the Nazis took my parents I was scared. After they killed my best friend I was angry. After they ruined my thirteenth birthday I was determined. To get to the forest. To join forces with Gabriek and Yuli. To be a family. To defeat the Nazis after all.

NOW

Once I didn't know about my grandfather Felix's scary childhood. Then I found out what the Nazis did to his best friend Zelda. Now I understand why Felix does the things he does. At least he's got me. My name is Zelda too. This is our story.

THEN

I had a plan for me and Zelda.
Pretend to be someone else.
Find new parents.
Be safe forever.
Then the Nazis came.

SOON

I hoped the Nazis would be defeated. And they were.
I hoped the war would be over.
And it was.
I hoped we would be safe.
But we aren't.

MAYBE

18 May 1946
Dear Zliv,
It's me you want, not Gabriek or Anya. I caused your brother's death, just me. But you'll have to come to the other side of the world to kill me, because that's where I'm going. If you don't believe me, check the newspapers.
Felix.

ABOUT THE AUTHOR

Morris Gleitzman grew up in England and came to Australia when he was sixteen. After university he worked for ten years as a screenwriter. Then he had a wonderful experience. He wrote a novel for young people. Now, with 44 books, he's one of Australia's most popular children's authors. He was appointed the Australian Children's Laureate for 2018–2019.

VISIT MORRIS AT HIS WEBSITE:

www.morrisgleitzman.com